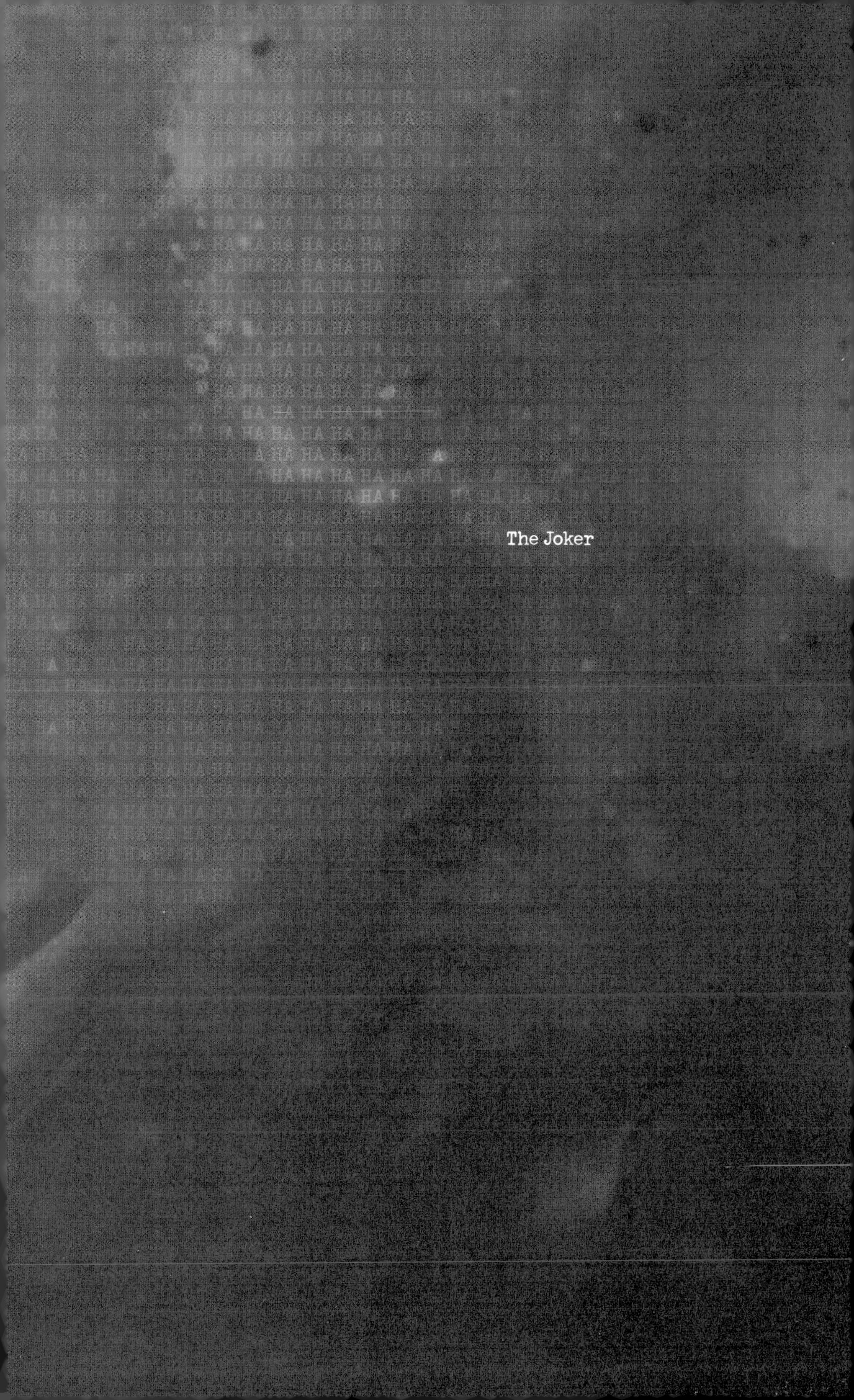

The Joker

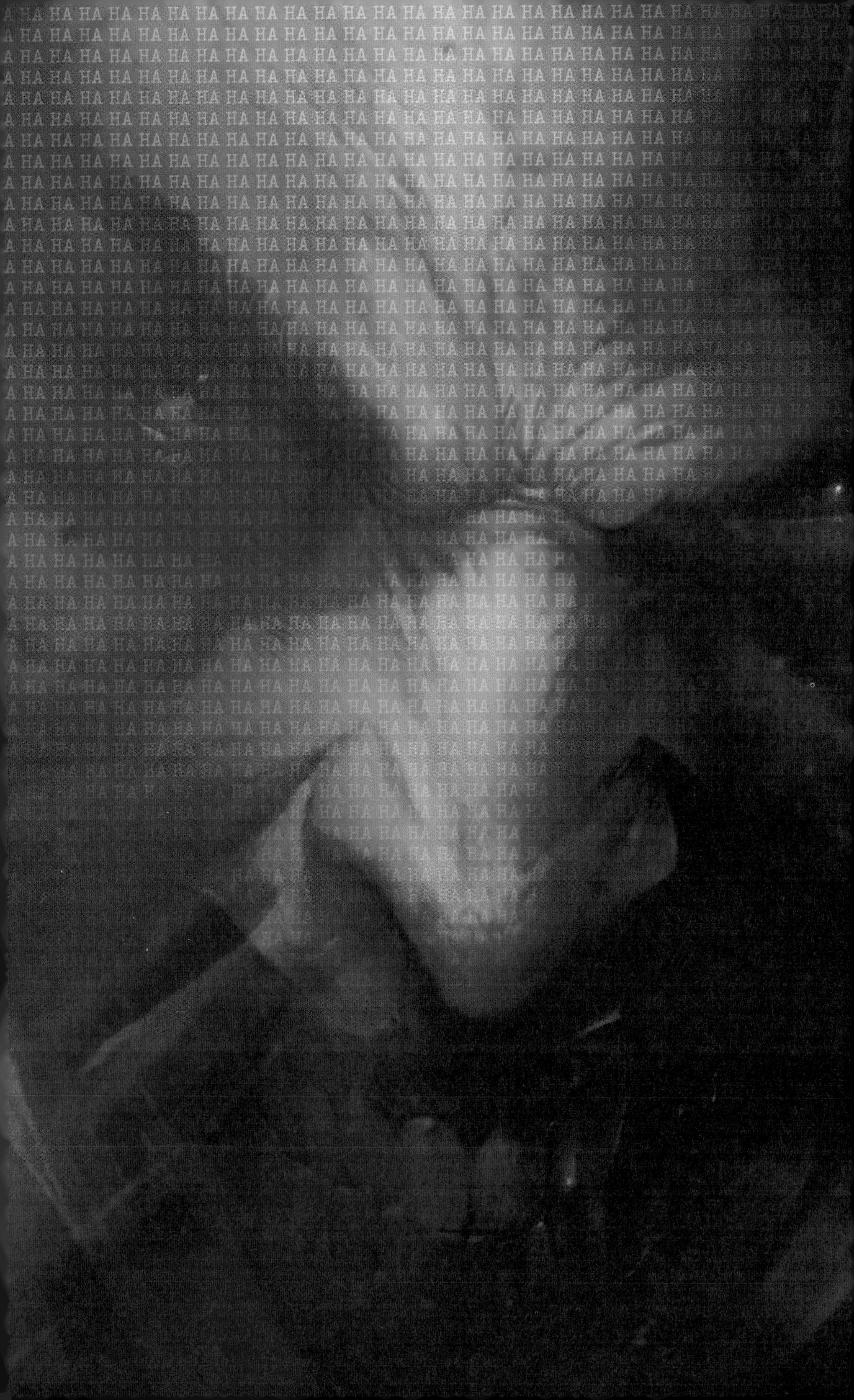

the Joker

Volume One

James Tynion IV with Matthew Rosenberg Writers
Guillem March and Francesco Francavilla Artists
Arif Prianto, Francesco Francavilla, and Tomeu Morey Colorists
Tom Napolitano and Clayton Cowles Letterers
Collection cover art by Guillem March and Tomeu Morey

Ben Abernathy Editor – Original Series & Collected Edition
Dave Wielgosz Associate Editor – Original Series
Steve Cook Design Director – Books
Louis Prandi Publication Design
Erin Vanover Publication Production

Marie Javins Editor-in-Chief, DC Comics

Daniel Cherry III Senior VP – General Manager
Jim Lee Publisher & Chief Creative Officer
Joen Choe VP – Global Brand & Creative Services
Don Falletti VP – Manufacturing Operations & Workflow Management
Lawrence Ganem VP – Talent Services
Alison Gill Senior VP – Manufacturing & Operations
Nick J. Napolitano VP – Manufacturing Administration & Design
Nancy Spears VP – Revenue

THE JOKER VOL. 1 Published by DC Comics. Compilation and all new material Copyright ©
2021 DC Comics. All Rights Reserved. Originally published in single magazine form in *The Joker* 1-5, *Batman*
100, and *Batman: The Joker War Zone*. Copyright © 2020, 2021 DC Comics. All Rights Reserved. All characters,
their distinctive likenesses, and related elements featured in this publication are trademarks of DC Comics.
The stories, characters, and incidents featured in this publication are entirely fictional. DC Comics does not
read or accept unsolicited submissions of ideas, stories, or artwork. DC – a WarnerMedia Company. DC Comics,
2900 West Alameda Ave., Burbank, CA 91505. Printed by Transcontinental Interglobe, Beauceville, QC,
Canada. 9/24/21. First Printing. ISBN: 978-1-77951-201-7

Library of Congress Cataloging-in-Publication Data is available.

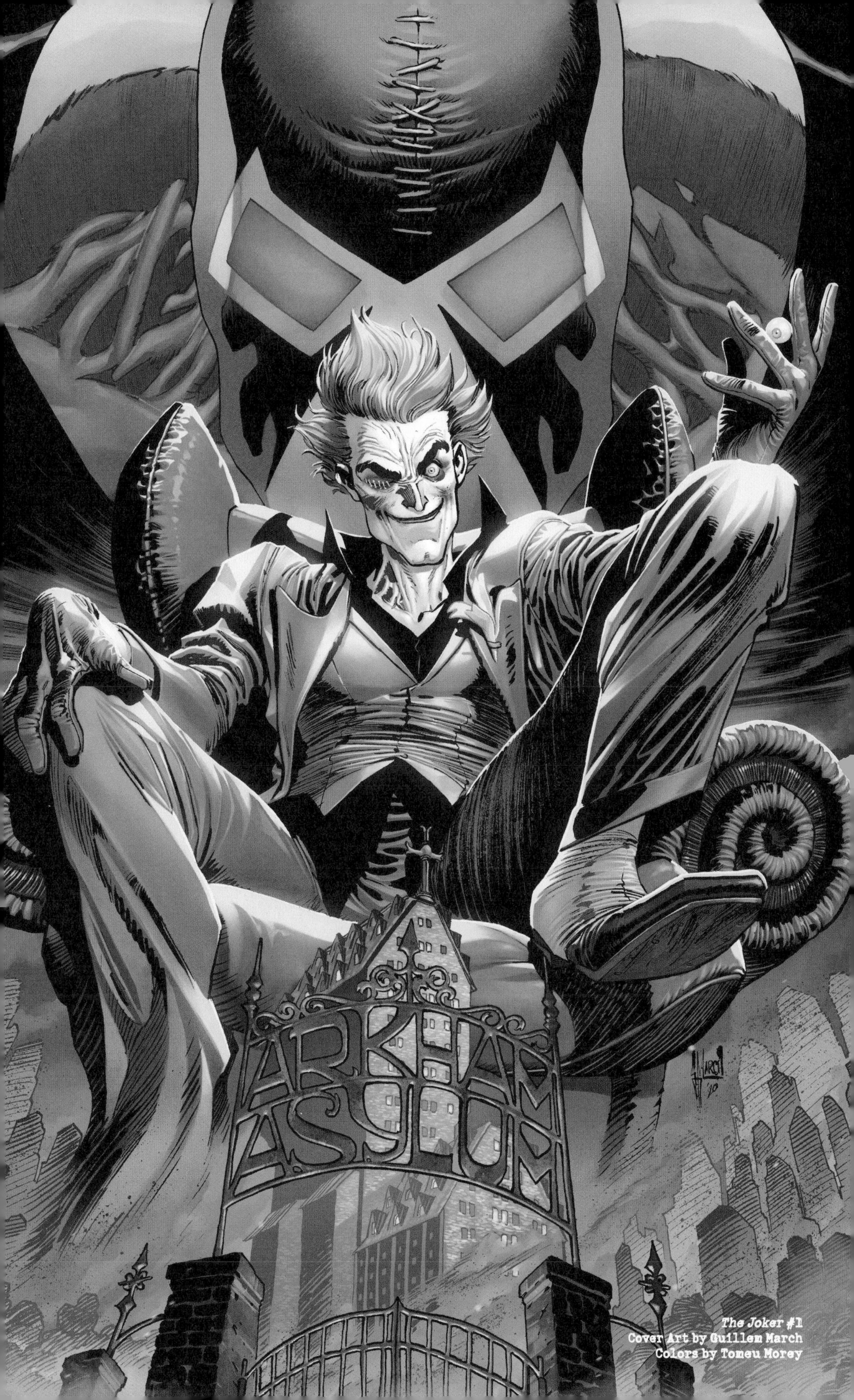
ARKHAM
ASYLUM

The Joker #1
Cover Art by Guillem March
Colors by Tomeu Morey

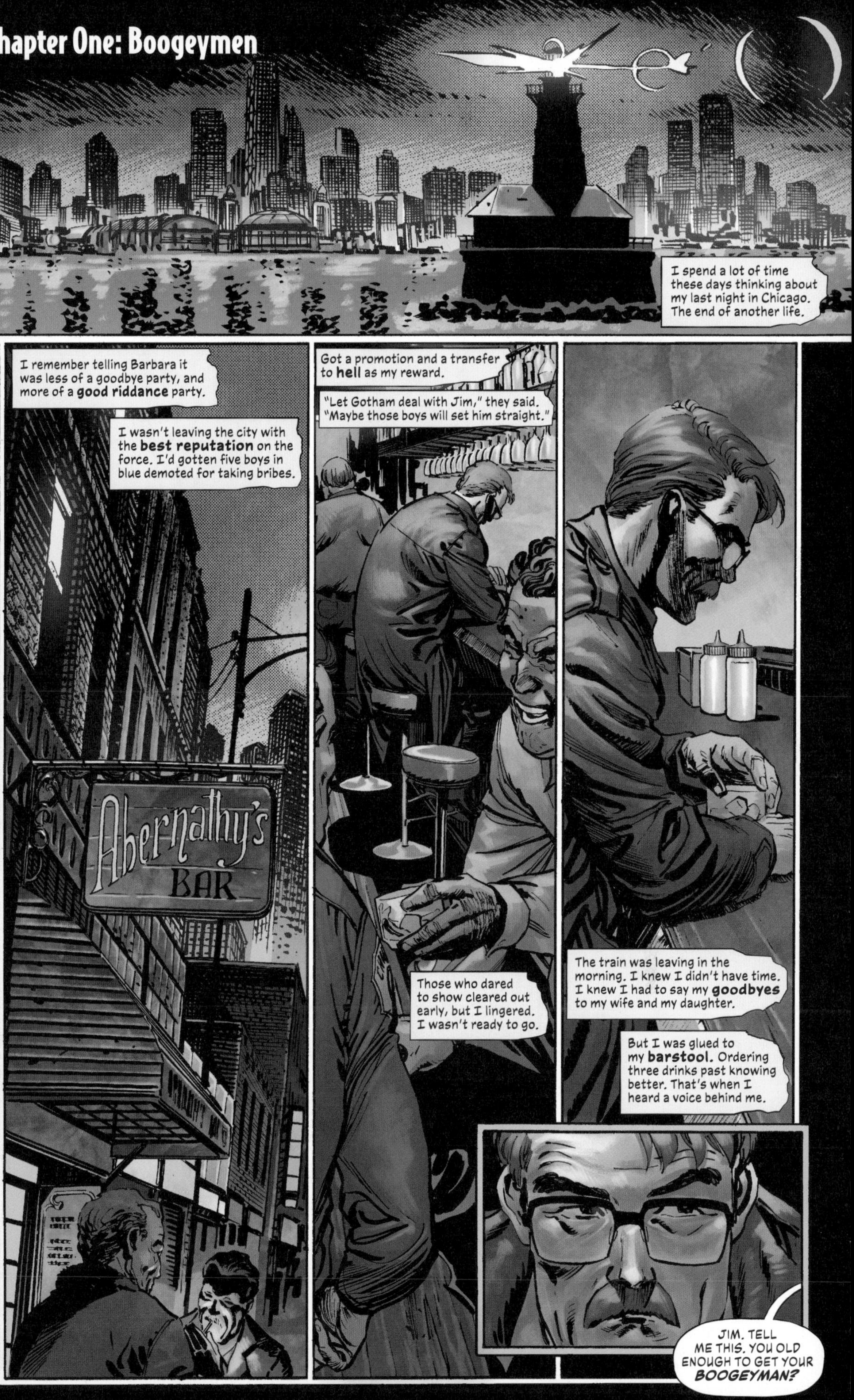
hapter One: Boogeymen
I spend a lot of time these days thinking about my last night in Chicago. The end of another life.
I remember telling Barbara it was less of a goodbye party, and more of a **good riddance** party.
I wasn't leaving the city with the **best reputation** on the force. I'd gotten five boys in blue demoted for taking bribes.
Abernathy's BAR
Got a promotion and a transfer to **hell** as my reward.
"Let Gotham deal with Jim," they said. "Maybe those boys will set him straight."
Those who dared to show cleared out early, but I lingered. I wasn't ready to go.
The train was leaving in the morning. I knew I didn't have time. I knew I had to say my **goodbyes** to my wife and my daughter.
But I was glued to my **barstool.** Ordering three drinks past knowing better. That's when I heard a voice behind me.
JIM. TELL ME THIS. YOU OLD ENOUGH TO GET YOUR ***BOOGEYMAN?***

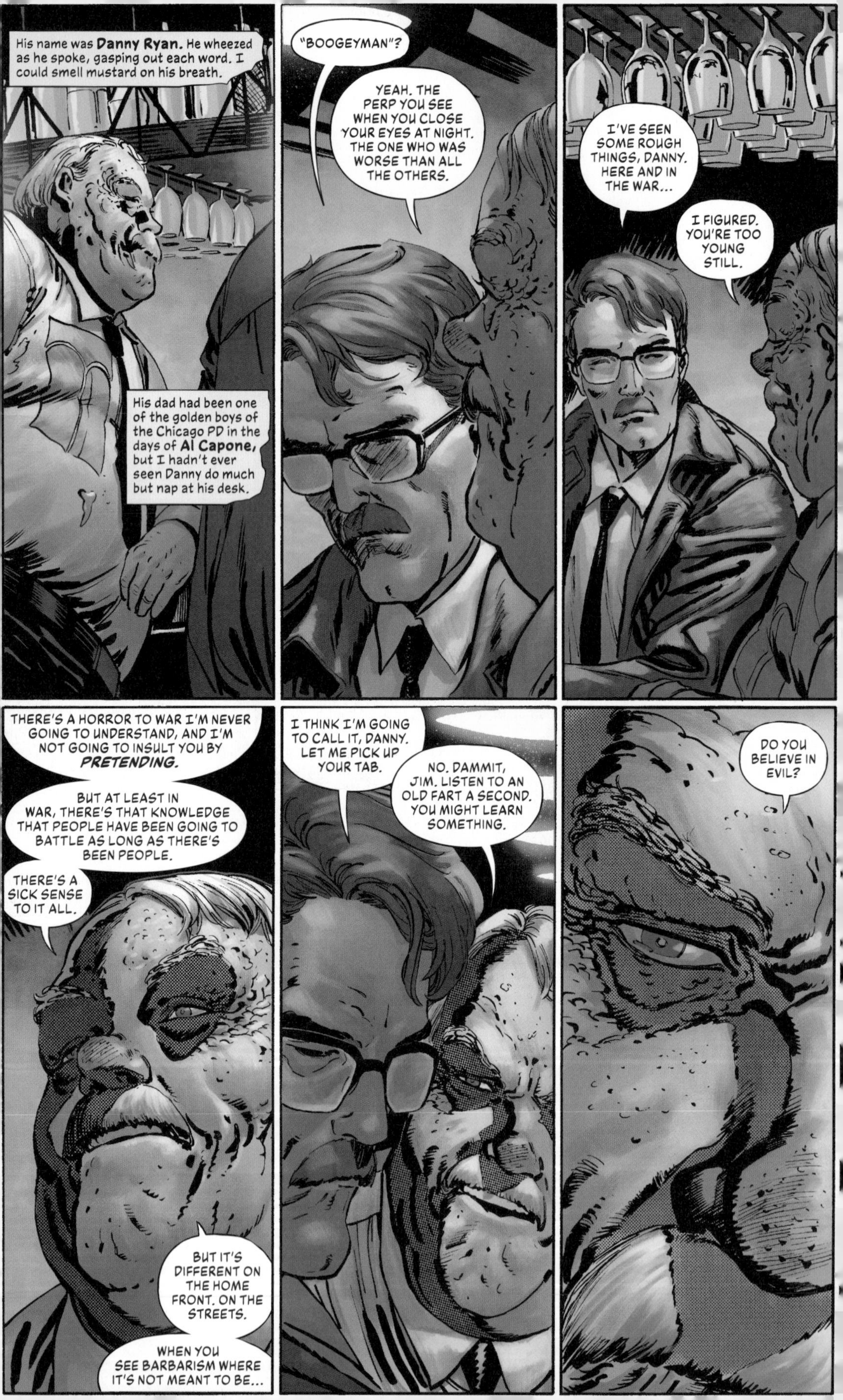
His name was Danny Ryan. He wheezed as he spoke, gasping out each word. I could smell mustard on his breath.
His dad had been one of the golden boys of the Chicago PD in the days of Al Capone, but I hadn't ever seen Danny do much but nap at his desk.
"BOOGEYMAN"?
YEAH. THE PERP YOU SEE WHEN YOU CLOSE YOUR EYES AT NIGHT. THE ONE WHO WAS WORSE THAN ALL THE OTHERS.
I'VE SEEN SOME ROUGH THINGS, DANNY. HERE AND IN THE WAR...
I FIGURED. YOU'RE TOO YOUNG STILL.
THERE'S A HORROR TO WAR I'M NEVER GOING TO UNDERSTAND, AND I'M NOT GOING TO INSULT YOU BY PRETENDING.
BUT AT LEAST IN WAR, THERE'S THAT KNOWLEDGE THAT PEOPLE HAVE BEEN GOING TO BATTLE AS LONG AS THERE'S BEEN PEOPLE.
THERE'S A SICK SENSE TO IT ALL.
BUT IT'S DIFFERENT ON THE HOME FRONT. ON THE STREETS.
WHEN YOU SEE BARBARISM WHERE IT'S NOT MEANT TO BE...
I THINK I'M GOING TO CALL IT, DANNY. LET ME PICK UP YOUR TAB.
NO. DAMMIT, JIM. LISTEN TO AN OLD FART A SECOND. YOU MIGHT LEARN SOMETHING.
DO YOU BELIEVE IN EVIL?

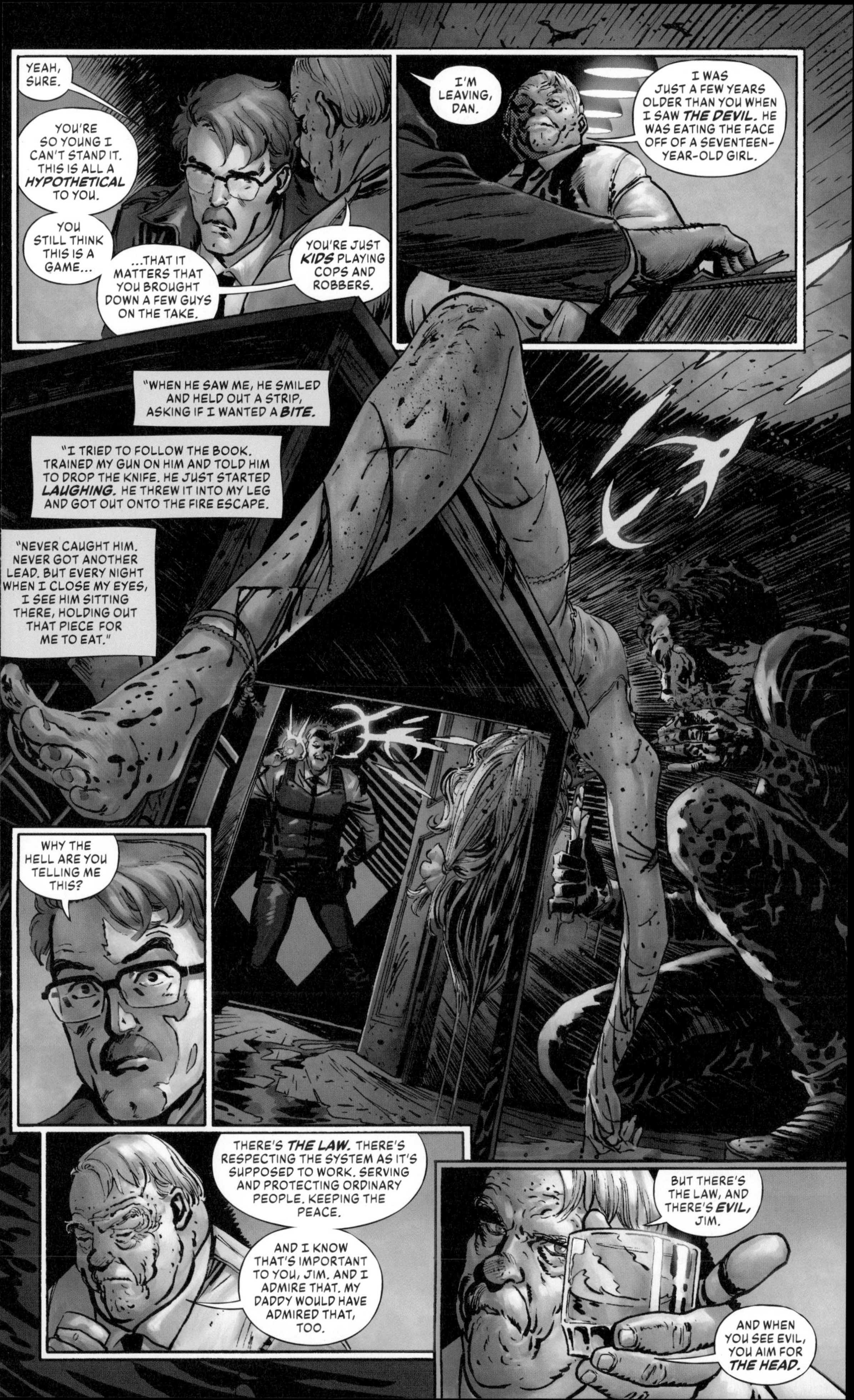
YEAH, SURE.
YOU'RE SO YOUNG I CAN'T STAND IT. THIS IS ALL A HYPOTHETICAL TO YOU.
YOU STILL THINK THIS IS A GAME...
...THAT IT MATTERS THAT YOU BROUGHT DOWN A FEW GUYS ON THE TAKE.
YOU'RE JUST KIDS PLAYING COPS AND ROBBERS.
I'M LEAVING, DAN.
I WAS JUST A FEW YEARS OLDER THAN YOU WHEN I SAW THE DEVIL. HE WAS EATING THE FACE OFF OF A SEVENTEEN-YEAR-OLD GIRL.
"WHEN HE SAW ME, HE SMILED AND HELD OUT A STRIP, ASKING IF I WANTED A BITE.
"I TRIED TO FOLLOW THE BOOK. TRAINED MY GUN ON HIM AND TOLD HIM TO DROP THE KNIFE. HE JUST STARTED LAUGHING. HE THREW IT INTO MY LEG AND GOT OUT ONTO THE FIRE ESCAPE.
"NEVER CAUGHT HIM. NEVER GOT ANOTHER LEAD. BUT EVERY NIGHT WHEN I CLOSE MY EYES, I SEE HIM SITTING THERE, HOLDING OUT THAT PIECE FOR ME TO EAT."
WHY THE HELL ARE YOU TELLING ME THIS?
THERE'S THE LAW. THERE'S RESPECTING THE SYSTEM AS IT'S SUPPOSED TO WORK. SERVING AND PROTECTING ORDINARY PEOPLE. KEEPING THE PEACE.
AND I KNOW THAT'S IMPORTANT TO YOU, JIM. AND I ADMIRE THAT. MY DADDY WOULD HAVE ADMIRED THAT, TOO.
BUT THERE'S THE LAW, AND THERE'S EVIL, JIM.
AND WHEN YOU SEE EVIL, YOU AIM FOR THE HEAD.

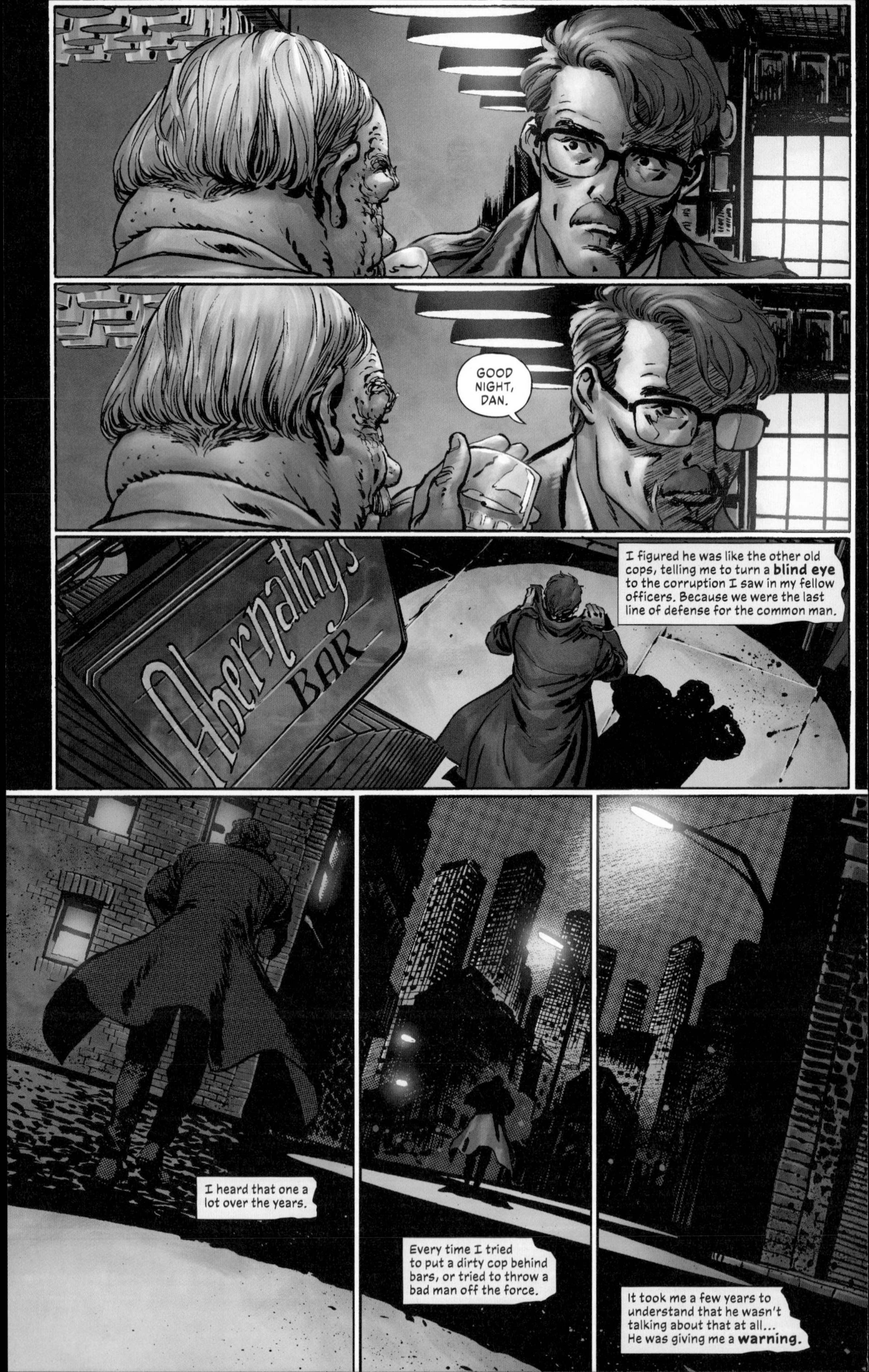
GOOD NIGHT, DAN.
Abernathy's BAR
I figured he was like the other old cops, telling me to turn a **blind eye** to the corruption I saw in my fellow officers. Because we were the last line of defense for the common man.
I heard that one a lot over the years.
Every time I tried to put a dirty cop behind bars, or tried to throw a bad man off the force.
It took me a few years to understand that he wasn't talking about that at all... He was giving me a **warning.**

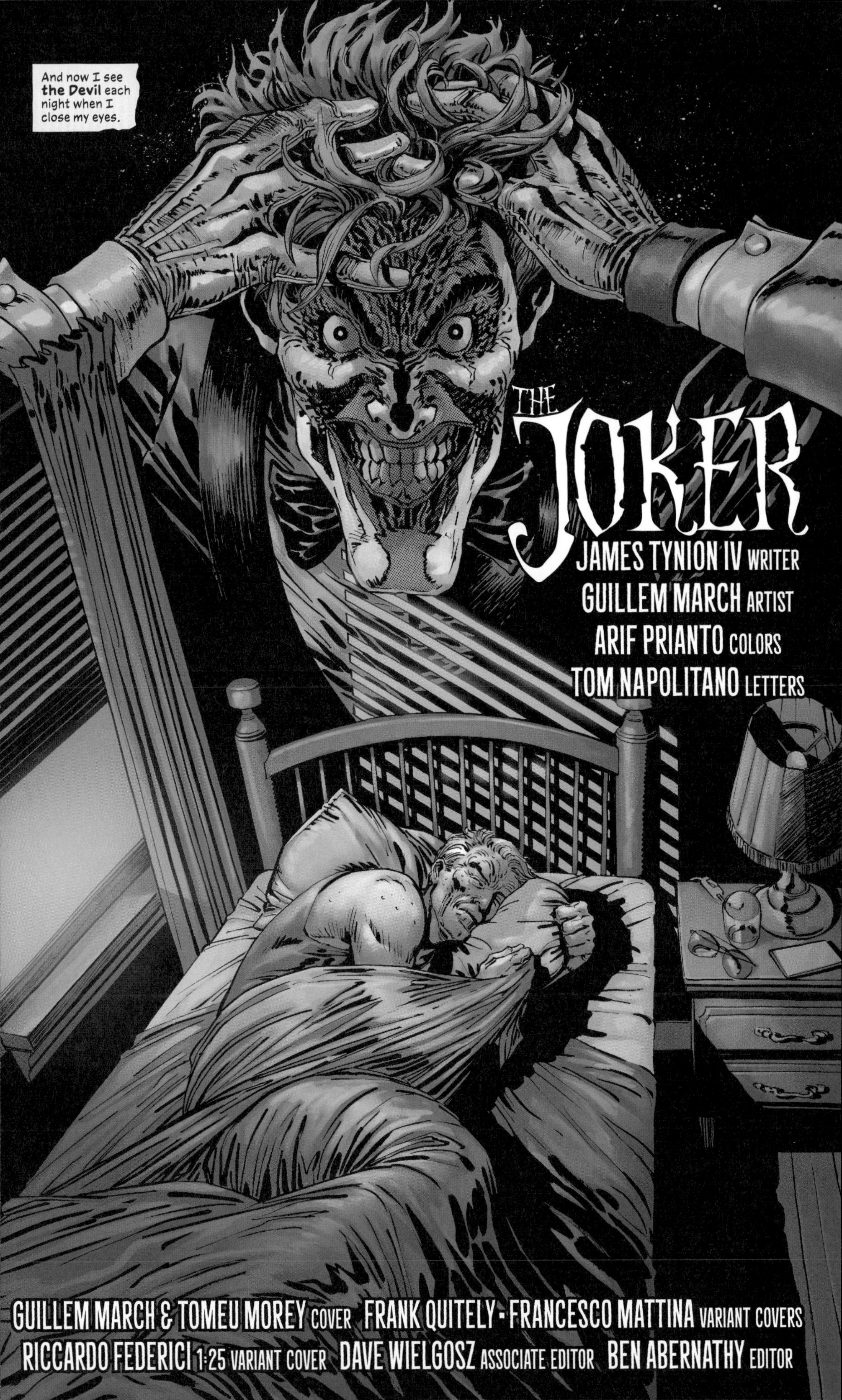
And now I see **the Devil** each night when I close my eyes.
THE JOKER
JAMES TYNION IV WRITER
GUILLEM MARCH ARTIST
ARIF PRIANTO COLORS
TOM NAPOLITANO LETTERS
GUILLEM MARCH & TOMEU MOREY COVER FRANK QUITELY • FRANCESCO MATTINA VARIANT COVERS
RICCARDO FEDERICI 1:25 VARIANT COVER DAVE WIELGOSZ ASSOCIATE EDITOR BEN ABERNATHY EDITOR

Chapter Two: Call It a Day

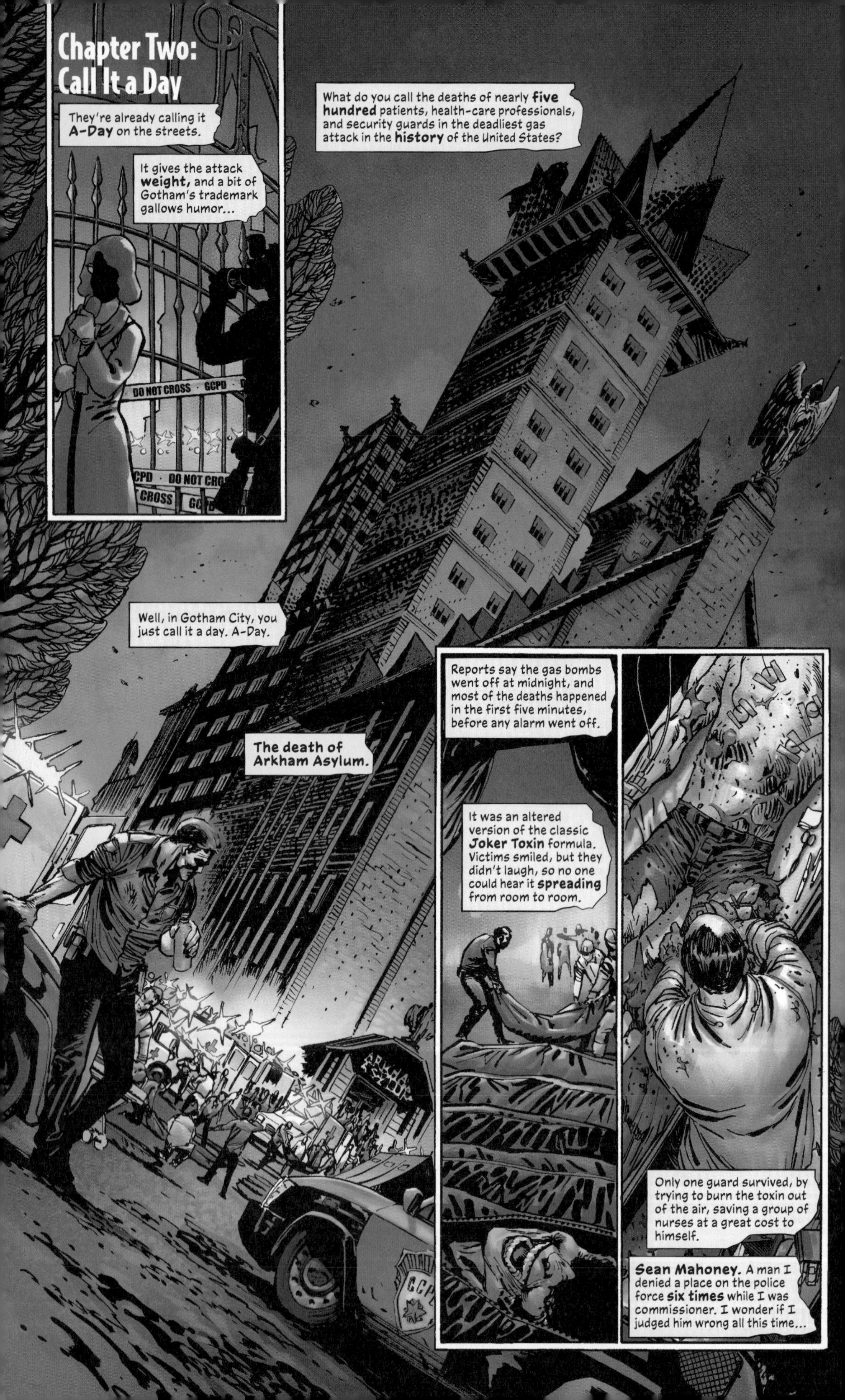

They're already calling it A-Day on the streets.
It gives the attack weight, and a bit of Gotham's trademark gallows humor...
DO NOT CROSS · GCPD
What do you call the deaths of nearly five hundred patients, health-care professionals, and security guards in the deadliest gas attack in the history of the United States?
Well, in Gotham City, you just call it a day. A-Day.
The death of Arkham Asylum.
Reports say the gas bombs went off at midnight, and most of the deaths happened in the first five minutes, before any alarm went off.
It was an altered version of the classic Joker Toxin formula. Victims smiled, but they didn't laugh, so no one could hear it spreading from room to room.
Only one guard survived, by trying to burn the toxin out of the air, saving a group of nurses at a great cost to himself.
Sean Mahoney. A man I denied a place on the police force six times while I was commissioner. I wonder if I judged him wrong all this time...

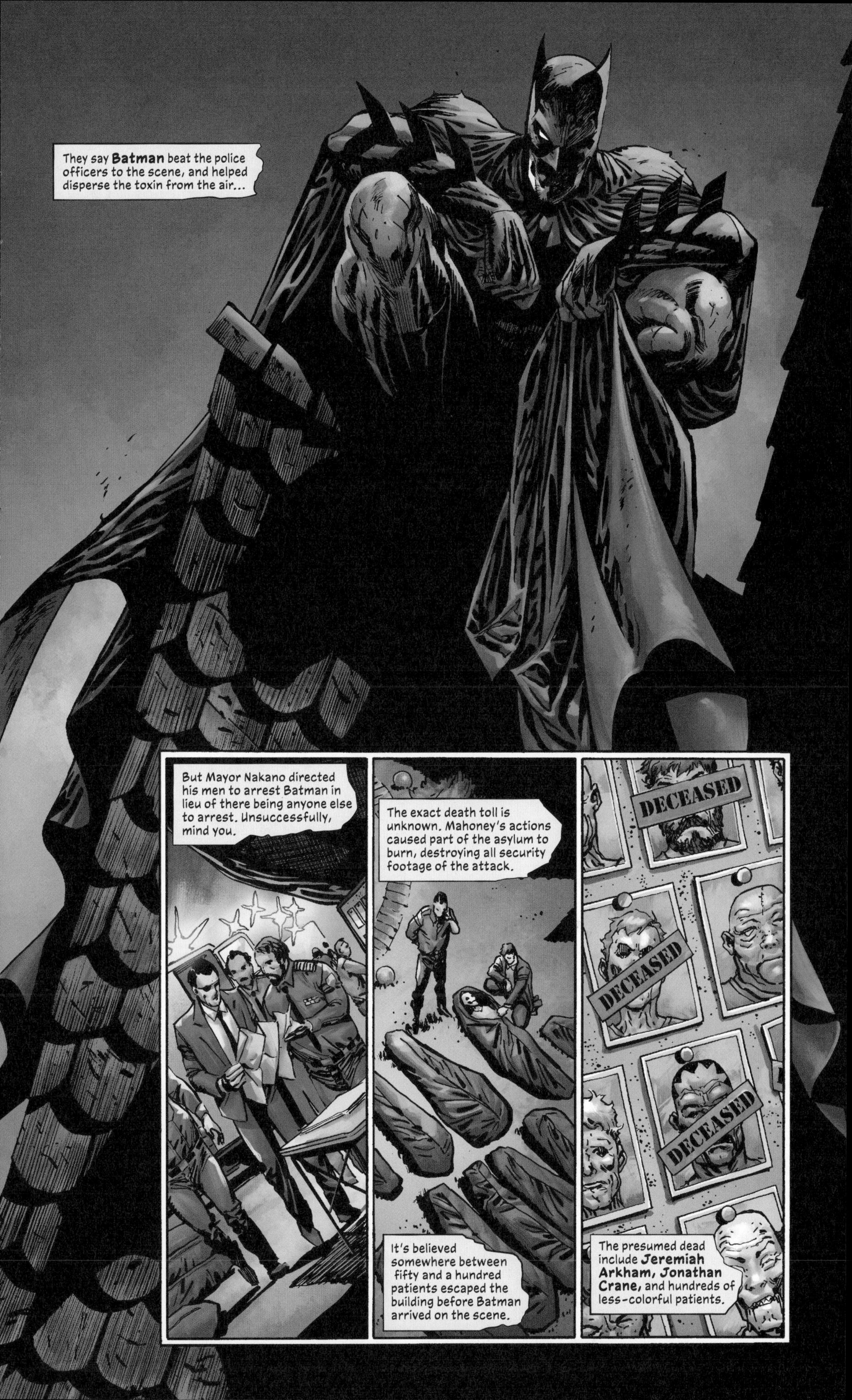
They say Batman beat the police officers to the scene, and helped disperse the toxin from the air...
But Mayor Nakano directed his men to arrest Batman in lieu of there being anyone else to arrest. Unsuccessfully, mind you.
The exact death toll is unknown. Mahoney's actions caused part of the asylum to burn, destroying all security footage of the attack.
It's believed somewhere between fifty and a hundred patients escaped the building before Batman arrived on the scene.
DECEASED
DECEASED
DECEASED
The presumed dead include Jeremiah Arkham, Jonathan Crane, and hundreds of less-colorful patients.

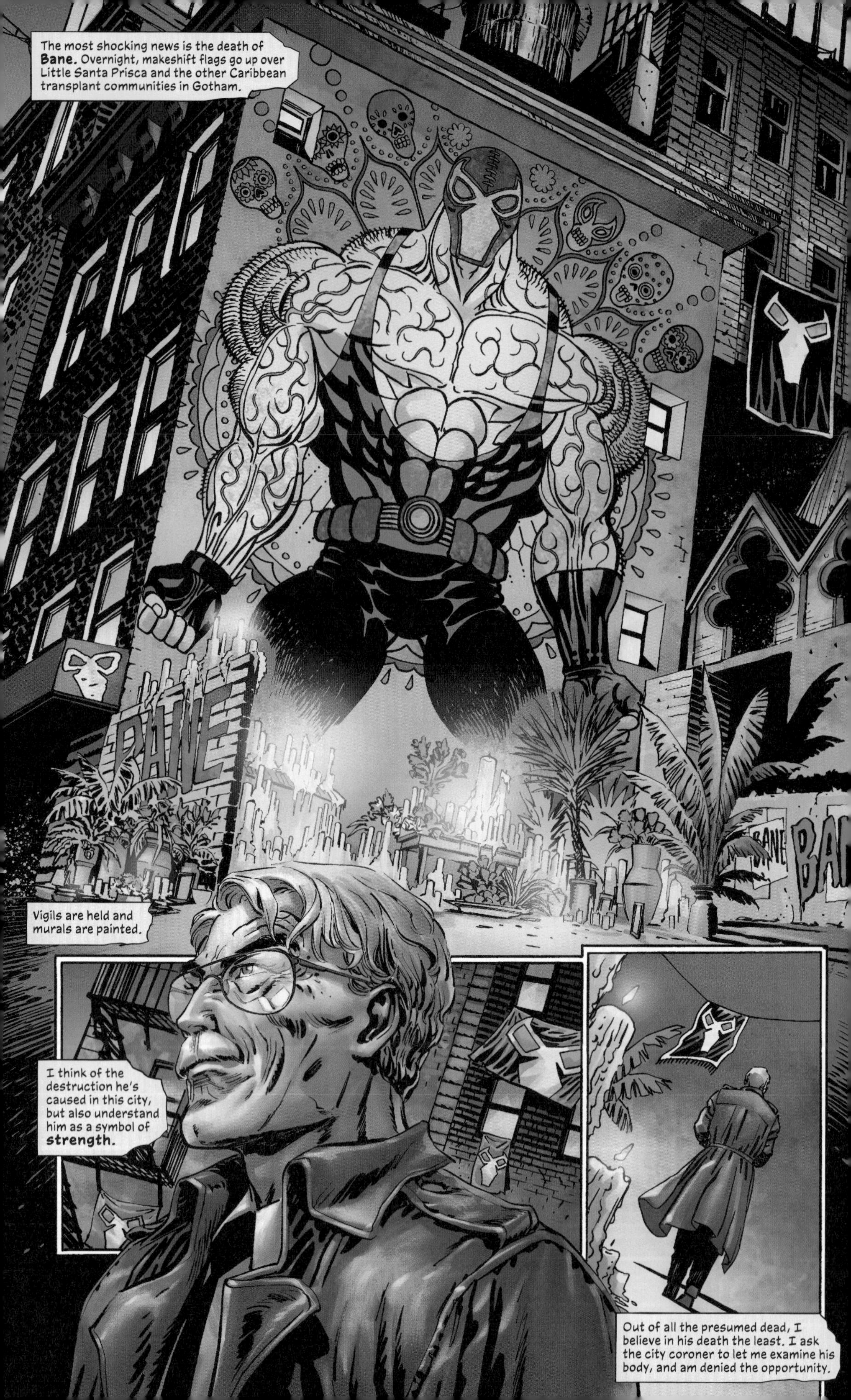
The most shocking news is the death of **Bane.** Overnight, makeshift flags go up over Little Santa Prisca and the other Caribbean transplant communities in Gotham.
BANE
BANE
Vigils are held and murals are painted.
I think of the destruction he's caused in this city, but also understand him as a symbol of **strength.**
Out of all the presumed dead, I believe in his death the least. I ask the city coroner to let me examine his body, and am denied the opportunity.

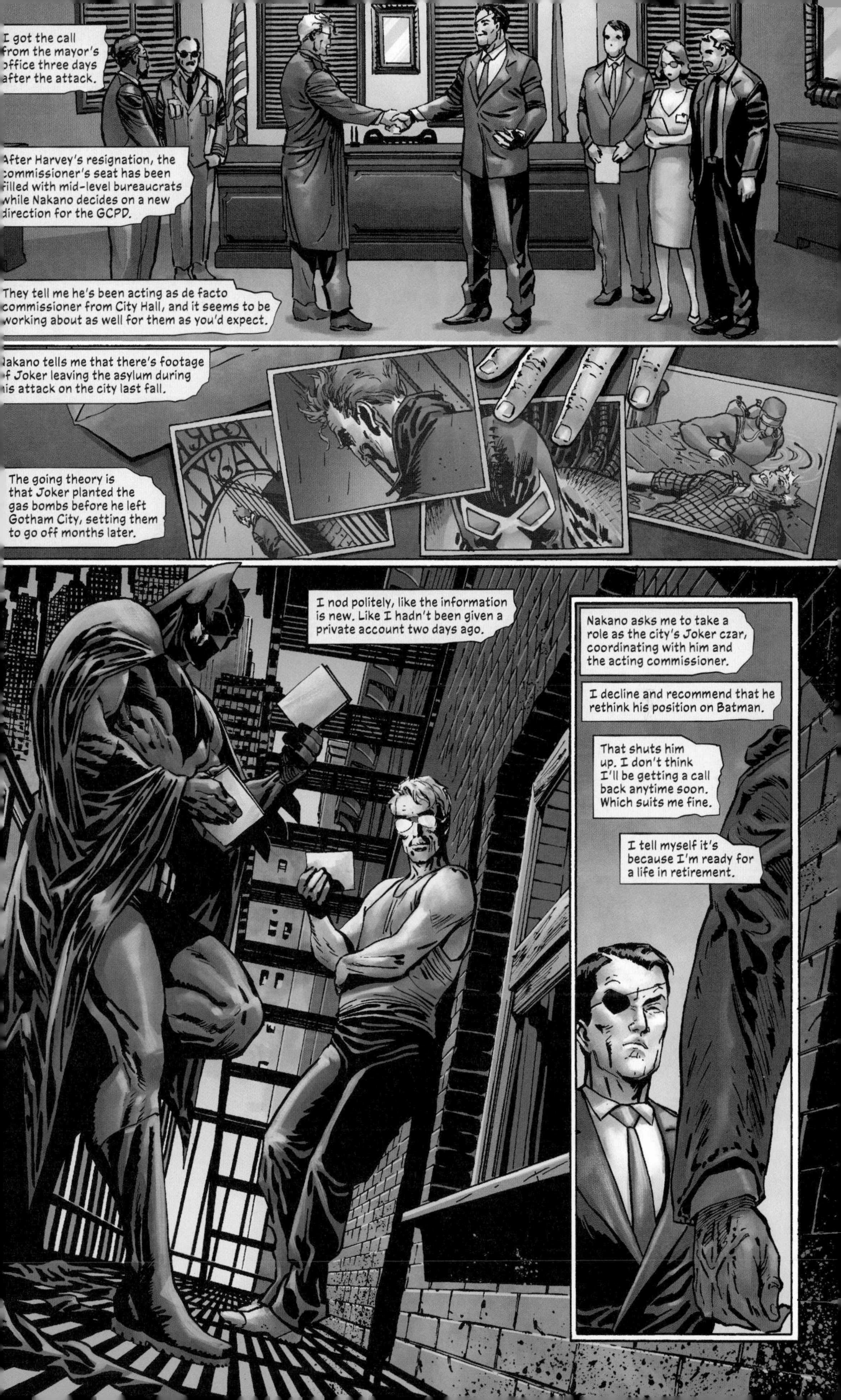
I got the call from the mayor's office three days after the attack.
After Harvey's resignation, the commissioner's seat has been filled with mid-level bureaucrats while Nakano decides on a new direction for the GCPD.
They tell me he's been acting as de facto commissioner from City Hall, and it seems to be working about as well for them as you'd expect.
Nakano tells me that there's footage of Joker leaving the asylum during his attack on the city last fall.
The going theory is that Joker planted the gas bombs before he left Gotham City, setting them to go off months later.
I nod politely, like the information is new. Like I hadn't been given a private account two days ago.
Nakano asks me to take a role as the city's Joker czar, coordinating with him and the acting commissioner.
I decline and recommend that he rethink his position on Batman.
That shuts him up. I don't think I'll be getting a call back anytime soon. Which suits me fine.
I tell myself it's because I'm ready for a life in retirement.

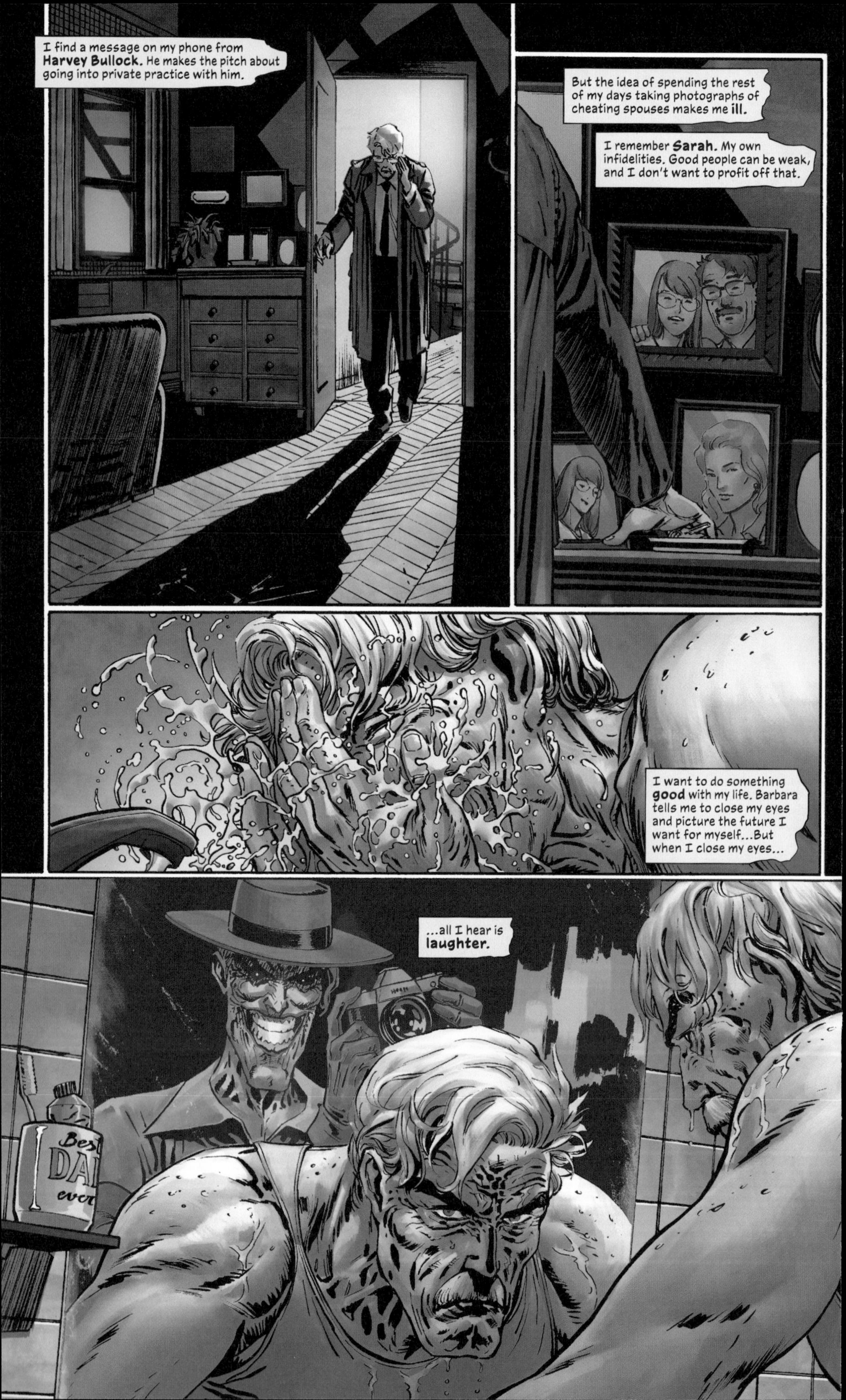
I find a message on my phone from **Harvey Bullock.** He makes the pitch about going into private practice with him.
But the idea of spending the rest of my days taking photographs of cheating spouses makes me **ill.**
I remember **Sarah.** My own infidelities. Good people can be weak, and I don't want to profit off that.
I want to do something **good** with my life. Barbara tells me to close my eyes and picture the future I want for myself...But when I close my eyes...
...all I hear is **laughter.**

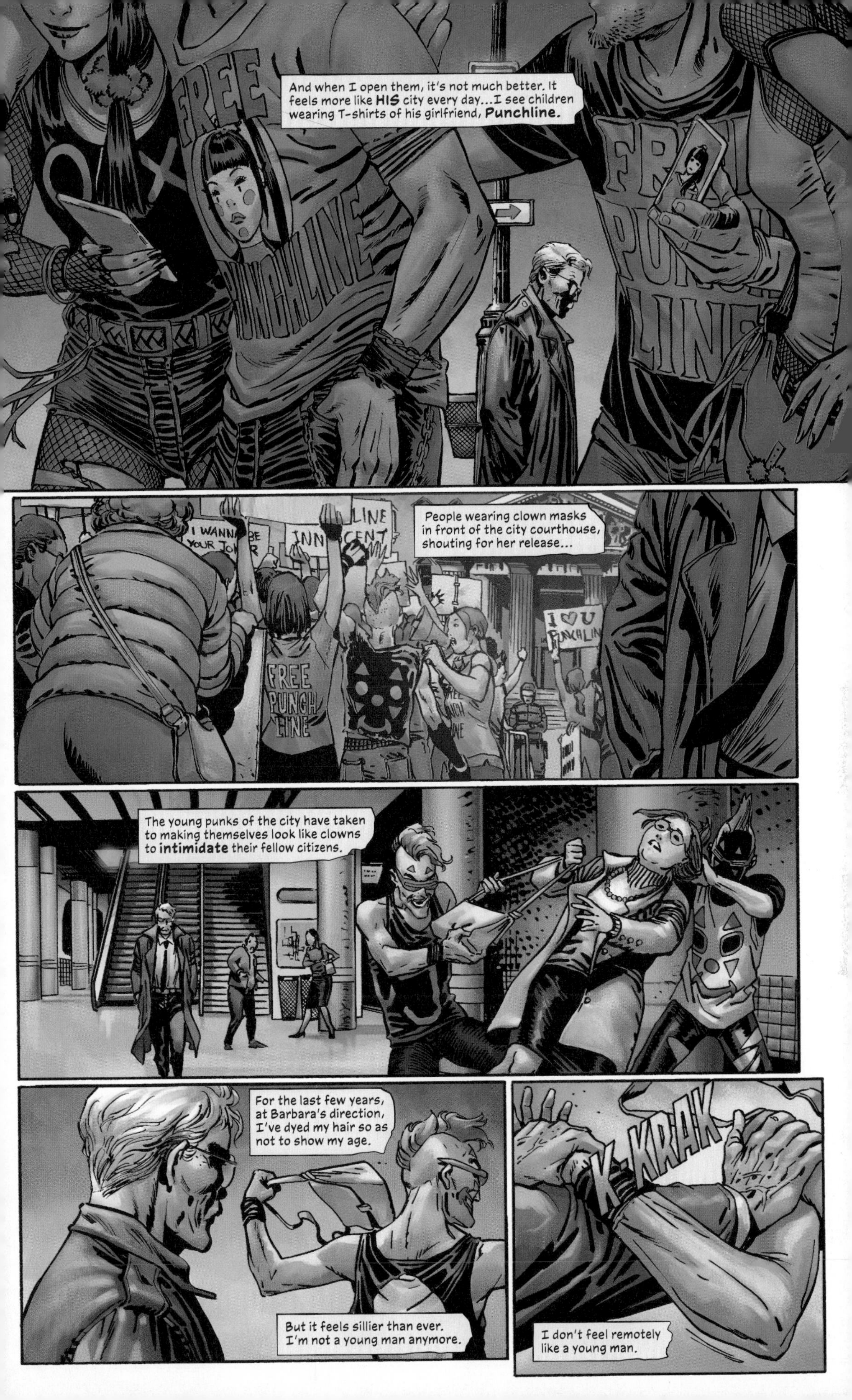

FREE
PUNCHLINE
And when I open them, it's not much better. It feels more like HIS city every day... I see children wearing T-shirts of his girlfriend, Punchline.
I WANNA BE YOUR JOKER
LINE
INNOCENT
People wearing clown masks in front of the city courthouse, shouting for her release...
I ♥ U PUNCHLINE
FREE PUNCH LINE
The young punks of the city have taken to making themselves look like clowns to intimidate their fellow citizens.
For the last few years, at Barbara's direction, I've dyed my hair so as not to show my age.
But it feels sillier than ever. I'm not a young man anymore.
K-KRAK
I don't feel remotely like a young man.

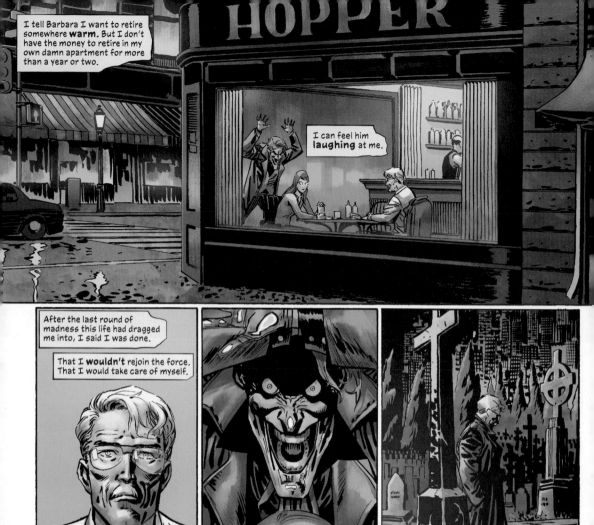

I tell Barbara I want to retire somewhere **warm**. But I don't have the money to retire in my own damn apartment for more than a year or two.

I can feel him **laughing** at me.

After the last round of madness this life had dragged me into, I said I was done.

That I **wouldn't** rejoin the force. That I would take care of myself.

I remember when I heard the news of a new Joker attack. But I told myself it was in everyone else's hands now.

I let myself go back to sleep.

What he did to Barbara nearly broke me, but she lived, and learned to thrive...It's knowing that he played a hand in tipping my son over the line one last time...

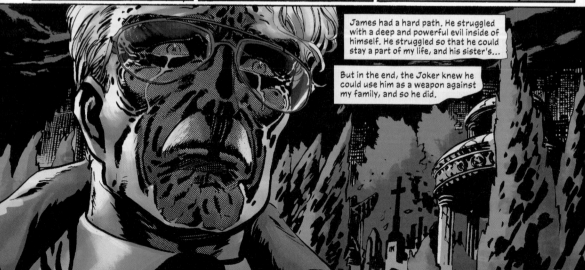

James had a hard path. He struggled with a deep and powerful evil inside of himself. He struggled so that he could stay a part of my life, and his sister's...

But in the end, the Joker knew he could use him as a weapon against my family, and so he did.

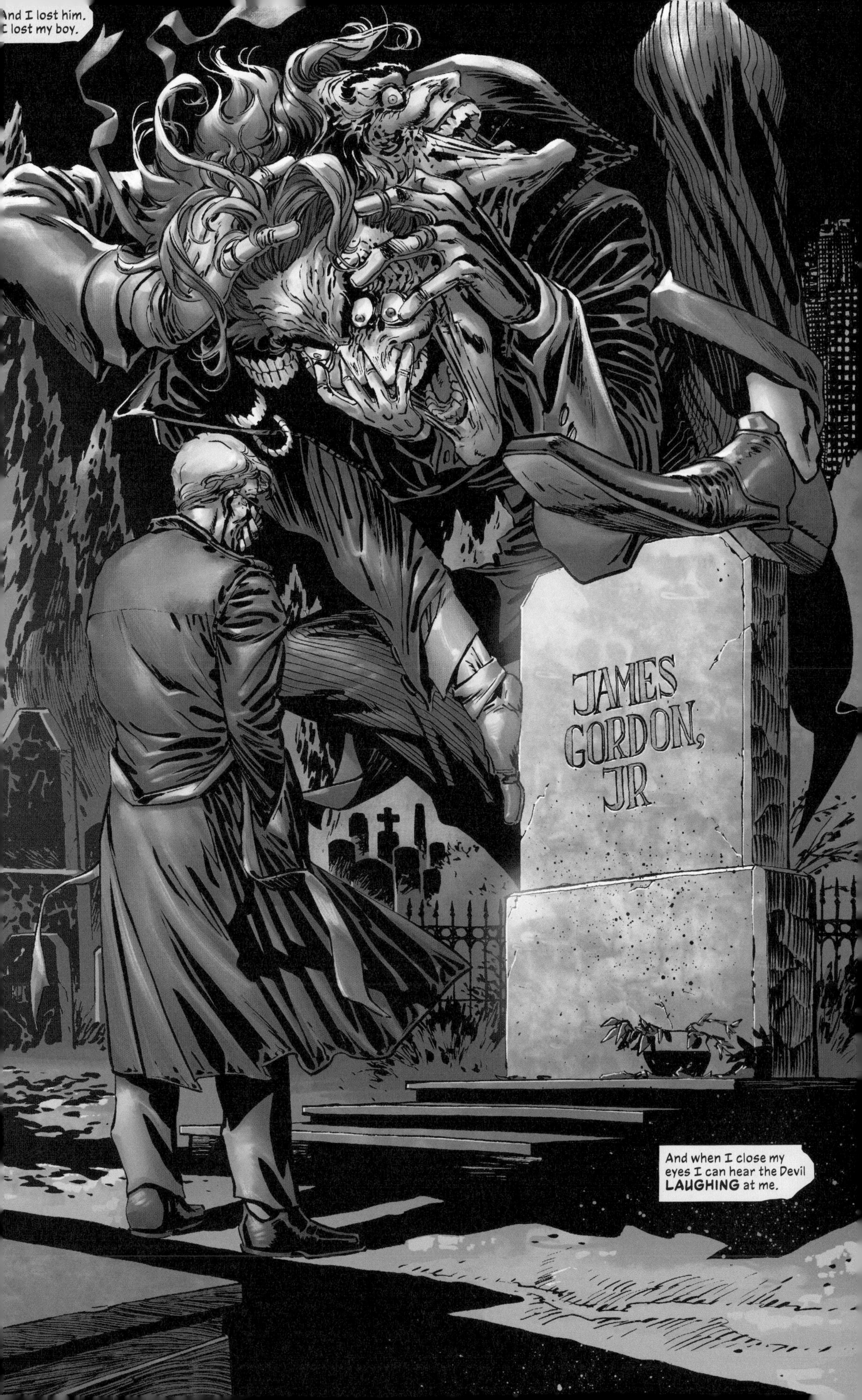
And I lost him. I lost my boy.
JAMES GORDON, JR
And when I close my eyes I can hear the Devil **LAUGHING** at me.

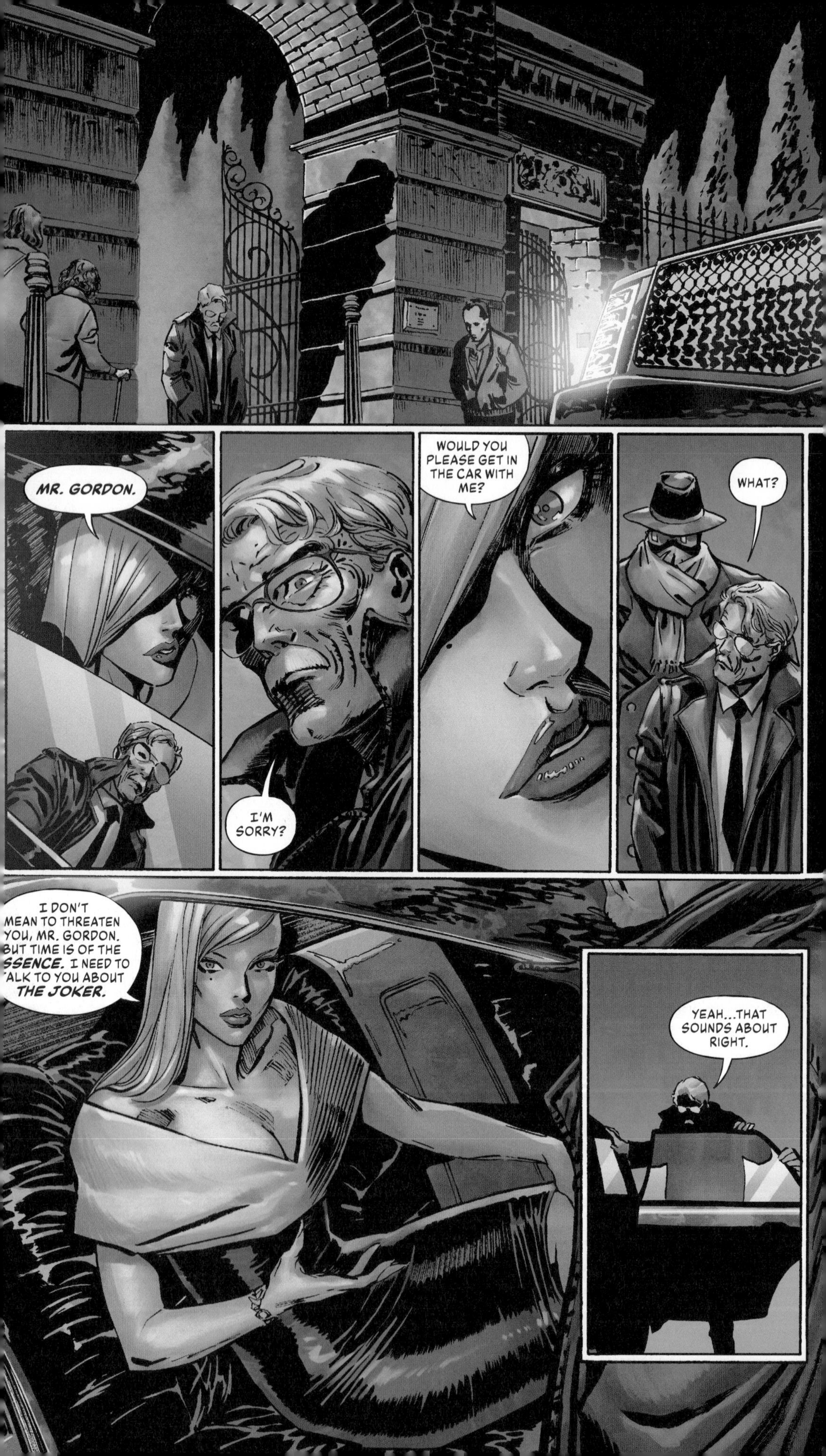

MR. GORDON.
I'M SORRY?
WOULD YOU PLEASE GET IN THE CAR WITH ME?
WHAT?
I DON'T MEAN TO THREATEN YOU, MR. GORDON. BUT TIME IS OF THE SSENCE. I NEED TO ALK TO YOU ABOUT THE JOKER.
YEAH...THAT SOUNDS ABOUT RIGHT.

Chapter Three: All That Glitters

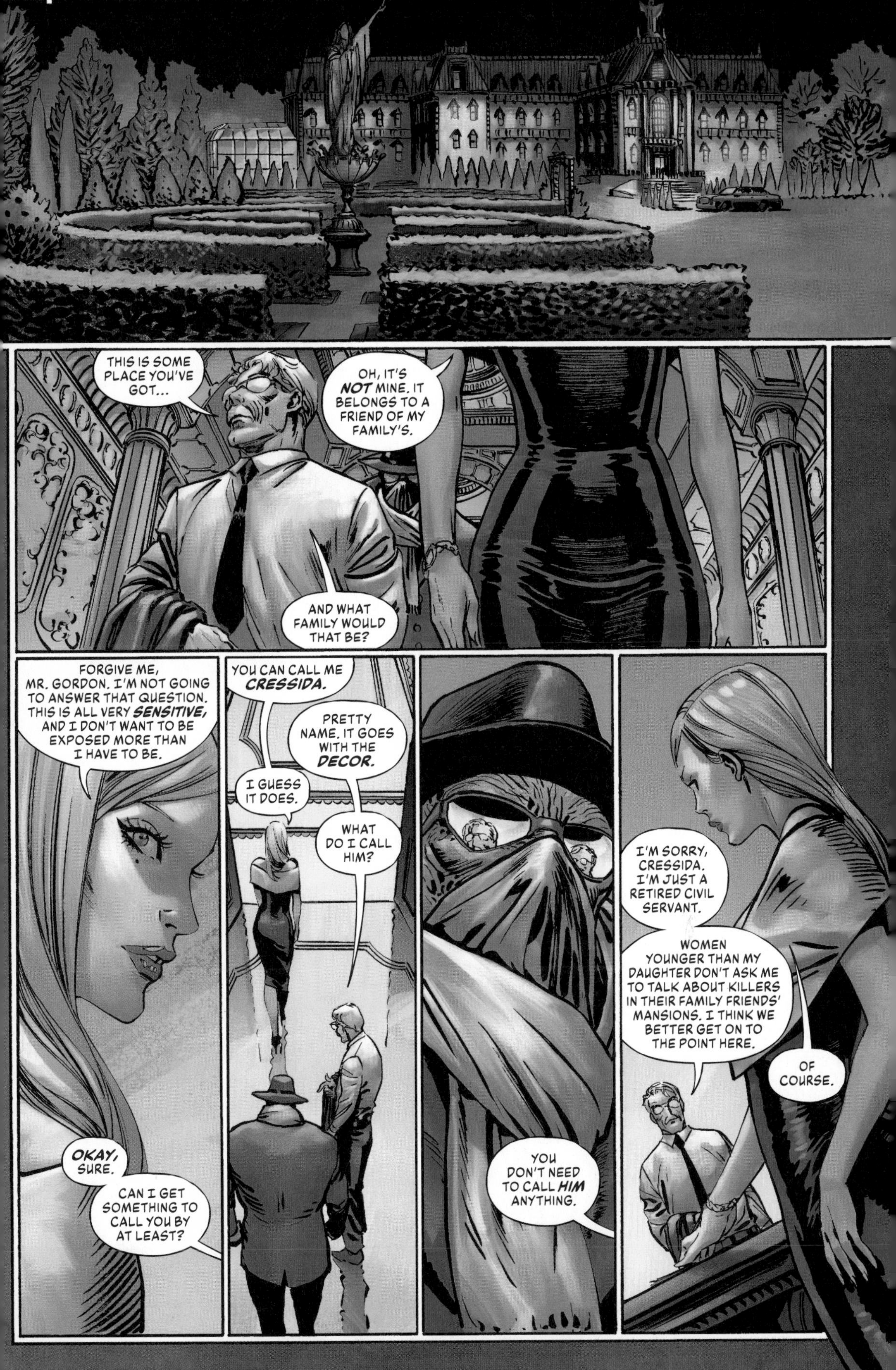
THIS IS SOME PLACE YOU'VE GOT...
OH, IT'S NOT MINE. IT BELONGS TO A FRIEND OF MY FAMILY'S.
AND WHAT FAMILY WOULD THAT BE?
FORGIVE ME, MR. GORDON. I'M NOT GOING TO ANSWER THAT QUESTION. THIS IS ALL VERY SENSITIVE, AND I DON'T WANT TO BE EXPOSED MORE THAN I HAVE TO BE.
OKAY, SURE.
CAN I GET SOMETHING TO CALL YOU BY AT LEAST?
YOU CAN CALL ME CRESSIDA.
PRETTY NAME. IT GOES WITH THE DECOR.
I GUESS IT DOES.
WHAT DO I CALL HIM?
YOU DON'T NEED TO CALL HIM ANYTHING.
I'M SORRY, CRESSIDA. I'M JUST A RETIRED CIVIL SERVANT.
WOMEN YOUNGER THAN MY DAUGHTER DON'T ASK ME TO TALK ABOUT KILLERS IN THEIR FAMILY FRIENDS' MANSIONS. I THINK WE BETTER GET ON TO THE POINT HERE.
OF COURSE.

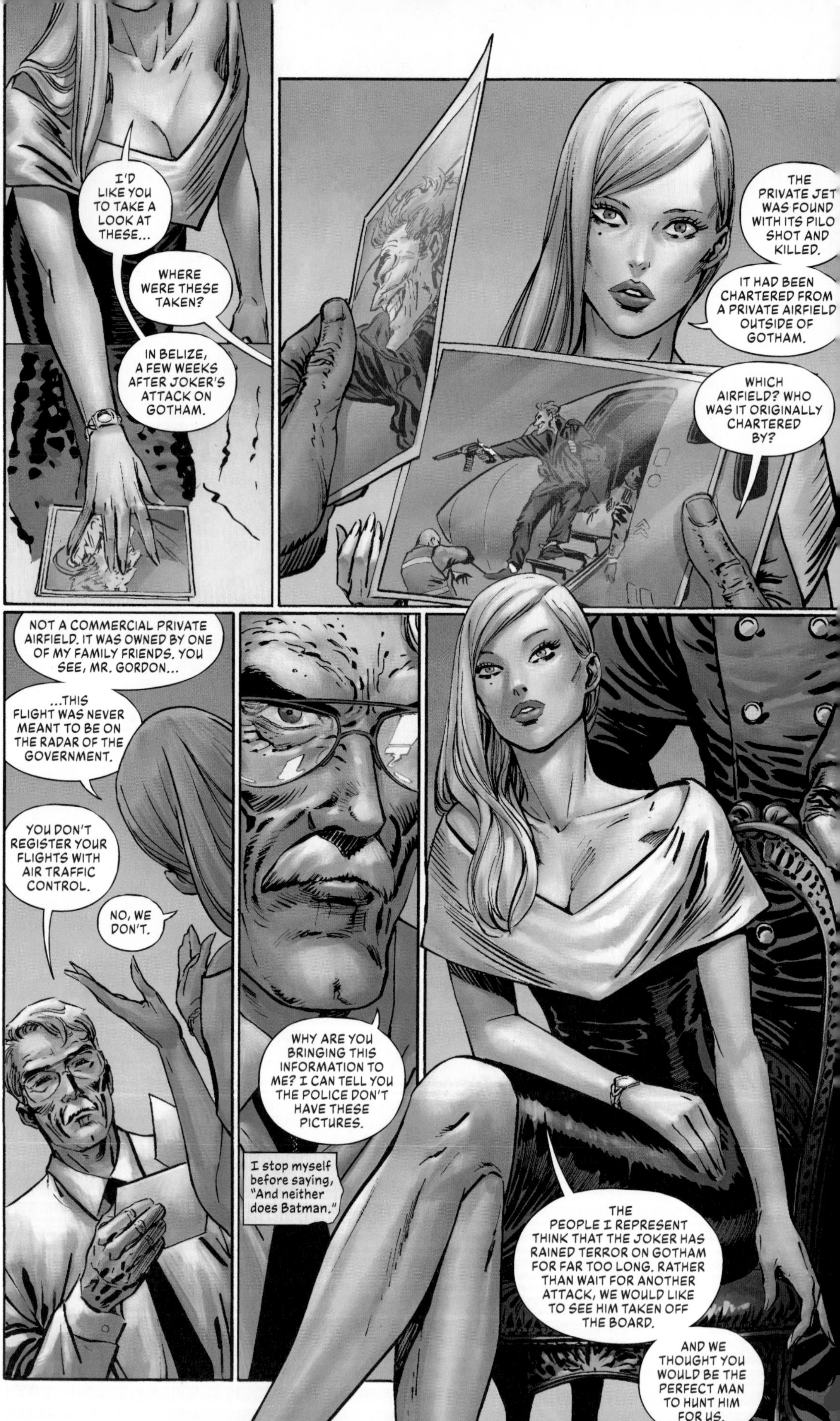
I'D LIKE YOU TO TAKE A LOOK AT THESE...
WHERE WERE THESE TAKEN?
IN BELIZE, A FEW WEEKS AFTER JOKER'S ATTACK ON GOTHAM.
THE PRIVATE JET WAS FOUND WITH ITS PILO SHOT AND KILLED.
IT HAD BEEN CHARTERED FROM A PRIVATE AIRFIELD OUTSIDE OF GOTHAM.
WHICH AIRFIELD? WHO WAS IT ORIGINALLY CHARTERED BY?
NOT A COMMERCIAL PRIVATE AIRFIELD. IT WAS OWNED BY ONE OF MY FAMILY FRIENDS. YOU SEE, MR. GORDON...
...THIS FLIGHT WAS NEVER MEANT TO BE ON THE RADAR OF THE GOVERNMENT.
YOU DON'T REGISTER YOUR FLIGHTS WITH AIR TRAFFIC CONTROL.
NO, WE DON'T.
WHY ARE YOU BRINGING THIS INFORMATION TO ME? I CAN TELL YOU THE POLICE DON'T HAVE THESE PICTURES.
I stop myself before saying, "And neither does Batman."
THE PEOPLE I REPRESENT THINK THAT THE JOKER HAS RAINED TERROR ON GOTHAM FOR FAR TOO LONG. RATHER THAN WAIT FOR ANOTHER ATTACK, WE WOULD LIKE TO SEE HIM TAKEN OFF THE BOARD.
AND WE THOUGHT YOU WOULD BE THE PERFECT MAN TO HUNT HIM FOR US.

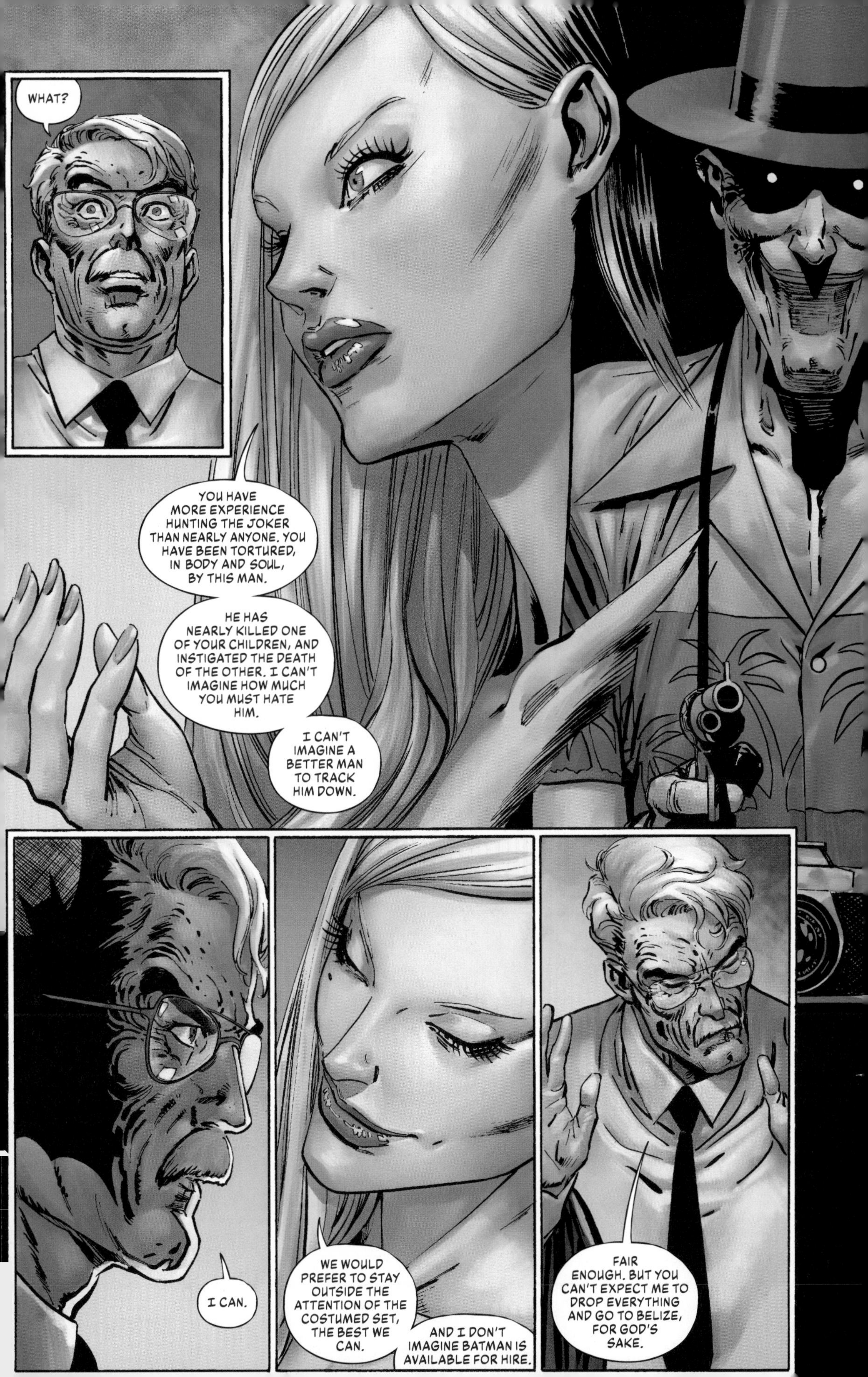
WHAT?
YOU HAVE MORE EXPERIENCE HUNTING THE JOKER THAN NEARLY ANYONE. YOU HAVE BEEN TORTURED, IN BODY AND SOUL, BY THIS MAN.
HE HAS NEARLY KILLED ONE OF YOUR CHILDREN, AND INSTIGATED THE DEATH OF THE OTHER. I CAN'T IMAGINE HOW MUCH YOU MUST HATE HIM.
I CAN'T IMAGINE A BETTER MAN TO TRACK HIM DOWN.
I CAN.
WE WOULD PREFER TO STAY OUTSIDE THE ATTENTION OF THE COSTUMED SET, THE BEST WE CAN.
AND I DON'T IMAGINE BATMAN IS AVAILABLE FOR HIRE.
FAIR ENOUGH. BUT YOU CAN'T EXPECT ME TO DROP EVERYTHING AND GO TO BELIZE, FOR GOD'S SAKE.

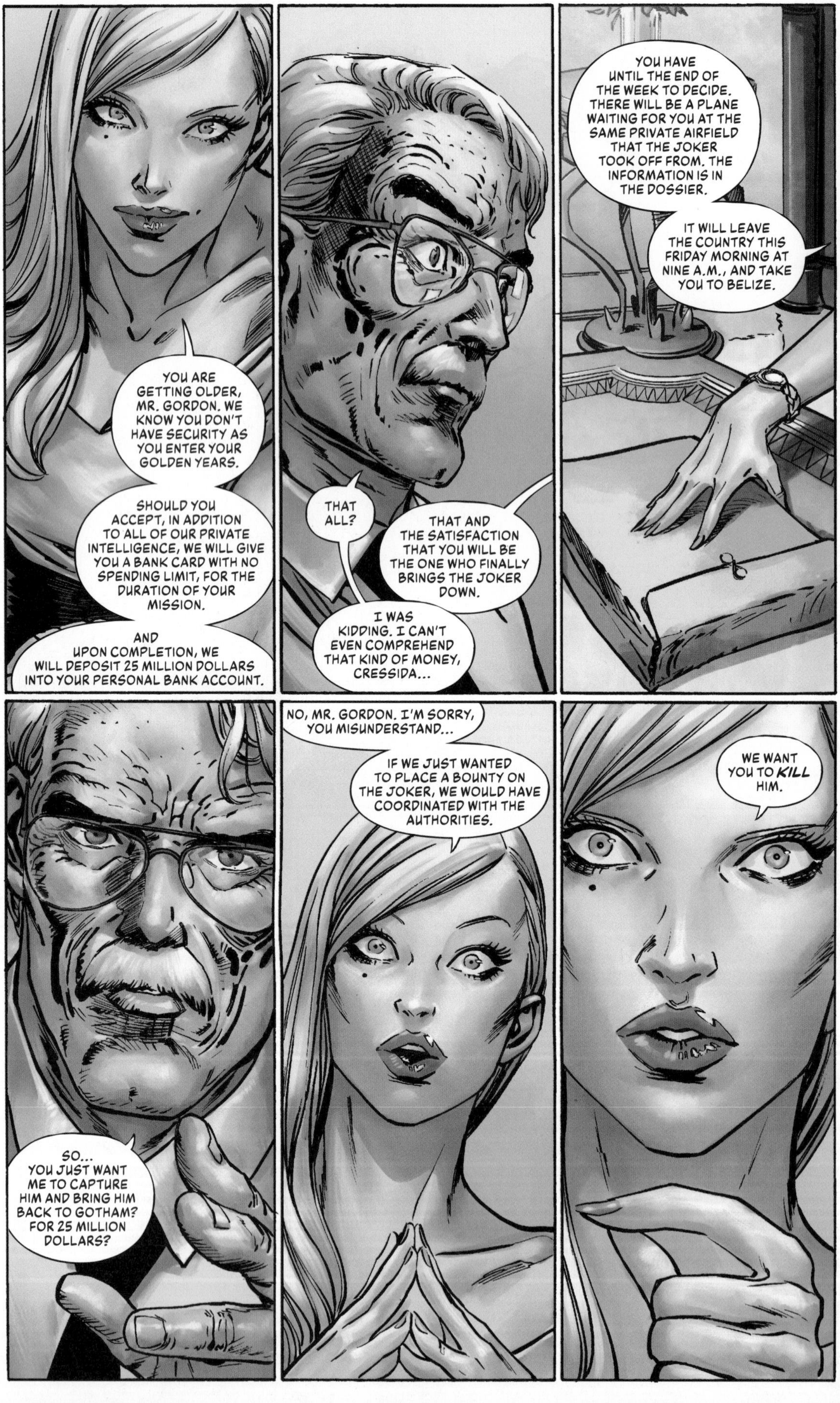
YOU ARE GETTING OLDER, MR. GORDON. WE KNOW YOU DON'T HAVE SECURITY AS YOU ENTER YOUR GOLDEN YEARS.
SHOULD YOU ACCEPT, IN ADDITION TO ALL OF OUR PRIVATE INTELLIGENCE, WE WILL GIVE YOU A BANK CARD WITH NO SPENDING LIMIT, FOR THE DURATION OF YOUR MISSION.
AND UPON COMPLETION, WE WILL DEPOSIT 25 MILLION DOLLARS INTO YOUR PERSONAL BANK ACCOUNT.
THAT ALL?
THAT AND THE SATISFACTION THAT YOU WILL BE THE ONE WHO FINALLY BRINGS THE JOKER DOWN.
I WAS KIDDING. I CAN'T EVEN COMPREHEND THAT KIND OF MONEY, CRESSIDA...
YOU HAVE UNTIL THE END OF THE WEEK TO DECIDE. THERE WILL BE A PLANE WAITING FOR YOU AT THE SAME PRIVATE AIRFIELD THAT THE JOKER TOOK OFF FROM. THE INFORMATION IS IN THE DOSSIER.
IT WILL LEAVE THE COUNTRY THIS FRIDAY MORNING AT NINE A.M., AND TAKE YOU TO BELIZE.
SO... YOU JUST WANT ME TO CAPTURE HIM AND BRING HIM BACK TO GOTHAM? FOR 25 MILLION DOLLARS?
NO, MR. GORDON. I'M SORRY, YOU MISUNDERSTAND...
IF WE JUST WANTED TO PLACE A BOUNTY ON THE JOKER, WE WOULD HAVE COORDINATED WITH THE AUTHORITIES.
WE WANT YOU TO KILL HIM.

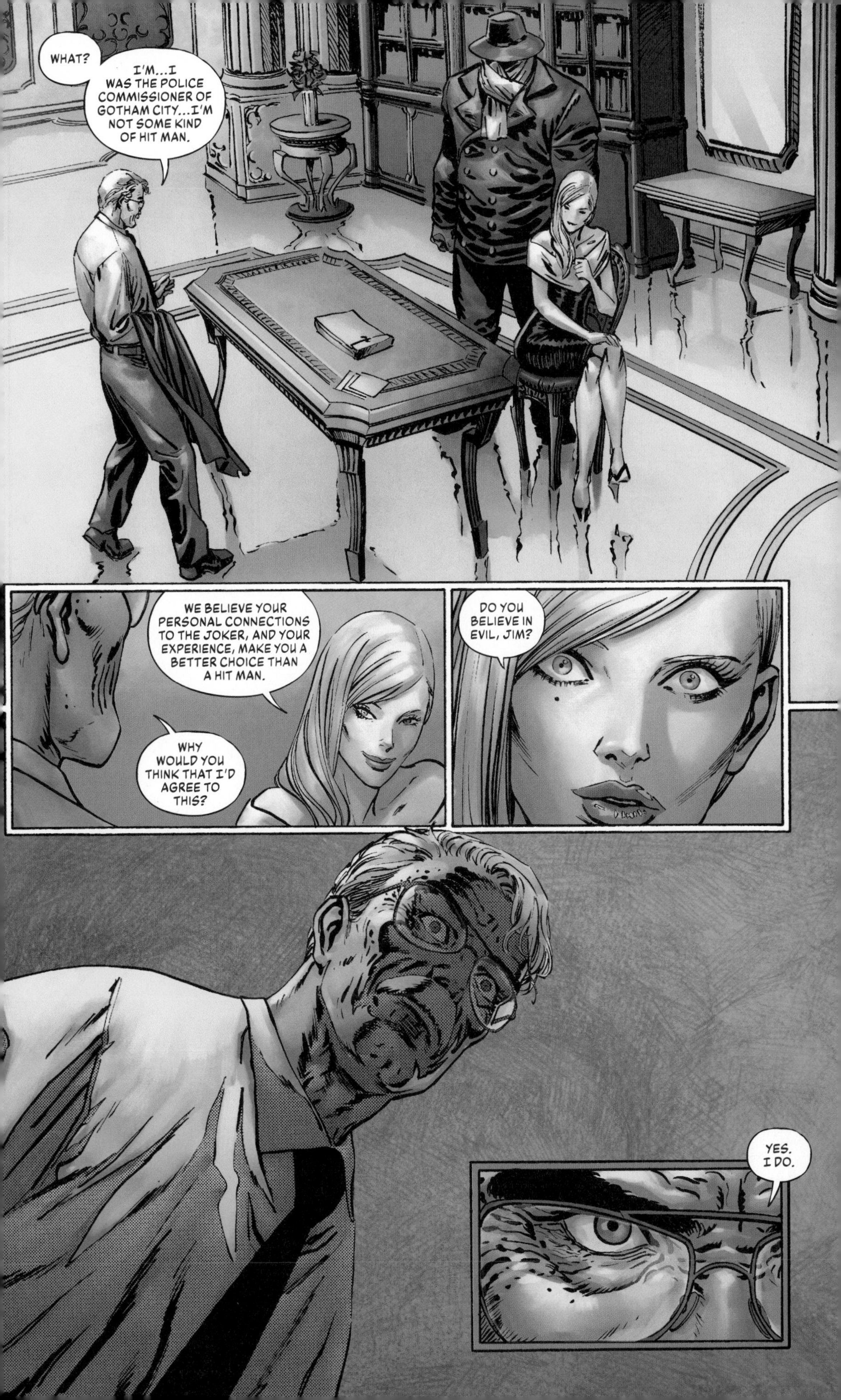
WHAT?
I'M...I WAS THE POLICE COMMISSIONER OF GOTHAM CITY...I'M NOT SOME KIND OF HIT MAN.
WE BELIEVE YOUR PERSONAL CONNECTIONS TO THE JOKER, AND YOUR EXPERIENCE, MAKE YOU A BETTER CHOICE THAN A HIT MAN.
WHY WOULD YOU THINK THAT I'D AGREE TO THIS?
DO YOU BELIEVE IN EVIL, JIM?
YES. I DO.

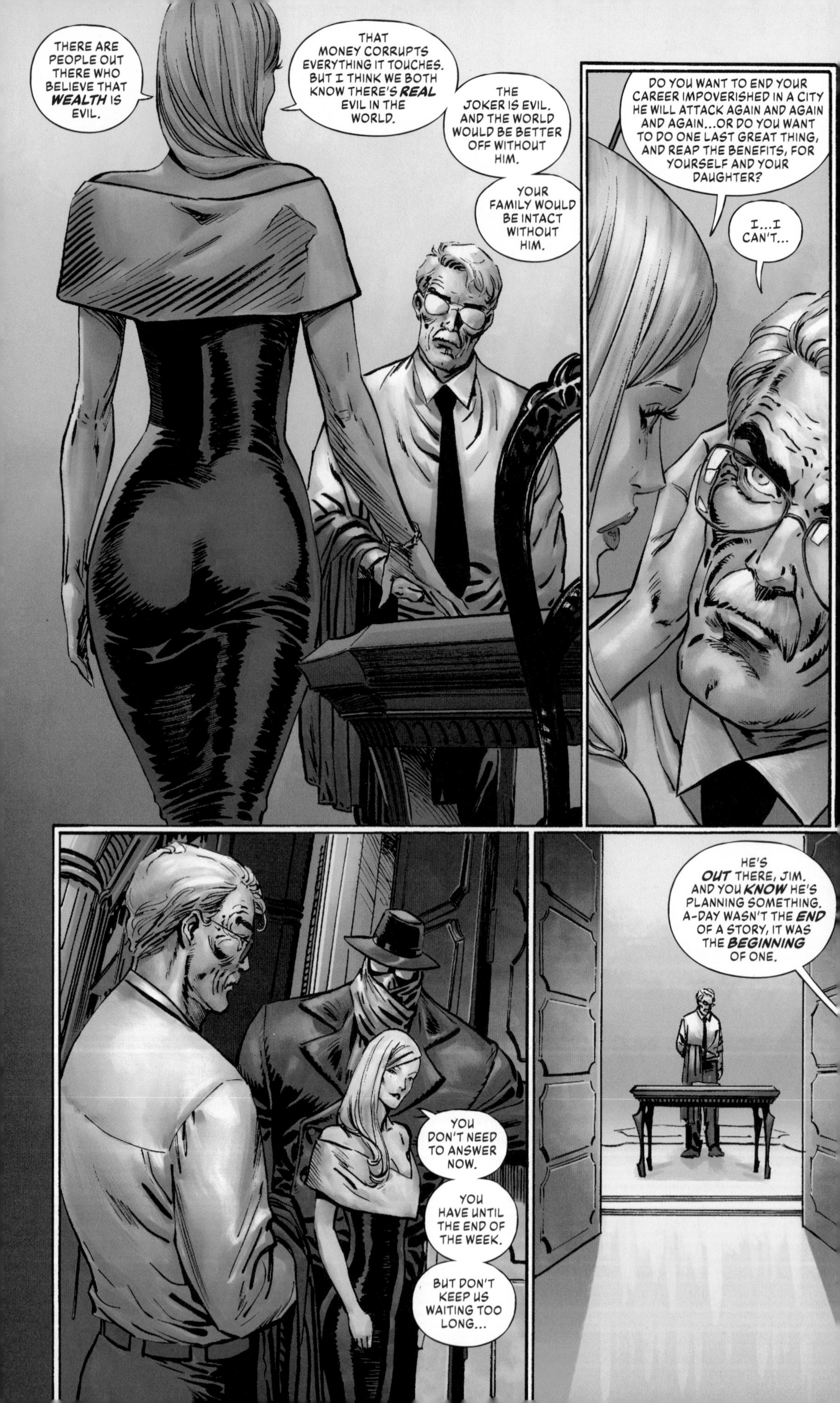
THERE ARE PEOPLE OUT THERE WHO BELIEVE THAT WEALTH IS EVIL.
THAT MONEY CORRUPTS EVERYTHING IT TOUCHES. BUT I THINK WE BOTH KNOW THERE'S REAL EVIL IN THE WORLD.
THE JOKER IS EVIL. AND THE WORLD WOULD BE BETTER OFF WITHOUT HIM.
YOUR FAMILY WOULD BE INTACT WITHOUT HIM.
DO YOU WANT TO END YOUR CAREER IMPOVERISHED IN A CITY HE WILL ATTACK AGAIN AND AGAIN AND AGAIN...OR DO YOU WANT TO DO ONE LAST GREAT THING, AND REAP THE BENEFITS, FOR YOURSELF AND YOUR DAUGHTER?
I...I CAN'T...
YOU DON'T NEED TO ANSWER NOW.
YOU HAVE UNTIL THE END OF THE WEEK.
BUT DON'T KEEP US WAITING TOO LONG...
HE'S OUT THERE, JIM. AND YOU KNOW HE'S PLANNING SOMETHING. A-DAY WASN'T THE END OF A STORY, IT WAS THE BEGINNING OF ONE.

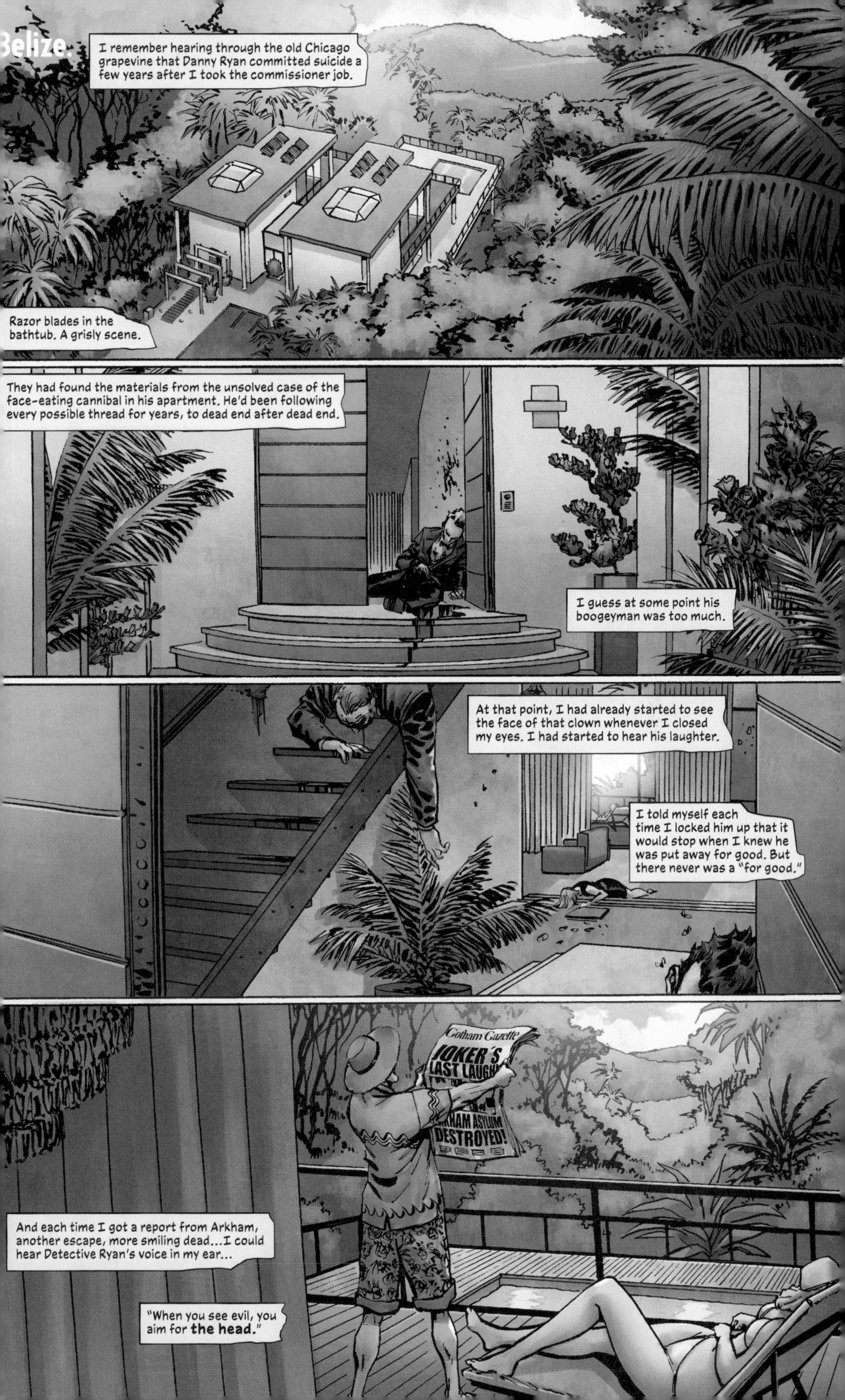
Belize.
I remember hearing through the old Chicago grapevine that Danny Ryan committed suicide a few years after I took the commissioner job.
Razor blades in the bathtub. A grisly scene.
They had found the materials from the unsolved case of the face-eating cannibal in his apartment. He'd been following every possible thread for years, to dead end after dead end.
I guess at some point his boogeyman was too much.
At that point, I had already started to see the face of that clown whenever I closed my eyes. I had started to hear his laughter.
I told myself each time I locked him up that it would stop when I knew he was put away for good. But there never was a "for good."
Gotham Gazette
JOKER'S LAST LAUGH
DESTROYED!
And each time I got a report from Arkham, another escape, more smiling dead...I could hear Detective Ryan's voice in my ear...
"When you see evil, you aim for **the head.**"

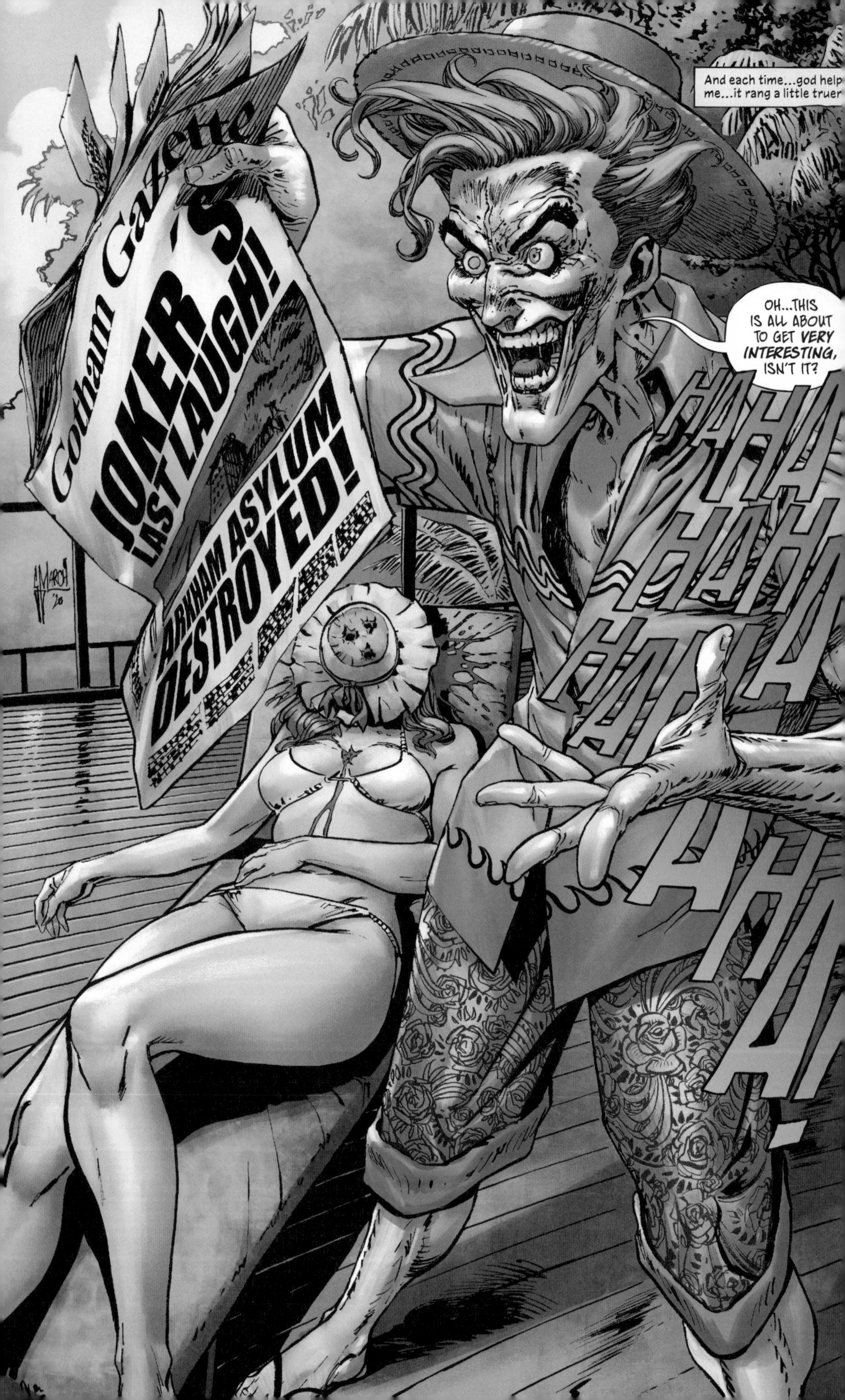
And each time...god help me...it rang a little truer
Gotham Gazette
JOKER'S LAST LAUGH!
ARKHAM ASYLUM DESTROYED!
OH...THIS IS ALL ABOUT TO GET VERY INTERESTING, ISN'T IT?

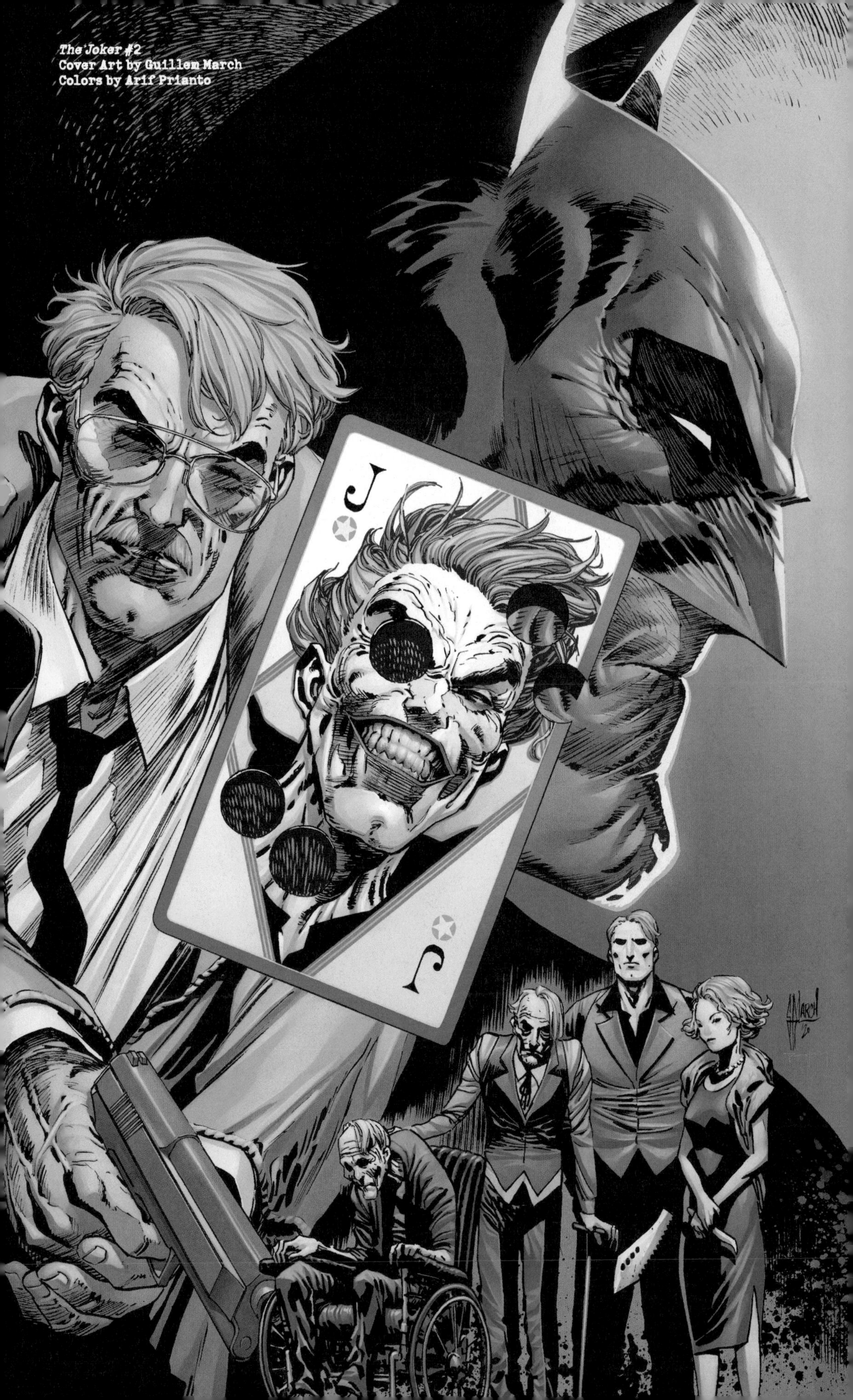

The Joker #2
Cover Art by Guillem March
Colors by Arif Prianto

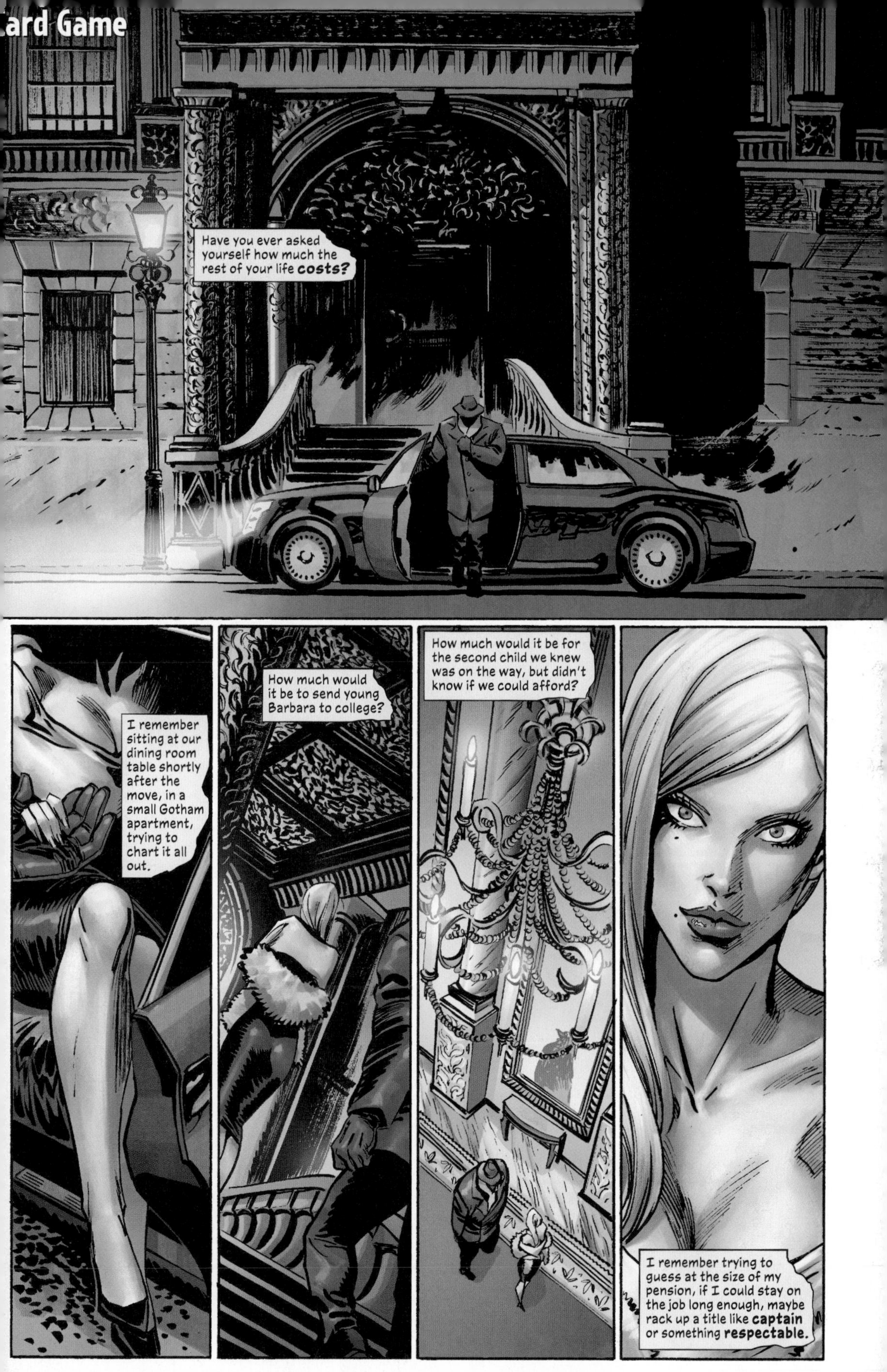
ard Game
Have you ever asked yourself how much the rest of your life costs?
I remember sitting at our dining room table shortly after the move, in a small Gotham apartment, trying to chart it all out.
How much would it be to send young Barbara to college?
How much would it be for the second child we knew was on the way, but didn't know if we could afford?
I remember trying to guess at the size of my pension, if I could stay on the job long enough, maybe rack up a title like captain or something respectable.

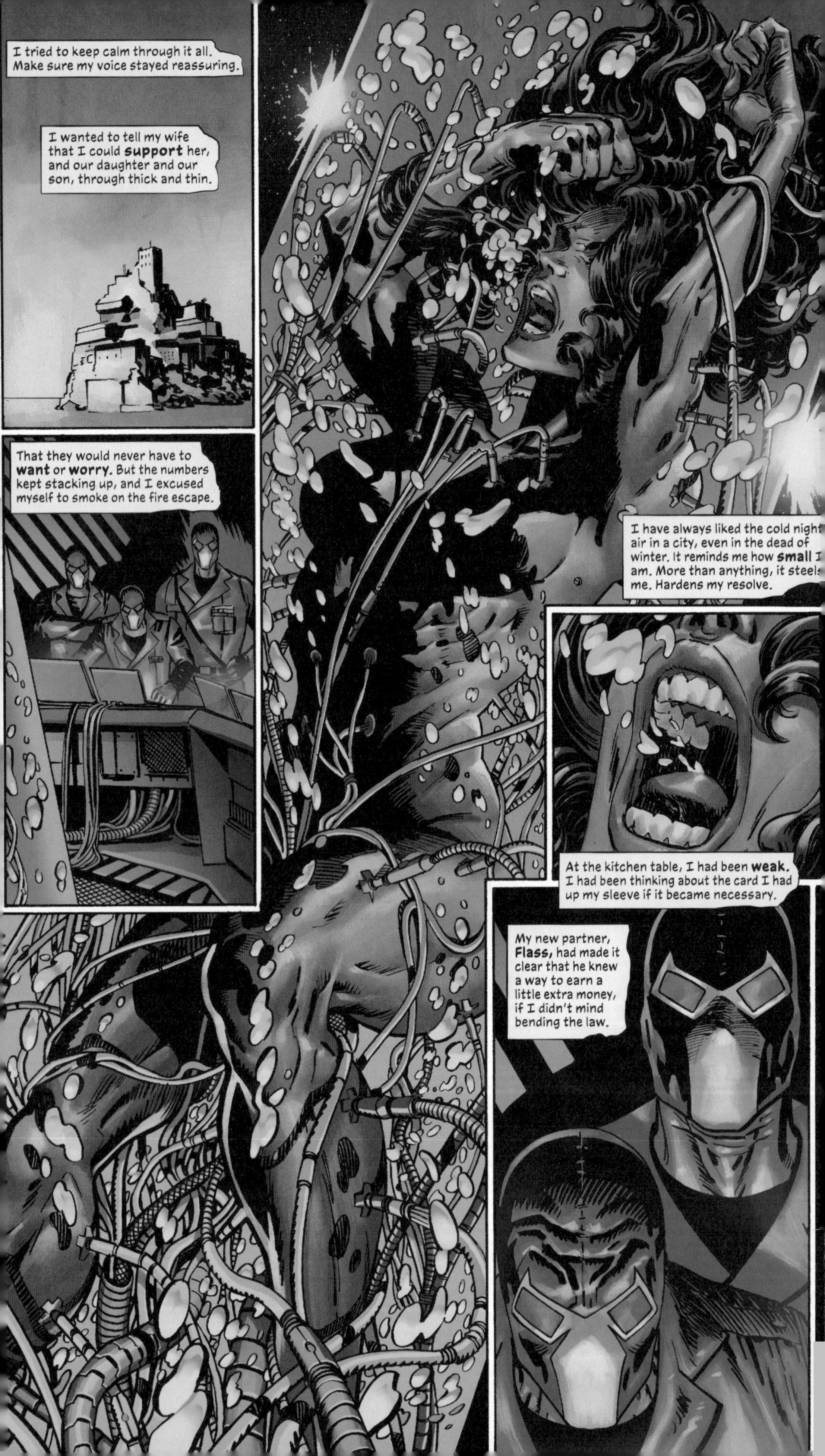
I tried to keep calm through it all. Make sure my voice stayed reassuring.
I wanted to tell my wife that I could **support** her, and our daughter and our son, through thick and thin.
That they would never have to **want** or **worry.** But the numbers kept stacking up, and I excused myself to smoke on the fire escape.
I have always liked the cold night air in a city, even in the dead of winter. It reminds me how **small** I am. More than anything, it steels me. Hardens my resolve.
At the kitchen table, I had been **weak.** I had been thinking about the card I had up my sleeve if it became necessary.
My new partner, **Flass,** had made it clear that he knew a way to earn a little extra money, if I didn't mind bending the law.

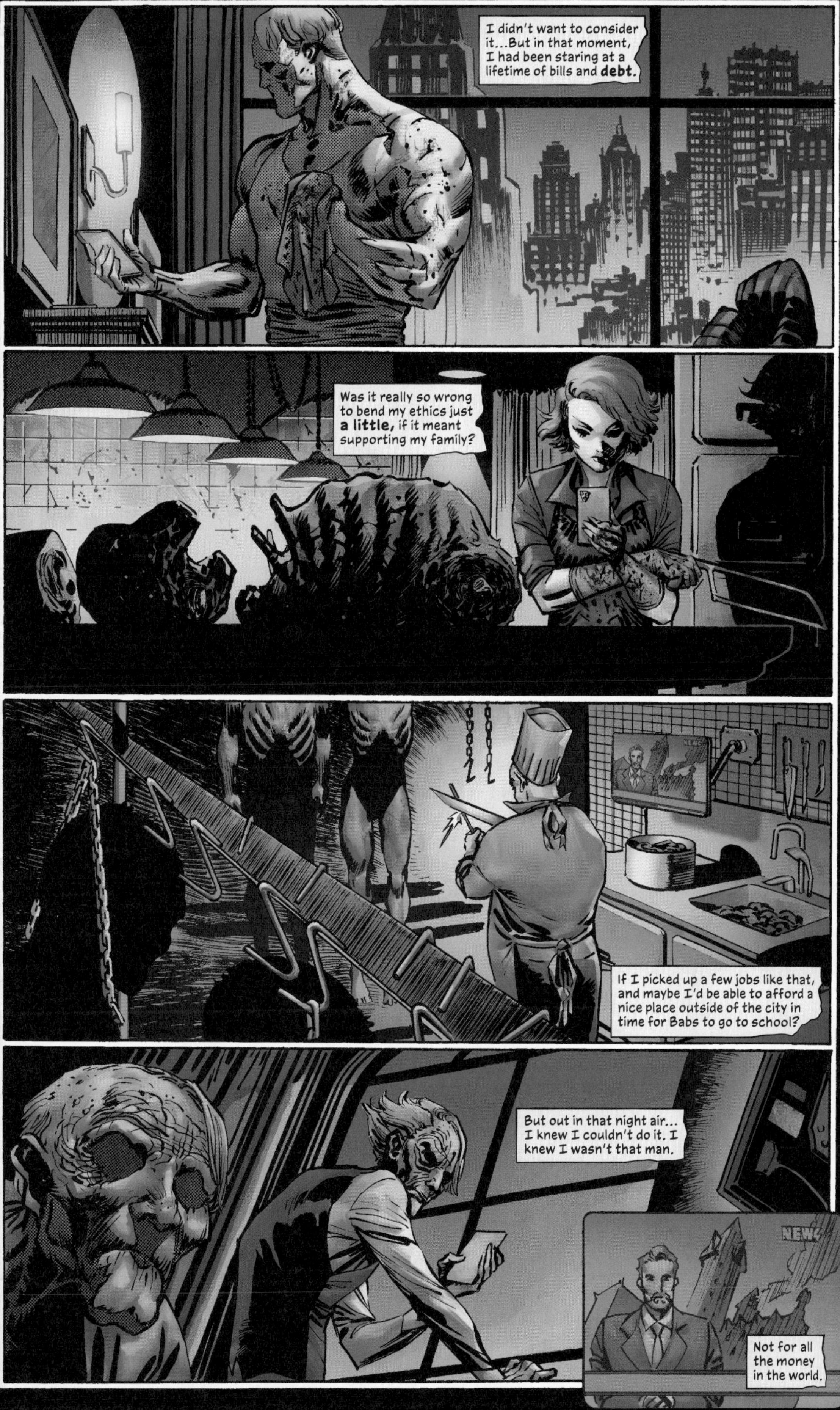
I didn't want to consider it...But in that moment, I had been staring at a lifetime of bills and **debt.**
Was it really so wrong to bend my ethics just **a little,** if it meant supporting my family?
If I picked up a few jobs like that, and maybe I'd be able to afford a nice place outside of the city in time for Babs to go to school?
But out in that night air... I knew I couldn't do it. I knew I wasn't that man.
NEWS
Not for all the money in the world.

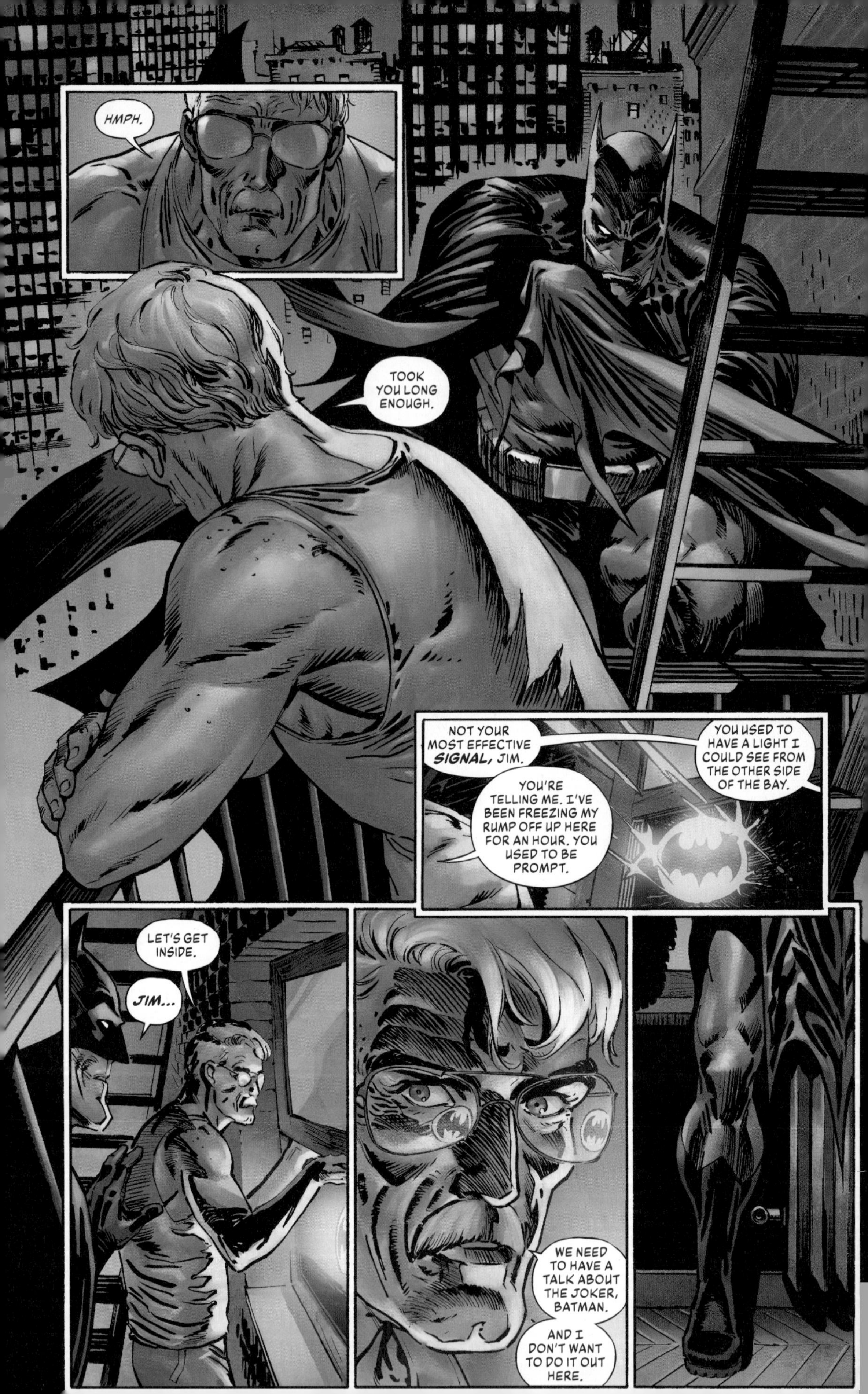
HMPH.
TOOK YOU LONG ENOUGH.
NOT YOUR MOST EFFECTIVE SIGNAL, JIM.
YOU USED TO HAVE A LIGHT I COULD SEE FROM THE OTHER SIDE OF THE BAY.
YOU'RE TELLING ME. I'VE BEEN FREEZING MY RUMP OFF UP HERE FOR AN HOUR. YOU USED TO BE PROMPT.
LET'S GET INSIDE.
JIM...
WE NEED TO HAVE A TALK ABOUT THE JOKER, BATMAN.
AND I DON'T WANT TO DO IT OUT HERE.

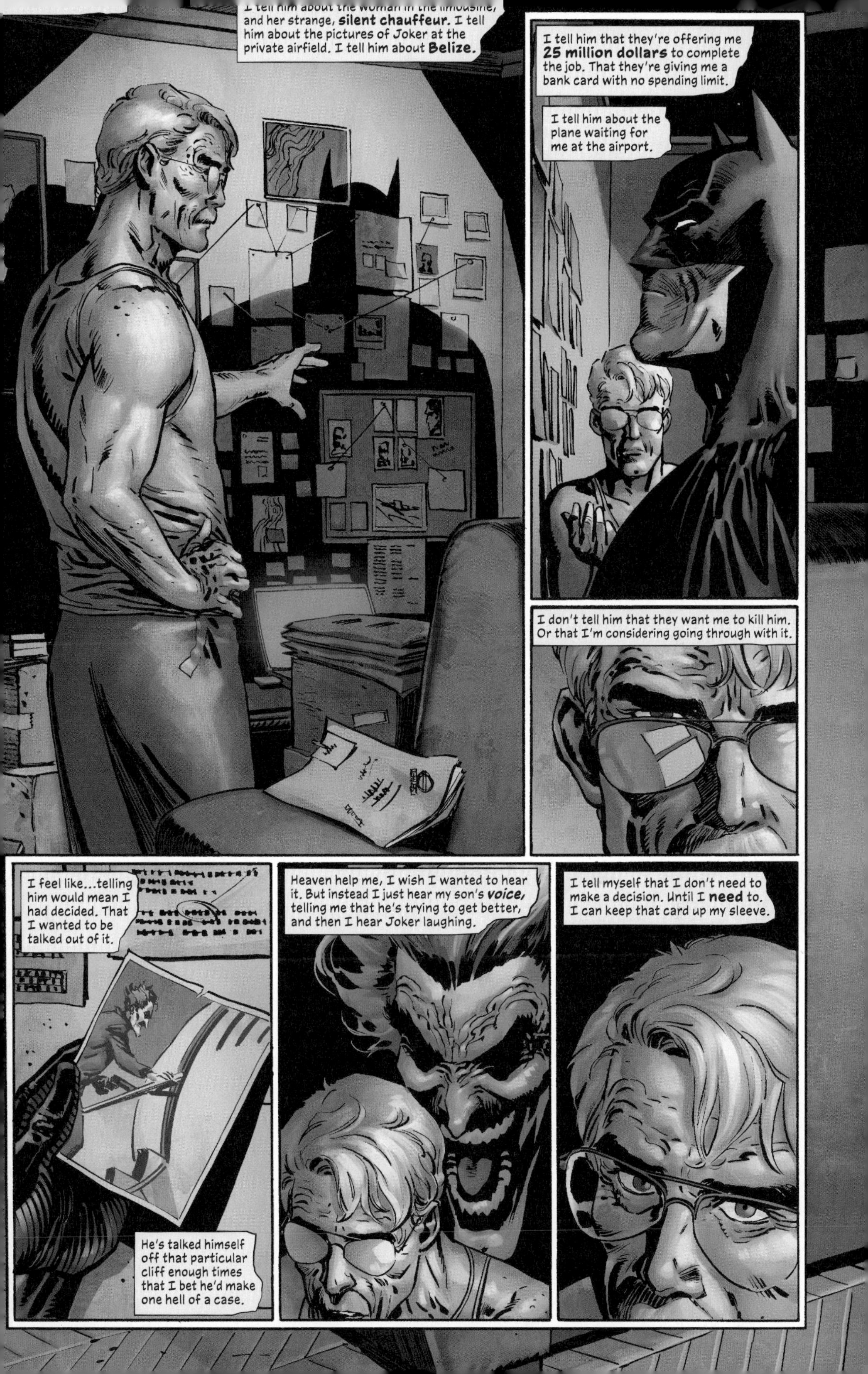
I tell him about the woman in the limousine, and her strange, **silent chauffeur.** I tell him about the pictures of Joker at the private airfield. I tell him about **Belize.**
I tell him that they're offering me **25 million dollars** to complete the job. That they're giving me a bank card with no spending limit.
I tell him about the plane waiting for me at the airport.
I don't tell him that they want me to kill him. Or that I'm considering going through with it.
I feel like...telling him would mean I had decided. That I wanted to be talked out of it.
He's talked himself off that particular cliff enough times that I bet he'd make one hell of a case.
Heaven help me, I wish I wanted to hear it. But instead I just hear my son's ***voice,*** telling me that he's trying to get better, and then I hear Joker laughing.
I tell myself that I don't need to make a decision. Until I **need** to. I can keep that card up my sleeve.

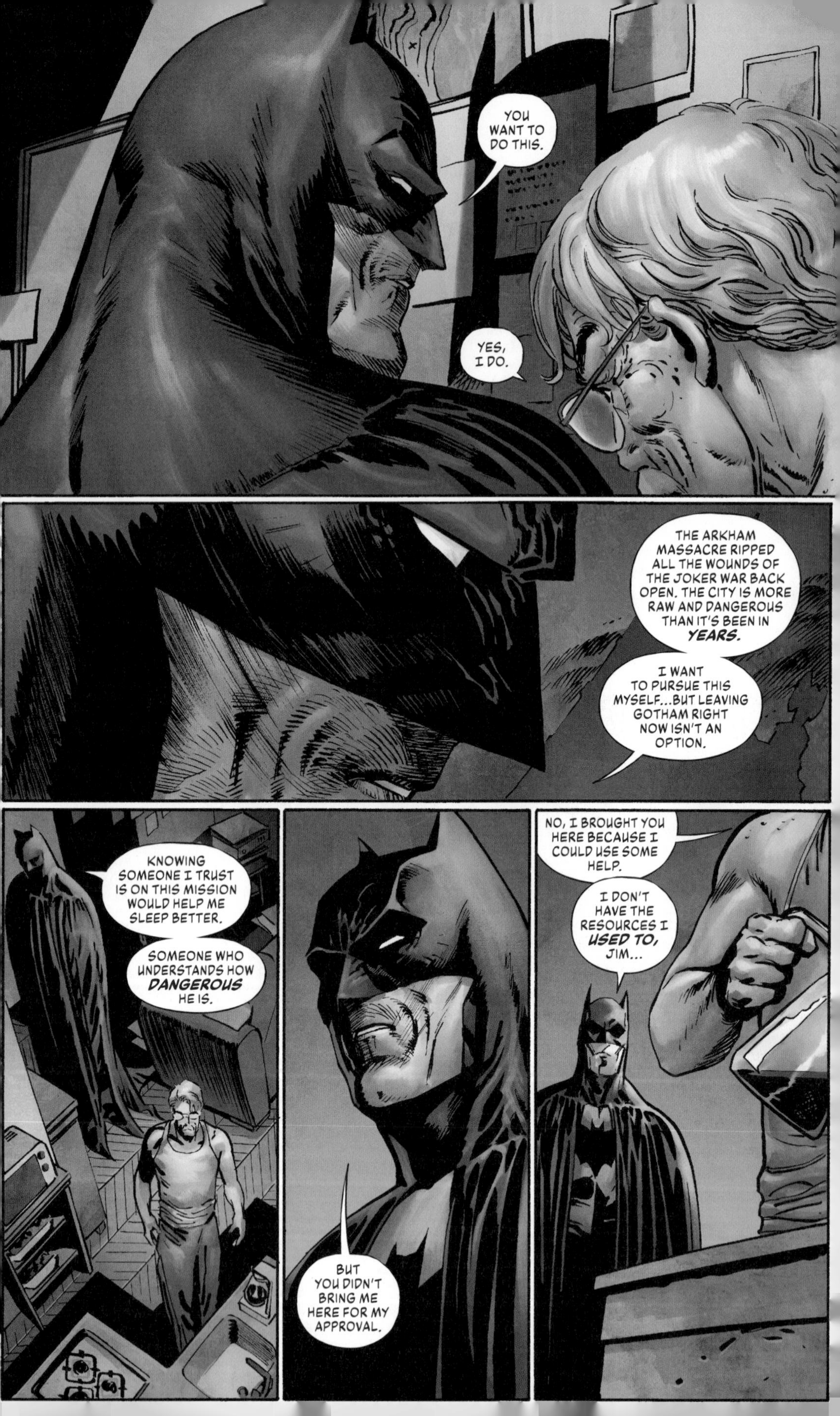
YOU WANT TO DO THIS.
YES, I DO.
THE ARKHAM MASSACRE RIPPED ALL THE WOUNDS OF THE JOKER WAR BACK OPEN. THE CITY IS MORE RAW AND DANGEROUS THAN IT'S BEEN IN YEARS.
I WANT TO PURSUE THIS MYSELF...BUT LEAVING GOTHAM RIGHT NOW ISN'T AN OPTION.
KNOWING SOMEONE I TRUST IS ON THIS MISSION WOULD HELP ME SLEEP BETTER.
SOMEONE WHO UNDERSTANDS HOW DANGEROUS HE IS.
BUT YOU DIDN'T BRING ME HERE FOR MY APPROVAL.
NO, I BROUGHT YOU HERE BECAUSE I COULD USE SOME HELP.
I DON'T HAVE THE RESOURCES I USED TO, JIM...

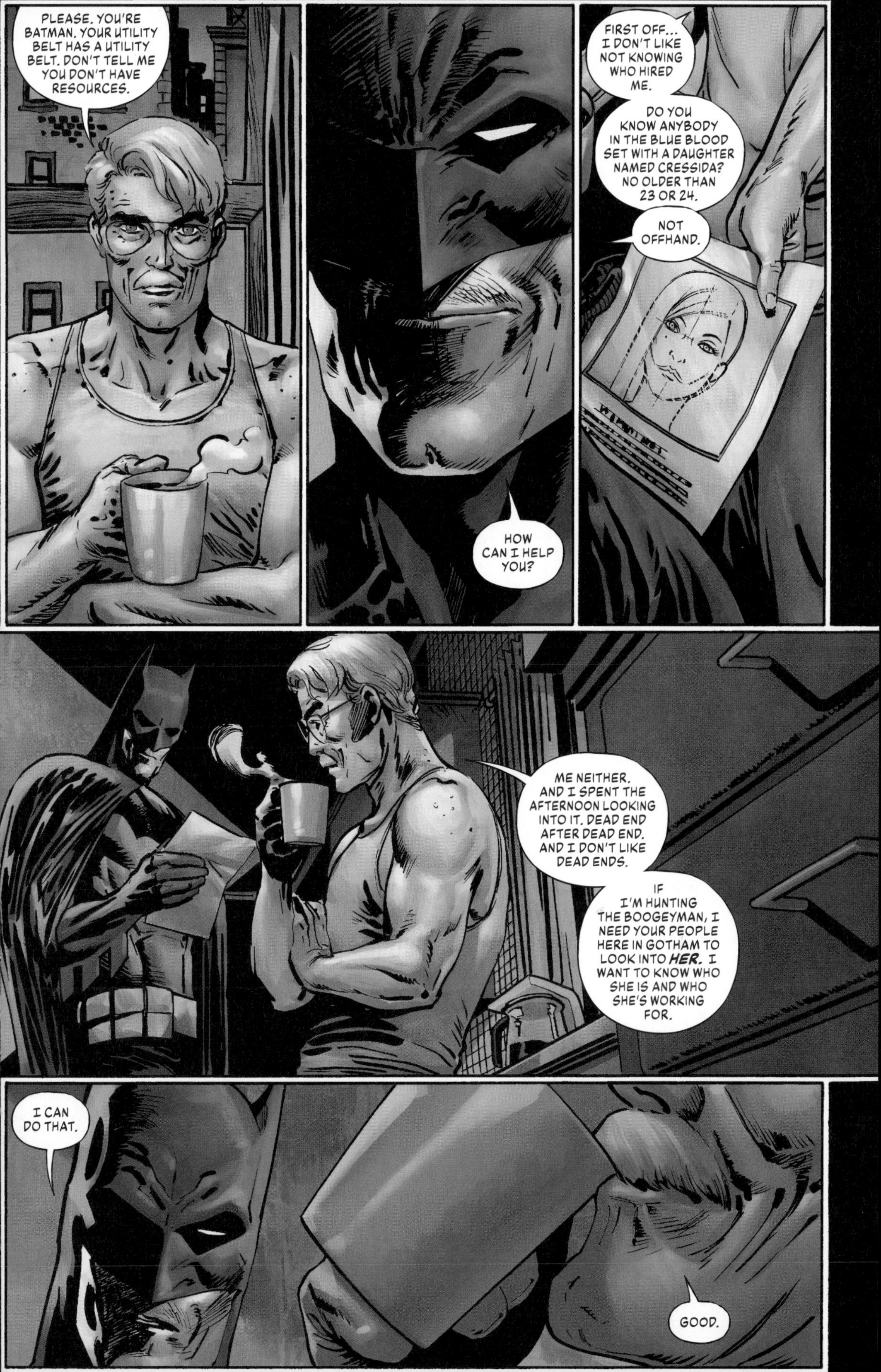
PLEASE. YOU'RE BATMAN. YOUR UTILITY BELT HAS A UTILITY BELT. DON'T TELL ME YOU DON'T HAVE RESOURCES.
HOW CAN I HELP YOU?
FIRST OFF... I DON'T LIKE NOT KNOWING WHO HIRED ME.
DO YOU KNOW ANYBODY IN THE BLUE BLOOD SET WITH A DAUGHTER NAMED CRESSIDA? NO OLDER THAN 23 OR 24.
NOT OFFHAND.
ME NEITHER. AND I SPENT THE AFTERNOON LOOKING INTO IT. DEAD END AFTER DEAD END. AND I DON'T LIKE DEAD ENDS.
IF I'M HUNTING THE BOOGEYMAN, I NEED YOUR PEOPLE HERE IN GOTHAM TO LOOK INTO HER. I WANT TO KNOW WHO SHE IS AND WHO SHE'S WORKING FOR.
I CAN DO THAT.
GOOD.

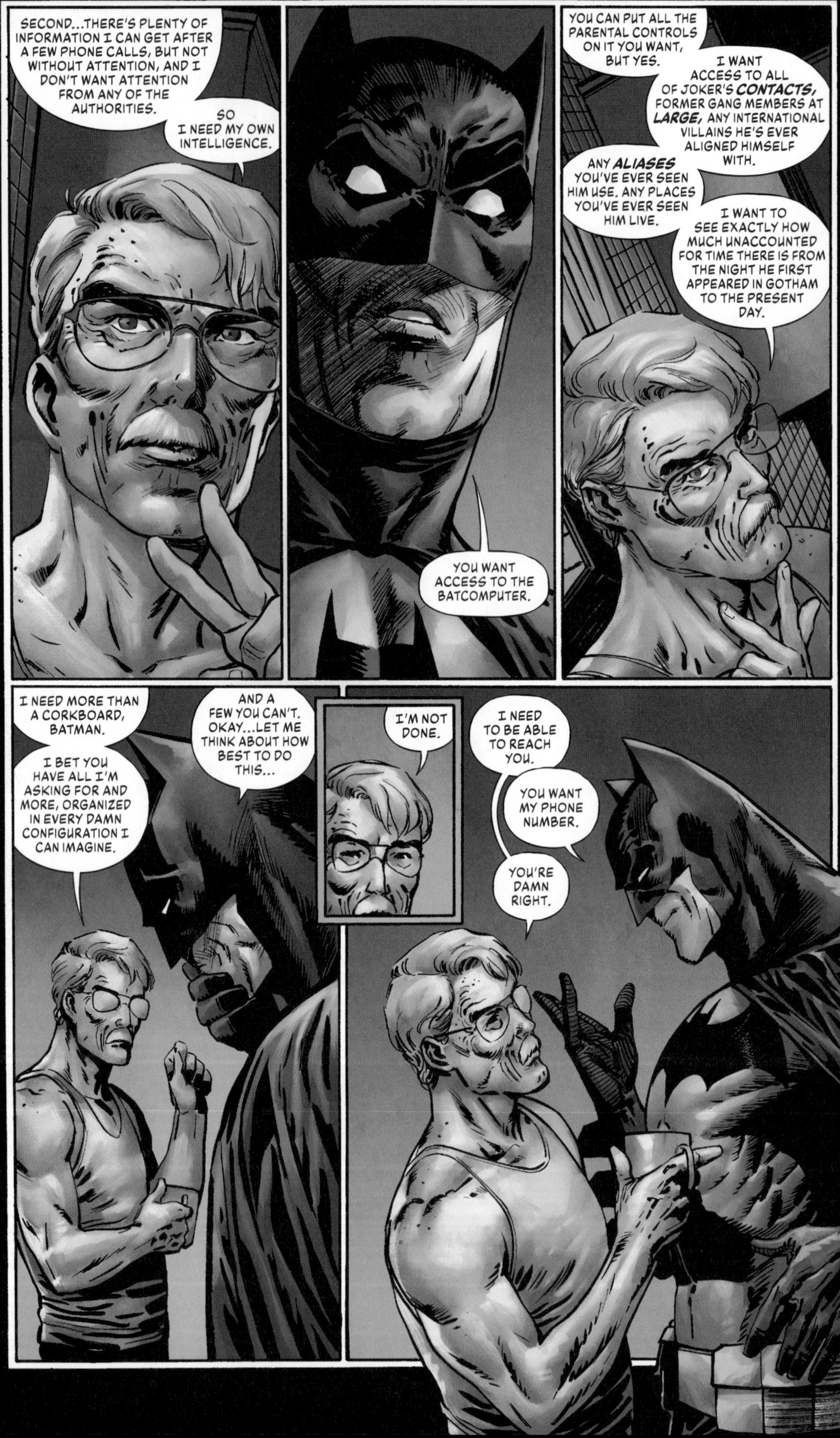
SECOND...THERE'S PLENTY OF INFORMATION I CAN GET AFTER A FEW PHONE CALLS, BUT NOT WITHOUT ATTENTION, AND I DON'T WANT ATTENTION FROM ANY OF THE AUTHORITIES.
SO I NEED MY OWN INTELLIGENCE.
YOU WANT ACCESS TO THE BATCOMPUTER.
YOU CAN PUT ALL THE PARENTAL CONTROLS ON IT YOU WANT, BUT YES.
I WANT ACCESS TO ALL OF JOKER'S ***CONTACTS,*** FORMER GANG MEMBERS AT ***LARGE,*** ANY INTERNATIONAL VILLAINS HE'S EVER ALIGNED HIMSELF WITH.
ANY ***ALIASES*** YOU'VE EVER SEEN HIM USE. ANY PLACES YOU'VE EVER SEEN HIM LIVE.
I WANT TO SEE EXACTLY HOW MUCH UNACCOUNTED FOR TIME THERE IS FROM THE NIGHT HE FIRST APPEARED IN GOTHAM TO THE PRESENT DAY.
I NEED MORE THAN A CORKBOARD, BATMAN.
I BET YOU HAVE ALL I'M ASKING FOR AND MORE, ORGANIZED IN EVERY DAMN CONFIGURATION I CAN IMAGINE.
AND A FEW YOU CAN'T. OKAY...LET ME THINK ABOUT HOW BEST TO DO THIS...
I'M NOT DONE.
I NEED TO BE ABLE TO REACH YOU.
YOU WANT MY PHONE NUMBER.
YOU'RE DAMN RIGHT.

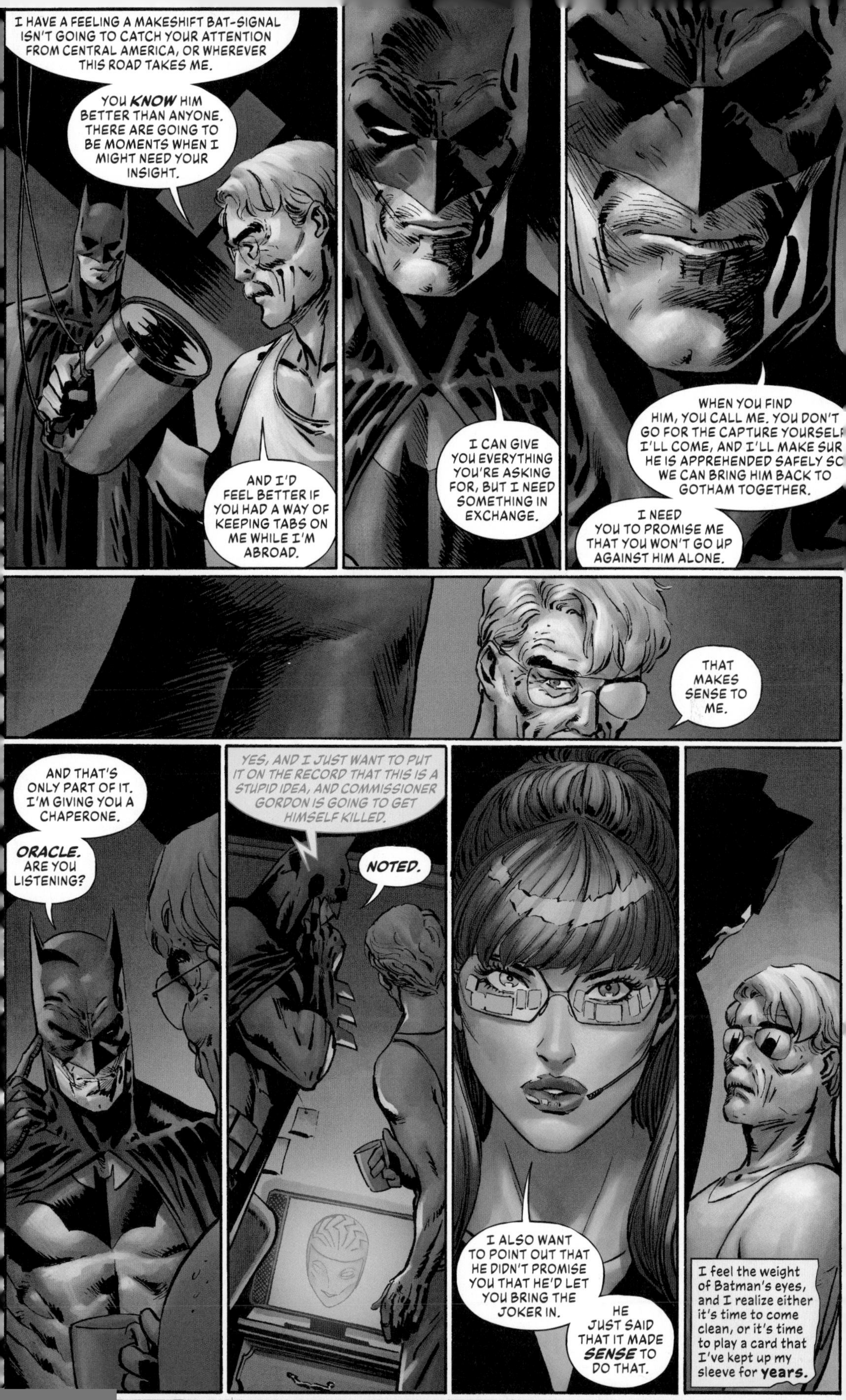
I HAVE A FEELING A MAKESHIFT BAT-SIGNAL ISN'T GOING TO CATCH YOUR ATTENTION FROM CENTRAL AMERICA, OR WHEREVER THIS ROAD TAKES ME.
YOU KNOW HIM BETTER THAN ANYONE. THERE ARE GOING TO BE MOMENTS WHEN I MIGHT NEED YOUR INSIGHT.
AND I'D FEEL BETTER IF YOU HAD A WAY OF KEEPING TABS ON ME WHILE I'M ABROAD.
I CAN GIVE YOU EVERYTHING YOU'RE ASKING FOR, BUT I NEED SOMETHING IN EXCHANGE.
I NEED YOU TO PROMISE ME THAT YOU WON'T GO UP AGAINST HIM ALONE.
WHEN YOU FIND HIM, YOU CALL ME. YOU DON'T GO FOR THE CAPTURE YOURSELF. I'LL COME, AND I'LL MAKE SURE HE IS APPREHENDED SAFELY SO WE CAN BRING HIM BACK TO GOTHAM TOGETHER.
THAT MAKES SENSE TO ME.
AND THAT'S ONLY PART OF IT. I'M GIVING YOU A CHAPERONE.
ORACLE. ARE YOU LISTENING?
YES, AND I JUST WANT TO PUT IT ON THE RECORD THAT THIS IS A STUPID IDEA, AND COMMISSIONER GORDON IS GOING TO GET HIMSELF KILLED.
NOTED.
I ALSO WANT TO POINT OUT THAT HE DIDN'T PROMISE YOU THAT HE'D LET YOU BRING THE JOKER IN.
HE JUST SAID THAT IT MADE SENSE TO DO THAT.
I feel the weight of Batman's eyes, and I realize either it's time to come clean, or it's time to play a card that I've kept up my sleeve for years.

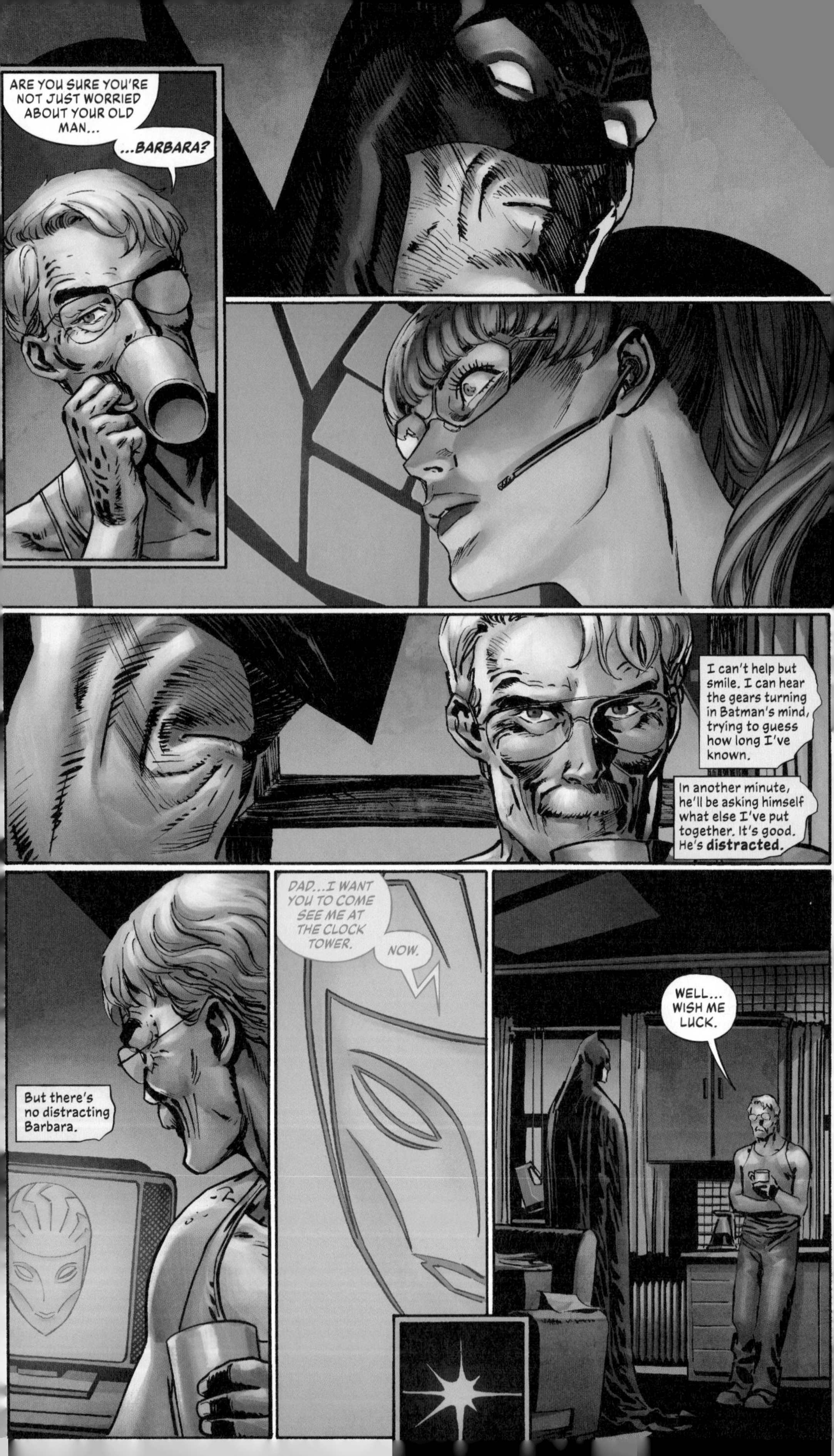
ARE YOU SURE YOU'RE NOT JUST WORRIED ABOUT YOUR OLD MAN...
...BARBARA?
I can't help but smile. I can hear the gears turning in Batman's mind, trying to guess how long I've known.
In another minute, he'll be asking himself what else I've put together. It's good. He's **distracted.**
But there's no distracting Barbara.
DAD...I WANT YOU TO COME SEE ME AT THE CLOCK TOWER.
NOW.
WELL... WISH ME LUCK.

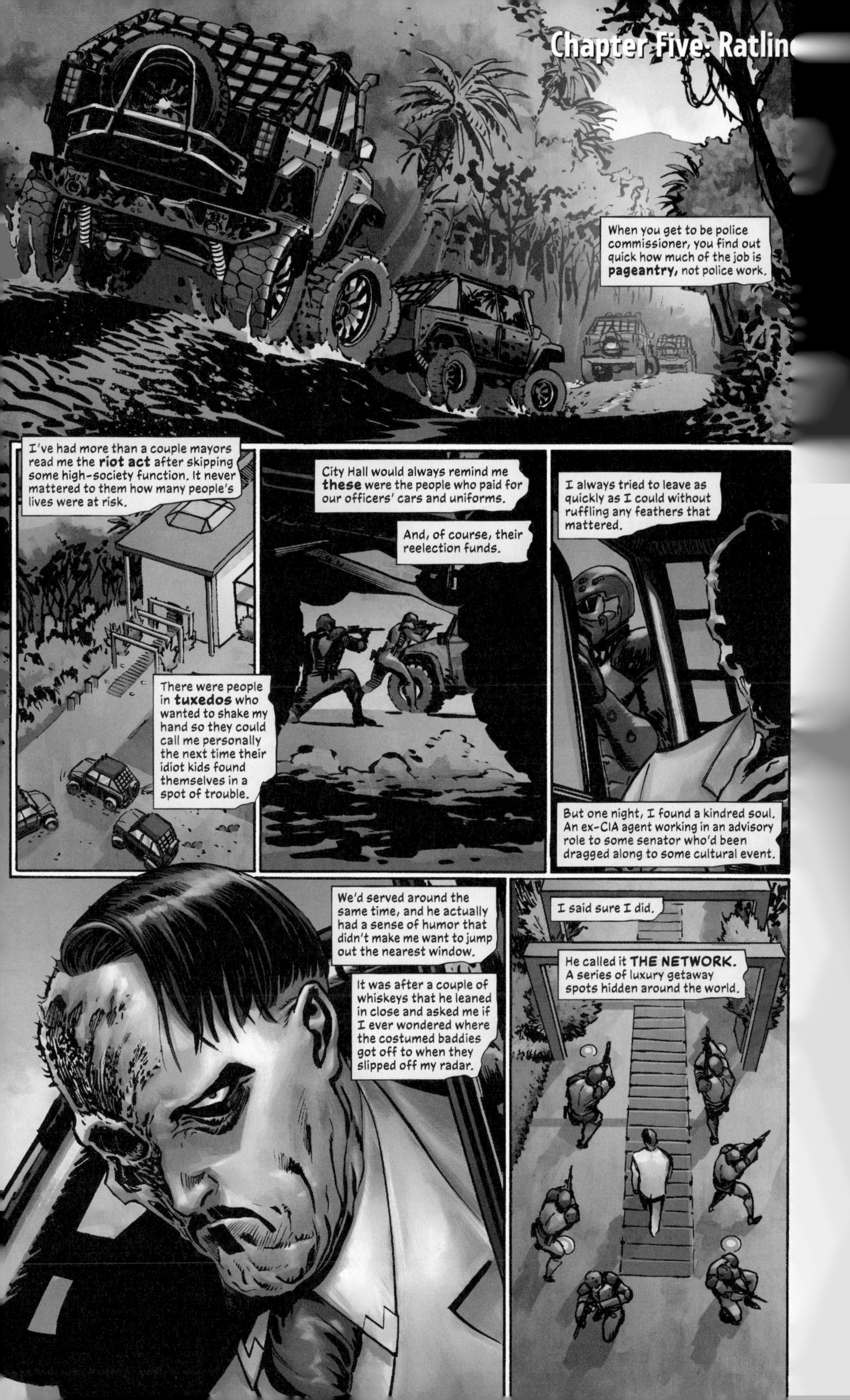

Chapter Five: Ratlin
When you get to be police commissioner, you find out quick how much of the job is pageantry, not police work.
I've had more than a couple mayors read me the riot act after skipping some high-society function. It never mattered to them how many people's lives were at risk.
There were people in tuxedos who wanted to shake my hand so they could call me personally the next time their idiot kids found themselves in a spot of trouble.
City Hall would always remind me these were the people who paid for our officers' cars and uniforms.
And, of course, their reelection funds.
I always tried to leave as quickly as I could without ruffling any feathers that mattered.
But one night, I found a kindred soul. An ex-CIA agent working in an advisory role to some senator who'd been dragged along to some cultural event.
We'd served around the same time, and he actually had a sense of humor that didn't make me want to jump out the nearest window.
It was after a couple of whiskeys that he leaned in close and asked me if I ever wondered where the costumed baddies got off to when they slipped off my radar.
I said sure I did.
He called it THE NETWORK. A series of luxury getaway spots hidden around the world.

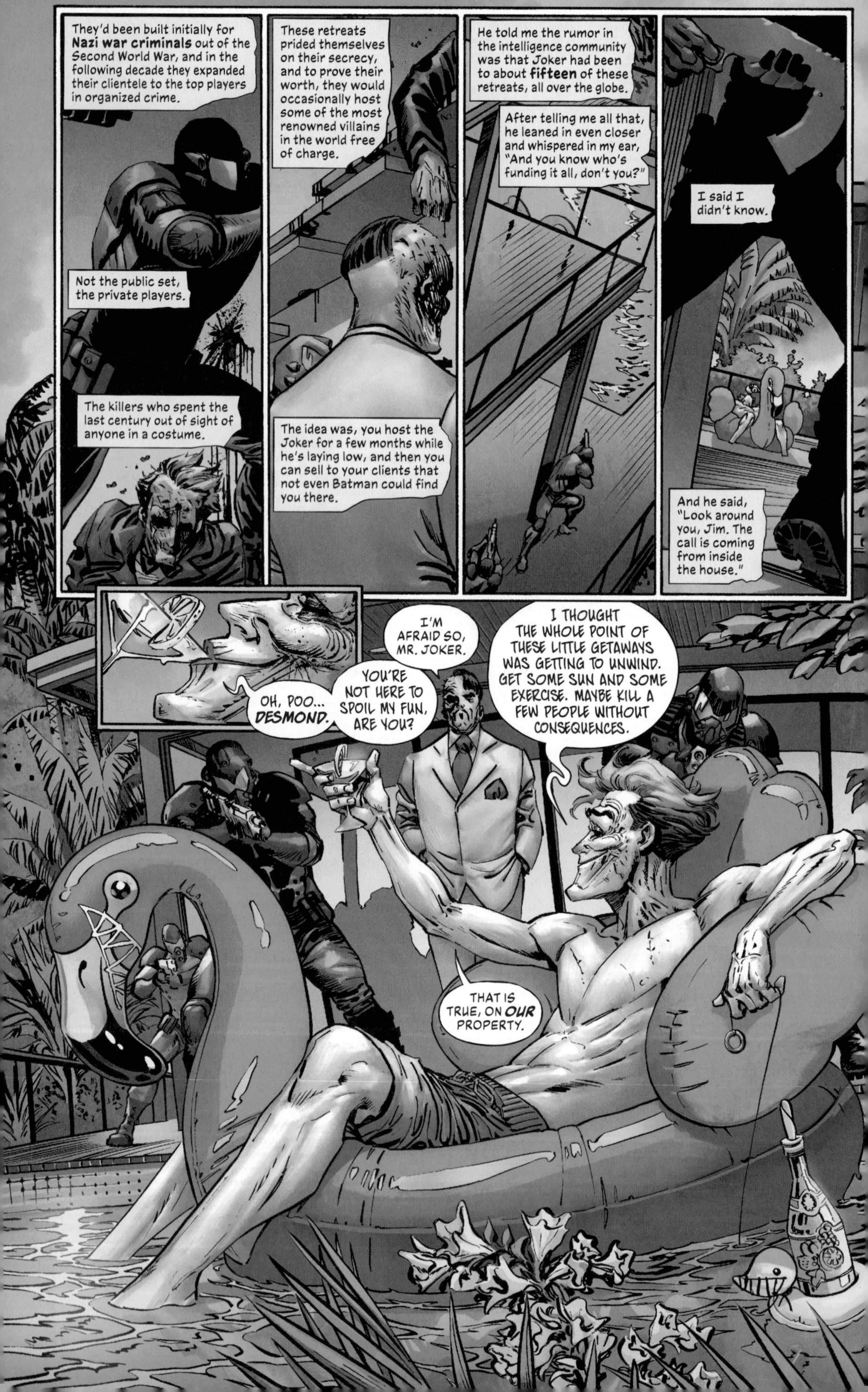
They'd been built initially for **Nazi war criminals** out of the Second World War, and in the following decade they expanded their clientele to the top players in organized crime.
Not the public set, the private players.
The killers who spent the last century out of sight of anyone in a costume.
These retreats prided themselves on their secrecy, and to prove their worth, they would occasionally host some of the most renowned villains in the world free of charge.
The idea was, you host the Joker for a few months while he's laying low, and then you can sell to your clients that not even Batman could find you there.
He told me the rumor in the intelligence community was that Joker had been to about **fifteen** of these retreats, all over the globe.
After telling me all that, he leaned in even closer and whispered in my ear, "And you know who's funding it all, don't you?"
I said I didn't know.
And he said, "Look around you, Jim. The call is coming from inside the house."
OH, POO... ***DESMOND.***
I'M AFRAID SO, MR. JOKER.
YOU'RE NOT HERE TO SPOIL MY FUN, ARE YOU?
I THOUGHT THE WHOLE POINT OF THESE LITTLE GETAWAYS WAS GETTING TO UNWIND. GET SOME SUN AND SOME EXERCISE. MAYBE KILL A FEW PEOPLE WITHOUT CONSEQUENCES.
THAT IS TRUE, ON ***OUR*** PROPERTY.

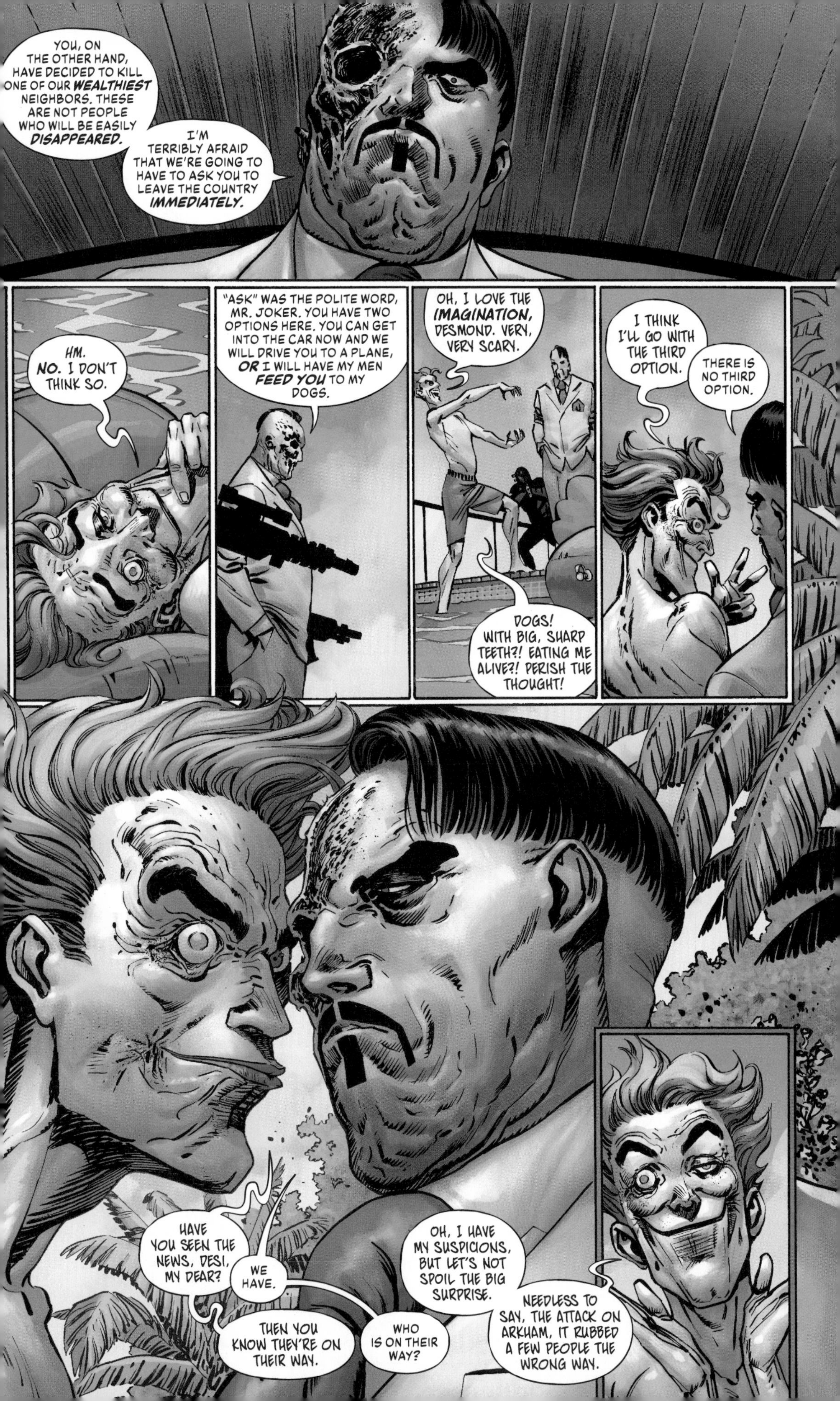

YOU, ON THE OTHER HAND, HAVE DECIDED TO KILL ONE OF OUR WEALTHIEST NEIGHBORS. THESE ARE NOT PEOPLE WHO WILL BE EASILY DISAPPEARED.
I'M TERRIBLY AFRAID THAT WE'RE GOING TO HAVE TO ASK YOU TO LEAVE THE COUNTRY IMMEDIATELY.
HM. NO. I DON'T THINK SO.
"ASK" WAS THE POLITE WORD, MR. JOKER. YOU HAVE TWO OPTIONS HERE. YOU CAN GET INTO THE CAR NOW AND WE WILL DRIVE YOU TO A PLANE, OR I WILL HAVE MY MEN FEED YOU TO MY DOGS.
OH, I LOVE THE IMAGINATION, DESMOND. VERY, VERY SCARY.
DOGS! WITH BIG, SHARP TEETH?! EATING ME ALIVE?! PERISH THE THOUGHT!
I THINK I'LL GO WITH THE THIRD OPTION.
THERE IS NO THIRD OPTION.
HAVE YOU SEEN THE NEWS, DESI, MY DEAR?
WE HAVE.
THEN YOU KNOW THEY'RE ON THEIR WAY.
WHO IS ON THEIR WAY?
OH, I HAVE MY SUSPICIONS, BUT LET'S NOT SPOIL THE BIG SURPRISE.
NEEDLESS TO SAY, THE ATTACK ON ARKHAM, IT RUBBED A FEW PEOPLE THE WRONG WAY.

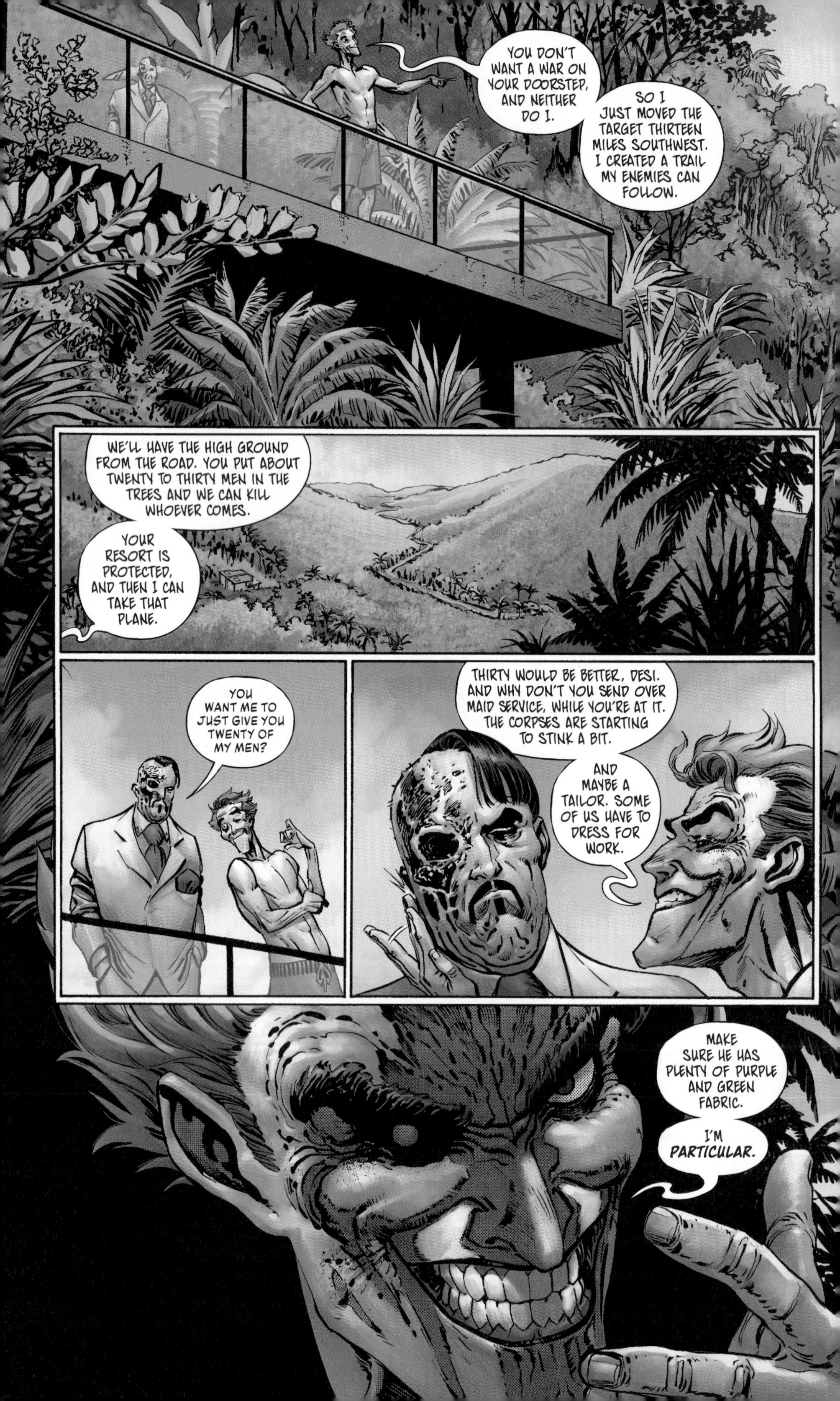

YOU DON'T WANT A WAR ON YOUR DOORSTEP, AND NEITHER DO I.
SO I JUST MOVED THE TARGET THIRTEEN MILES SOUTHWEST. I CREATED A TRAIL MY ENEMIES CAN FOLLOW.
WE'LL HAVE THE HIGH GROUND FROM THE ROAD. YOU PUT ABOUT TWENTY TO THIRTY MEN IN THE TREES AND WE CAN KILL WHOEVER COMES.
YOUR RESORT IS PROTECTED, AND THEN I CAN TAKE THAT PLANE.
YOU WANT ME TO JUST GIVE YOU TWENTY OF MY MEN?
THIRTY WOULD BE BETTER, DESI. AND WHY DON'T YOU SEND OVER MAID SERVICE, WHILE YOU'RE AT IT. THE CORPSES ARE STARTING TO STINK A BIT.
AND MAYBE A TAILOR. SOME OF US HAVE TO DRESS FOR WORK.
MAKE SURE HE HAS PLENTY OF PURPLE AND GREEN FABRIC.
I'M **PARTICULAR.**

hapter Six: Blood

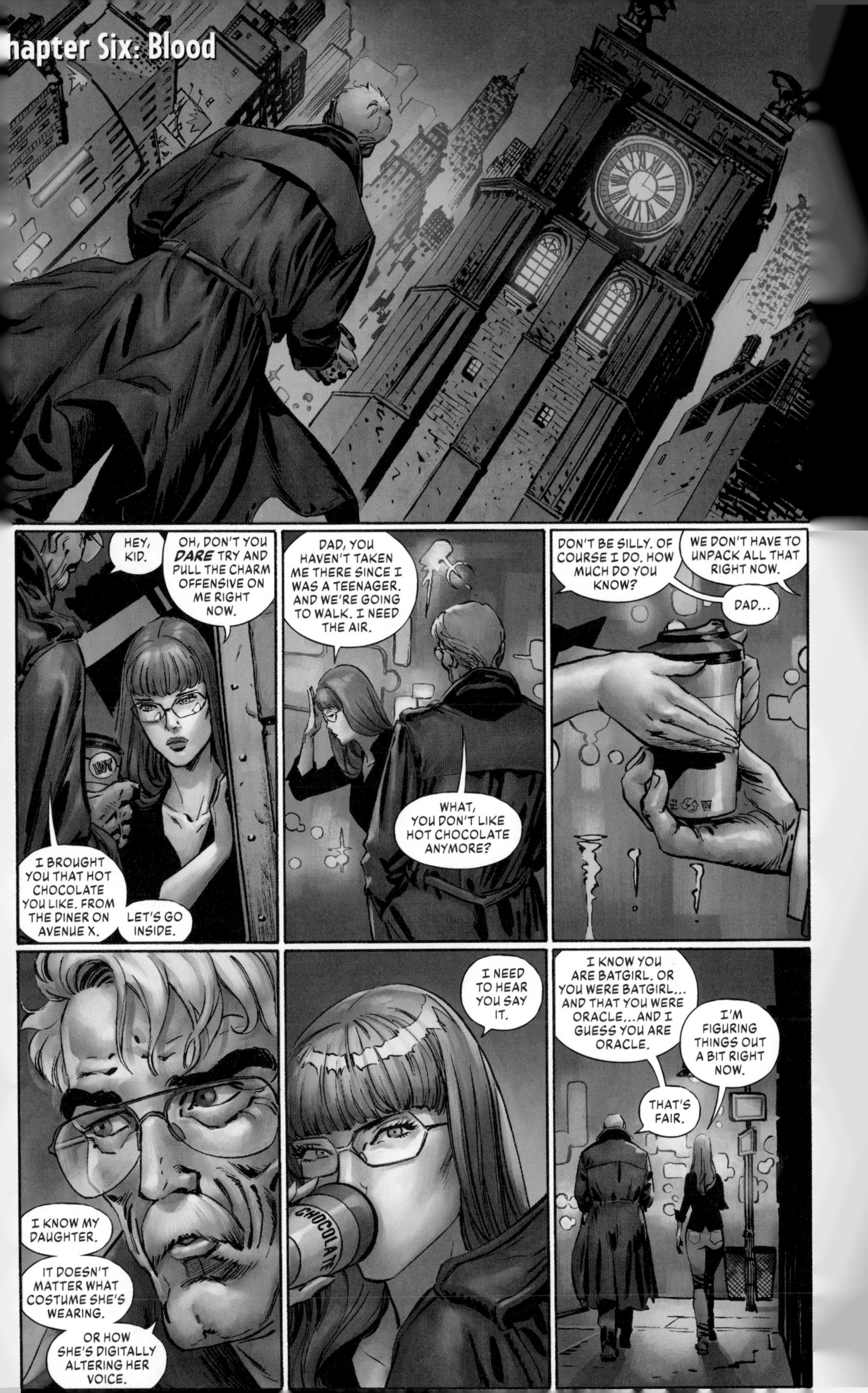
HEY, KID.
OH, DON'T YOU **DARE** TRY AND PULL THE CHARM OFFENSIVE ON ME RIGHT NOW.
HOT
I BROUGHT YOU THAT HOT CHOCOLATE YOU LIKE. FROM THE DINER ON AVENUE X.
LET'S GO INSIDE.
DAD, YOU HAVEN'T TAKEN ME THERE SINCE I WAS A TEENAGER. AND WE'RE GOING TO WALK. I NEED THE AIR.
WHAT, YOU DON'T LIKE HOT CHOCOLATE ANYMORE?
DON'T BE SILLY. OF COURSE I DO. HOW MUCH DO YOU KNOW?
WE DON'T HAVE TO UNPACK ALL THAT RIGHT NOW.
DAD...
I KNOW MY DAUGHTER.
IT DOESN'T MATTER WHAT COSTUME SHE'S WEARING.
OR HOW SHE'S DIGITALLY ALTERING HER VOICE.
CHOCOLATE
I NEED TO HEAR YOU SAY IT.
I KNOW YOU ARE BATGIRL. OR YOU WERE BATGIRL... AND THAT YOU WERE ORACLE...AND I GUESS YOU ARE ORACLE.
THAT'S FAIR.
I'M FIGURING THINGS OUT A BIT RIGHT NOW.

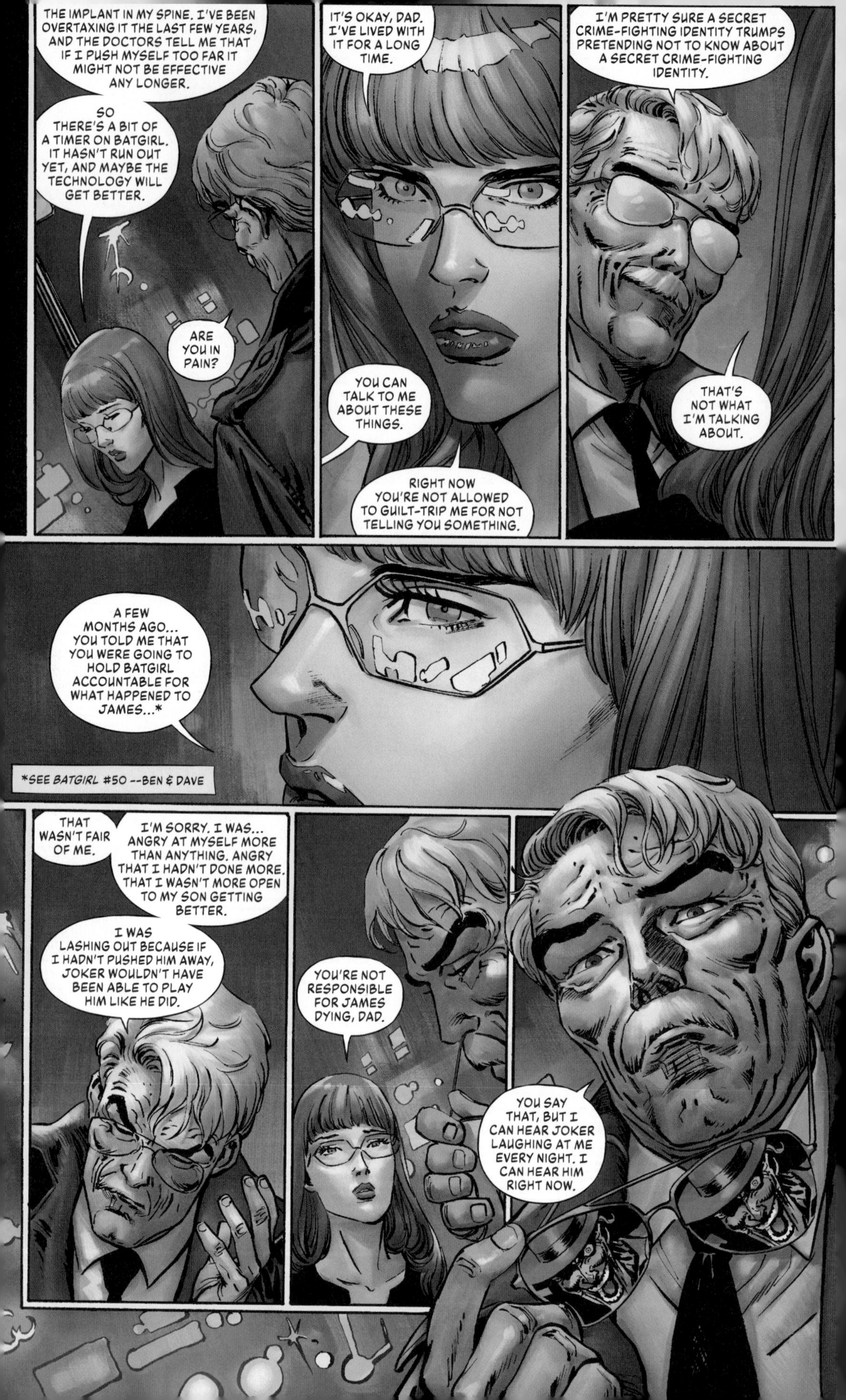
THE IMPLANT IN MY SPINE. I'VE BEEN OVERTAXING IT THE LAST FEW YEARS, AND THE DOCTORS TELL ME THAT IF I PUSH MYSELF TOO FAR IT MIGHT NOT BE EFFECTIVE ANY LONGER.
SO THERE'S A BIT OF A TIMER ON BATGIRL. IT HASN'T RUN OUT YET, AND MAYBE THE TECHNOLOGY WILL GET BETTER.
ARE YOU IN PAIN?
IT'S OKAY, DAD. I'VE LIVED WITH IT FOR A LONG TIME.
YOU CAN TALK TO ME ABOUT THESE THINGS.
RIGHT NOW YOU'RE NOT ALLOWED TO GUILT-TRIP ME FOR NOT TELLING YOU SOMETHING.
I'M PRETTY SURE A SECRET CRIME-FIGHTING IDENTITY TRUMPS PRETENDING NOT TO KNOW ABOUT A SECRET CRIME-FIGHTING IDENTITY.
THAT'S NOT WHAT I'M TALKING ABOUT.
A FEW MONTHS AGO... YOU TOLD ME THAT YOU WERE GOING TO HOLD BATGIRL ACCOUNTABLE FOR WHAT HAPPENED TO JAMES...*
*SEE BATGIRL #50 --BEN & DAVE
THAT WASN'T FAIR OF ME.
I'M SORRY. I WAS... ANGRY AT MYSELF MORE THAN ANYTHING. ANGRY THAT I HADN'T DONE MORE. THAT I WASN'T MORE OPEN TO MY SON GETTING BETTER.
I WAS LASHING OUT BECAUSE IF I HADN'T PUSHED HIM AWAY, JOKER WOULDN'T HAVE BEEN ABLE TO PLAY HIM LIKE HE DID.
YOU'RE NOT RESPONSIBLE FOR JAMES DYING, DAD.
YOU SAY THAT, BUT I CAN HEAR JOKER LAUGHING AT ME EVERY NIGHT. I CAN HEAR HIM RIGHT NOW.

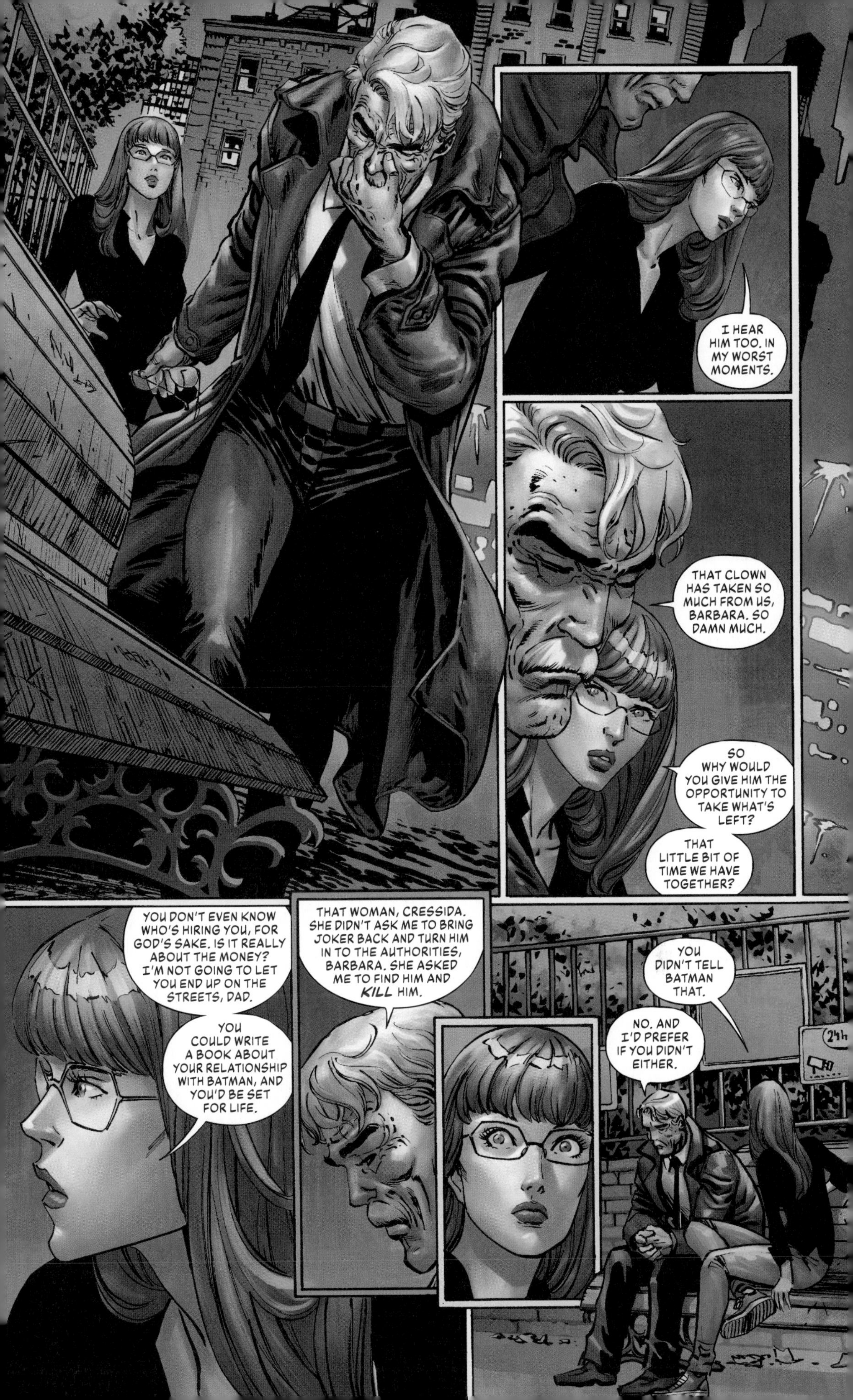

I HEAR HIM TOO. IN MY WORST MOMENTS.
THAT CLOWN HAS TAKEN SO MUCH FROM US, BARBARA. SO DAMN MUCH.
SO WHY WOULD YOU GIVE HIM THE OPPORTUNITY TO TAKE WHAT'S LEFT?
THAT LITTLE BIT OF TIME WE HAVE TOGETHER?
YOU DON'T EVEN KNOW WHO'S HIRING YOU, FOR GOD'S SAKE. IS IT REALLY ABOUT THE MONEY? I'M NOT GOING TO LET YOU END UP ON THE STREETS, DAD.
YOU COULD WRITE A BOOK ABOUT YOUR RELATIONSHIP WITH BATMAN, AND YOU'D BE SET FOR LIFE.
THAT WOMAN, CRESSIDA. SHE DIDN'T ASK ME TO BRING JOKER BACK AND TURN HIM IN TO THE AUTHORITIES, BARBARA. SHE ASKED ME TO FIND HIM AND *KILL* HIM.
YOU DIDN'T TELL BATMAN THAT.
NO. AND I'D PREFER IF YOU DIDN'T EITHER.
24h

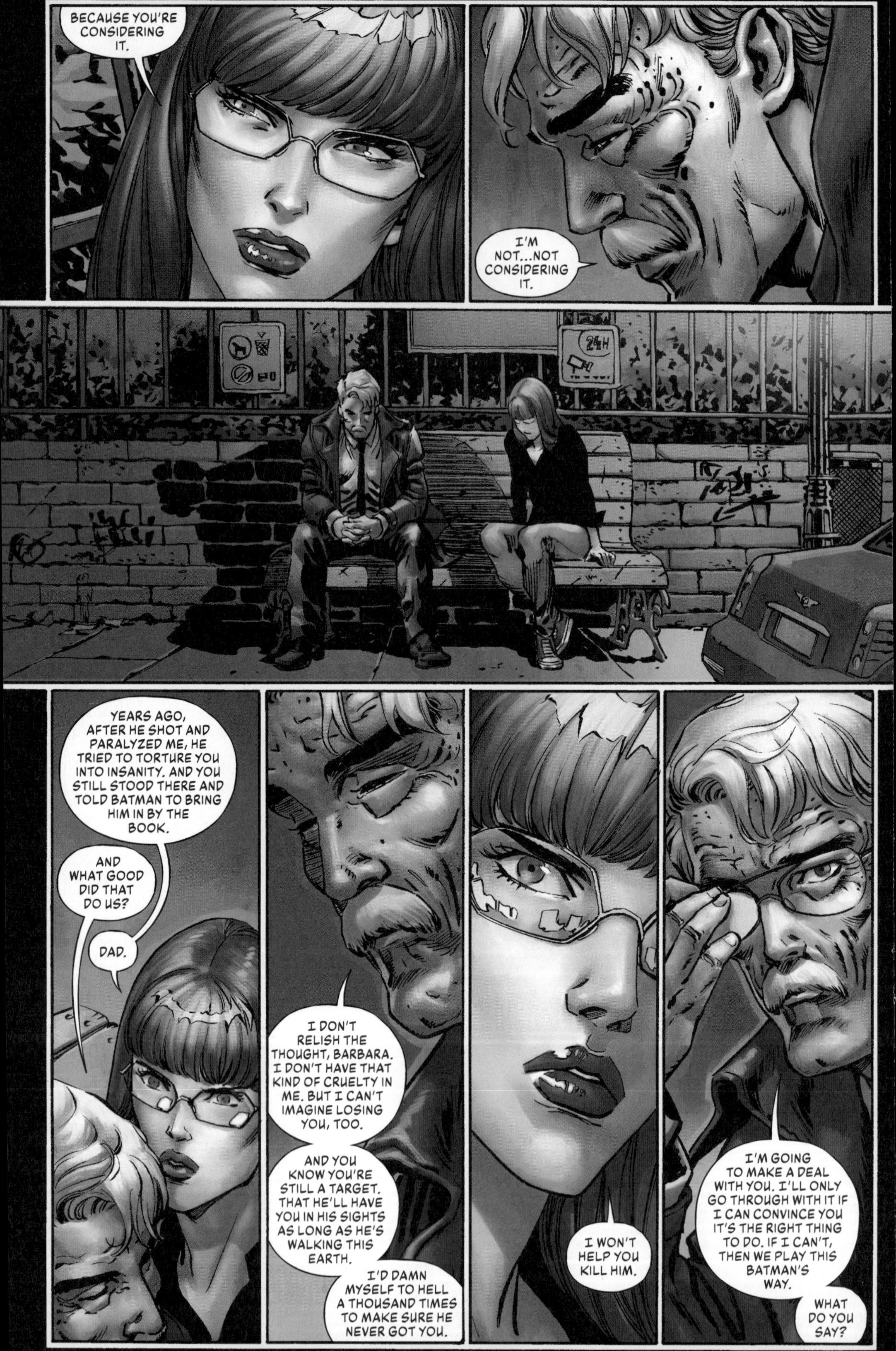
BECAUSE YOU'RE CONSIDERING IT.
I'M NOT...NOT CONSIDERING IT.
YEARS AGO, AFTER HE SHOT AND PARALYZED ME, HE TRIED TO TORTURE YOU INTO INSANITY. AND YOU STILL STOOD THERE AND TOLD BATMAN TO BRING HIM IN BY THE BOOK.
AND WHAT GOOD DID THAT DO US?
DAD.
I DON'T RELISH THE THOUGHT, BARBARA. I DON'T HAVE THAT KIND OF CRUELTY IN ME. BUT I CAN'T IMAGINE LOSING YOU, TOO.
AND YOU KNOW YOU'RE STILL A TARGET. THAT HE'LL HAVE YOU IN HIS SIGHTS AS LONG AS HE'S WALKING THIS EARTH.
I'D DAMN MYSELF TO HELL A THOUSAND TIMES TO MAKE SURE HE NEVER GOT YOU.
I WON'T HELP YOU KILL HIM.
I'M GOING TO MAKE A DEAL WITH YOU. I'LL ONLY GO THROUGH WITH IT IF I CAN CONVINCE YOU IT'S THE RIGHT THING TO DO. IF I CAN'T, THEN WE PLAY THIS BATMAN'S WAY.
WHAT DO YOU SAY?

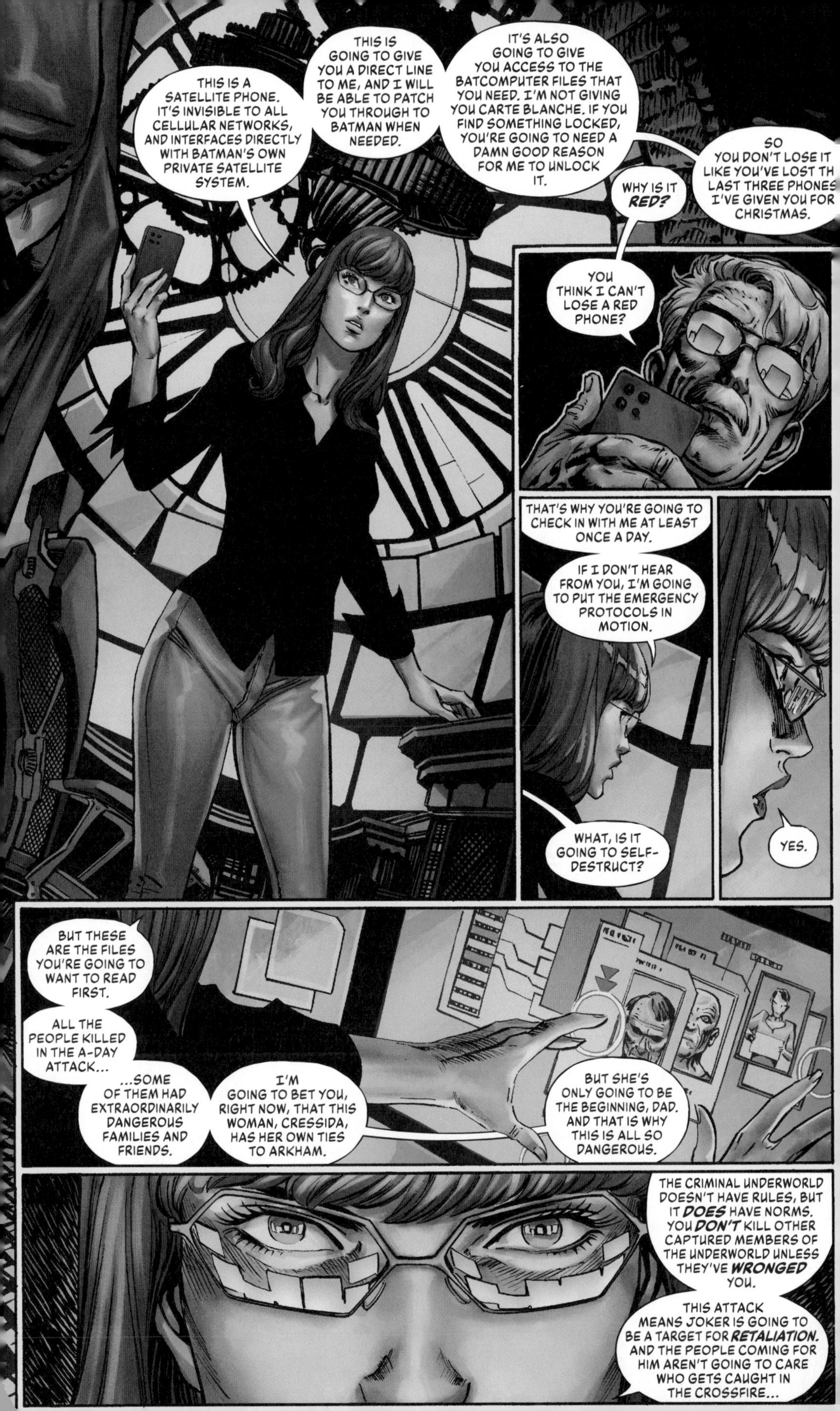
THIS IS A SATELLITE PHONE. IT'S INVISIBLE TO ALL CELLULAR NETWORKS, AND INTERFACES DIRECTLY WITH BATMAN'S OWN PRIVATE SATELLITE SYSTEM.
THIS IS GOING TO GIVE YOU A DIRECT LINE TO ME, AND I WILL BE ABLE TO PATCH YOU THROUGH TO BATMAN WHEN NEEDED.
IT'S ALSO GOING TO GIVE YOU ACCESS TO THE BATCOMPUTER FILES THAT YOU NEED. I'M NOT GIVING YOU CARTE BLANCHE. IF YOU FIND SOMETHING LOCKED, YOU'RE GOING TO NEED A DAMN GOOD REASON FOR ME TO UNLOCK IT.
WHY IS IT *RED?*
SO YOU DON'T LOSE IT LIKE YOU'VE LOST TH LAST THREE PHONES I'VE GIVEN YOU FOR CHRISTMAS.
YOU THINK I CAN'T LOSE A RED PHONE?
THAT'S WHY YOU'RE GOING TO CHECK IN WITH ME AT LEAST ONCE A DAY.
IF I DON'T HEAR FROM YOU, I'M GOING TO PUT THE EMERGENCY PROTOCOLS IN MOTION.
WHAT, IS IT GOING TO SELF-DESTRUCT?
YES.
BUT THESE ARE THE FILES YOU'RE GOING TO WANT TO READ FIRST.
ALL THE PEOPLE KILLED IN THE A-DAY ATTACK...
...SOME OF THEM HAD EXTRAORDINARILY DANGEROUS FAMILIES AND FRIENDS.
I'M GOING TO BET YOU, RIGHT NOW, THAT THIS WOMAN, CRESSIDA, HAS HER OWN TIES TO ARKHAM.
BUT SHE'S ONLY GOING TO BE THE BEGINNING, DAD. AND THAT IS WHY THIS IS ALL SO DANGEROUS.
THE CRIMINAL UNDERWORLD DOESN'T HAVE RULES, BUT IT *DOES* HAVE NORMS. YOU *DON'T* KILL OTHER CAPTURED MEMBERS OF THE UNDERWORLD UNLESS THEY'VE *WRONGED* YOU.
THIS ATTACK MEANS JOKER IS GOING TO BE A TARGET FOR *RETALIATION.* AND THE PEOPLE COMING FOR HIM AREN'T GOING TO CARE WHO GETS CAUGHT IN THE CROSSFIRE...

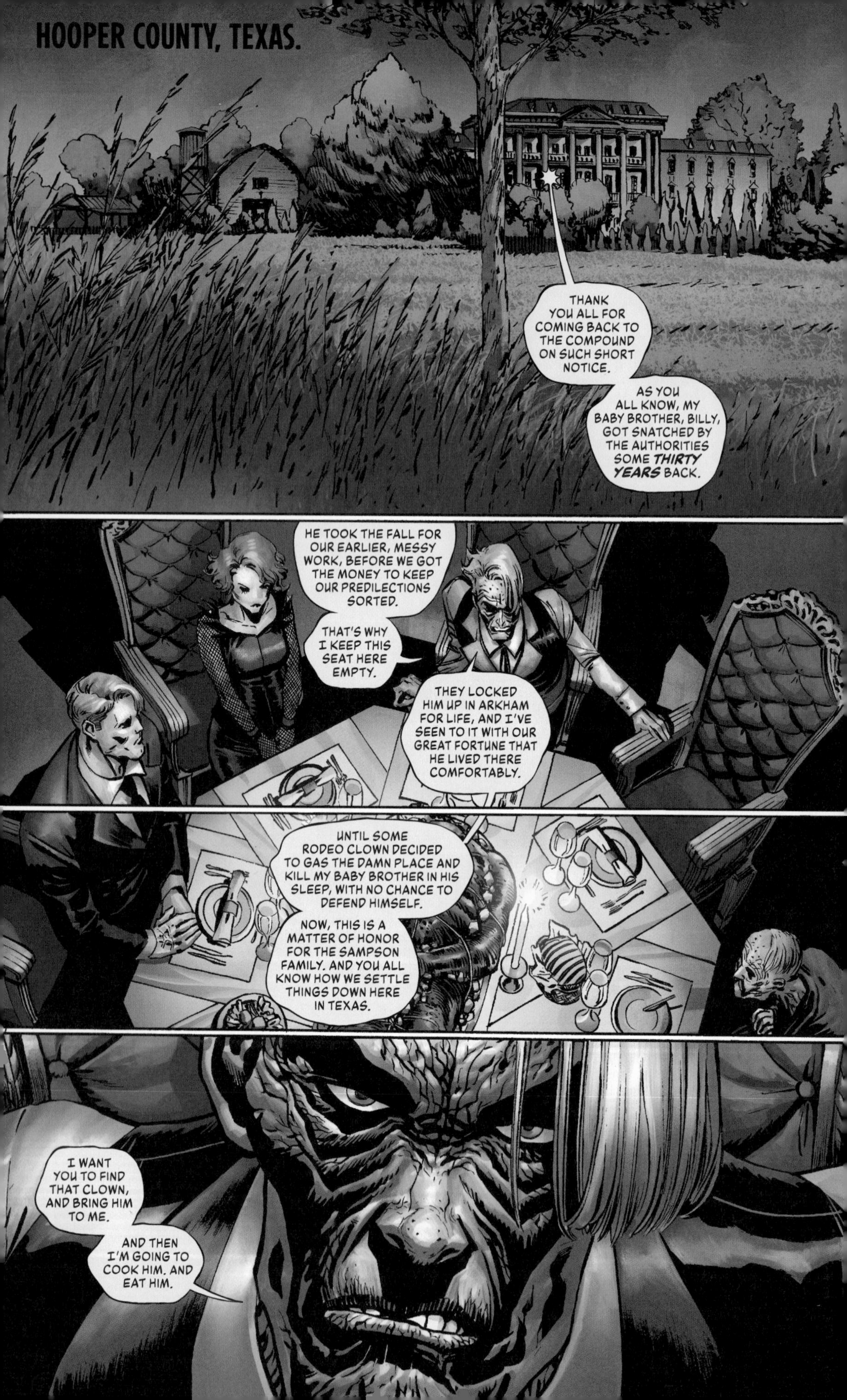
HOOPER COUNTY, TEXAS.
THANK YOU ALL FOR COMING BACK TO THE COMPOUND ON SUCH SHORT NOTICE.
AS YOU ALL KNOW, MY BABY BROTHER, BILLY, GOT SNATCHED BY THE AUTHORITIES SOME THIRTY YEARS BACK.
HE TOOK THE FALL FOR OUR EARLIER, MESSY WORK, BEFORE WE GOT THE MONEY TO KEEP OUR PREDILECTIONS SORTED.
THAT'S WHY I KEEP THIS SEAT HERE EMPTY.
THEY LOCKED HIM UP IN ARKHAM FOR LIFE, AND I'VE SEEN TO IT WITH OUR GREAT FORTUNE THAT HE LIVED THERE COMFORTABLY.
UNTIL SOME RODEO CLOWN DECIDED TO GAS THE DAMN PLACE AND KILL MY BABY BROTHER IN HIS SLEEP, WITH NO CHANCE TO DEFEND HIMSELF.
NOW, THIS IS A MATTER OF HONOR FOR THE SAMPSON FAMILY. AND YOU ALL KNOW HOW WE SETTLE THINGS DOWN HERE IN TEXAS.
I WANT YOU TO FIND THAT CLOWN, AND BRING HIM TO ME.
AND THEN I'M GOING TO COOK HIM. AND EAT HIM.

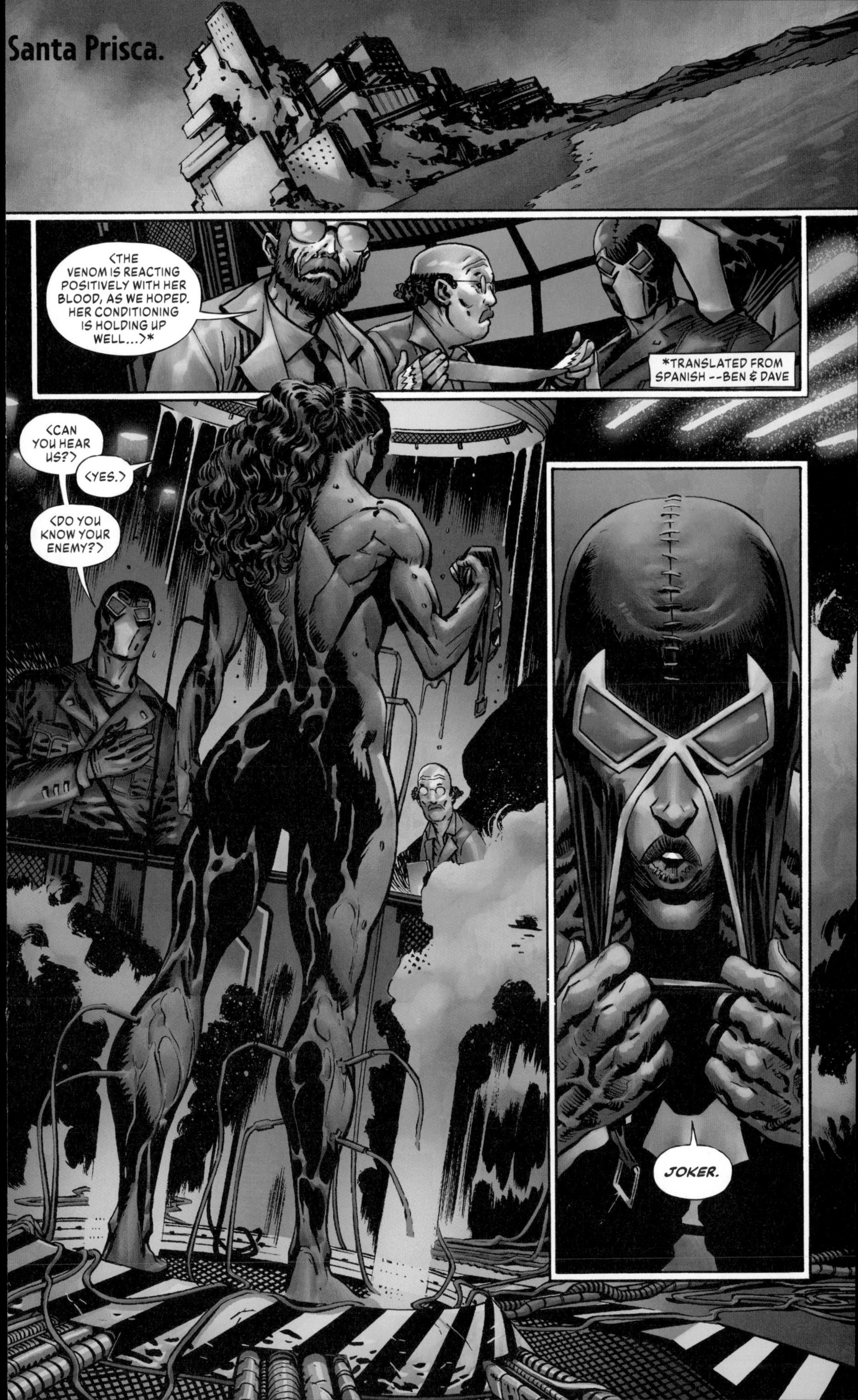
Santa Prisca.
<THE VENOM IS REACTING POSITIVELY WITH HER BLOOD, AS WE HOPED. HER CONDITIONING IS HOLDING UP WELL...>*
*TRANSLATED FROM SPANISH --BEN & DAVE
<CAN YOU HEAR US?>
<YES.>
<DO YOU KNOW YOUR ENEMY?>
JOKER.

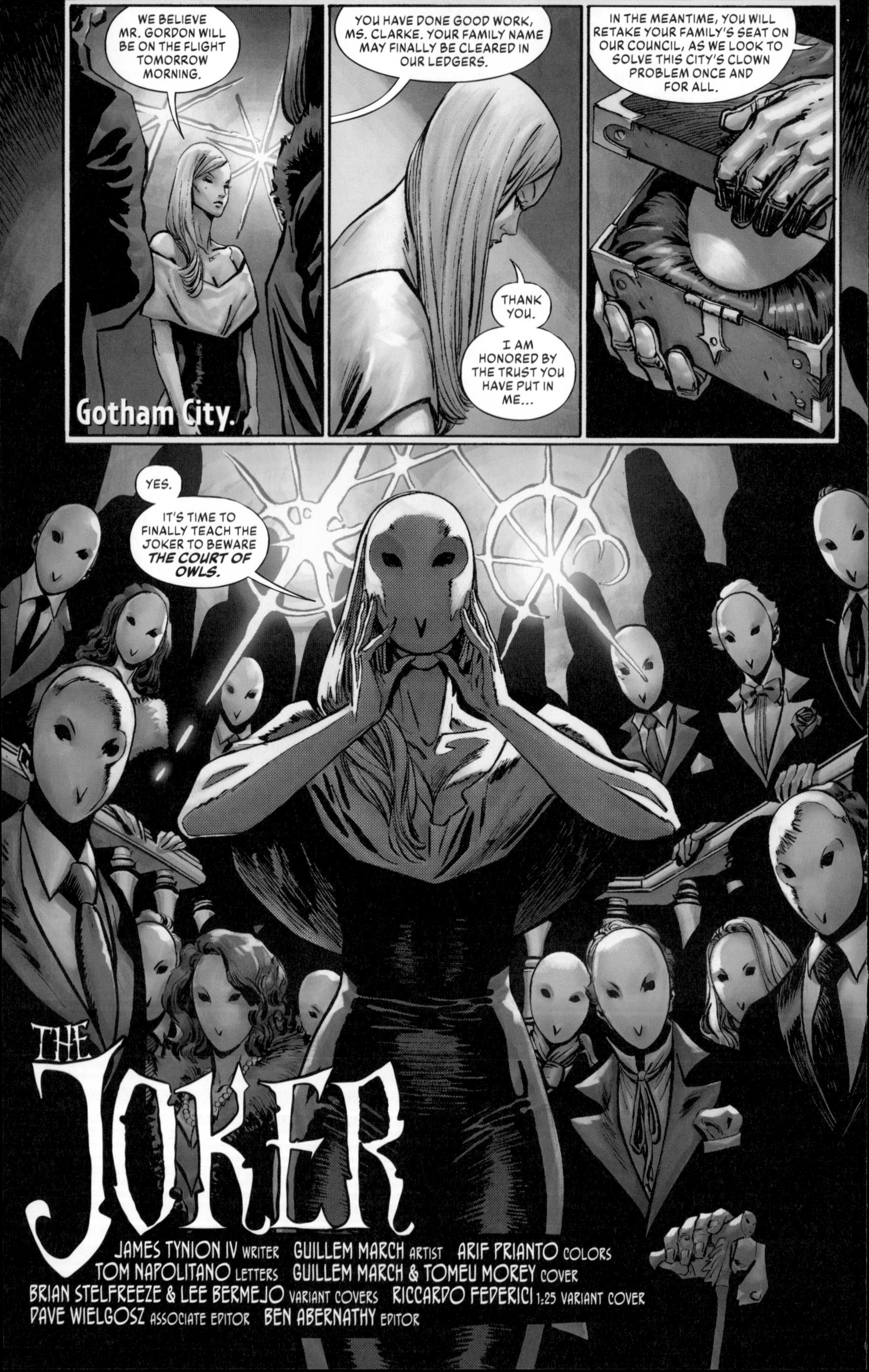
WE BELIEVE MR. GORDON WILL BE ON THE FLIGHT TOMORROW MORNING.
Gotham City.
YOU HAVE DONE GOOD WORK, MS. CLARKE. YOUR FAMILY NAME MAY FINALLY BE CLEARED IN OUR LEDGERS.
THANK YOU.
I AM HONORED BY THE TRUST YOU HAVE PUT IN ME...
IN THE MEANTIME, YOU WILL RETAKE YOUR FAMILY'S SEAT ON OUR COUNCIL, AS WE LOOK TO SOLVE THIS CITY'S CLOWN PROBLEM ONCE AND FOR ALL.
YES.
IT'S TIME TO FINALLY TEACH THE JOKER TO BEWARE *THE COURT OF OWLS.*
THE JOKER
JAMES TYNION IV WRITER GUILLEM MARCH ARTIST ARIF PRIANTO COLORS
TOM NAPOLITANO LETTERS GUILLEM MARCH & TOMEU MOREY COVER
BRIAN STELFREEZE & LEE BERMEJO VARIANT COVERS RICCARDO FEDERICI 1:25 VARIANT COVER
DAVE WIELGOSZ ASSOCIATE EDITOR BEN ABERNATHY EDITOR

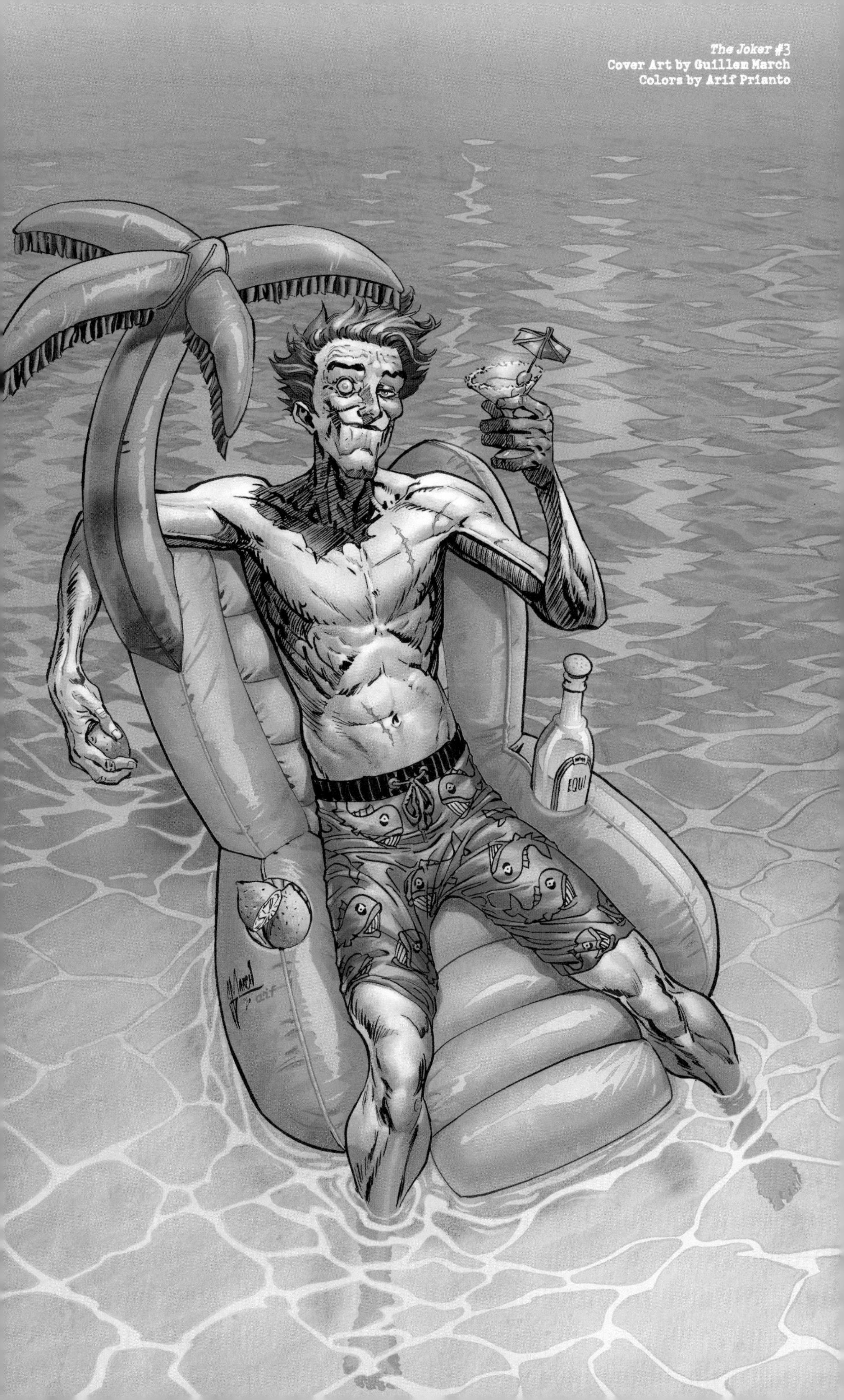
EQUI

The Joker #3
Cover Art by Guillem March
Colors by Arif Prianto

Chapter Seven: One Bad Day

I'm ashamed to admit it, but there are still nights when it all comes back to me. That night in **Amusement Mile**.

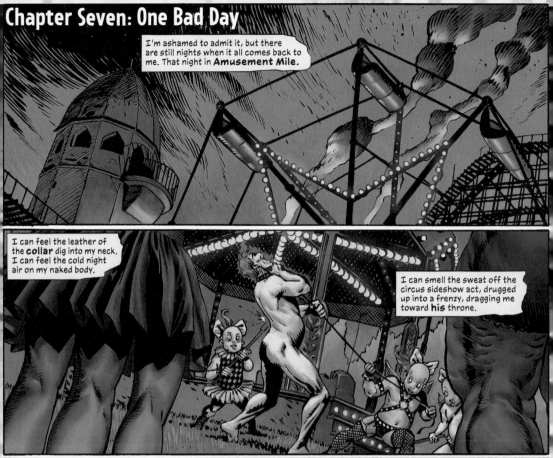

I can feel the leather of the **collar** dig into my neck. I can feel the cold night air on my naked body.

I can smell the sweat off the circus sideshow act, drugged up into a frenzy, dragging me toward **his** throne.

I remember the panic rising in my chest as I tried to grapple with what was happening around me.

I asked, delirious, what I was doing there. And then the voice of the Devil responded...

DOING?

YOU'RE DOING WHAT **ANY** SANE MAN IN YOUR APPALLING CIRCUMSTANCES WOULD DO.

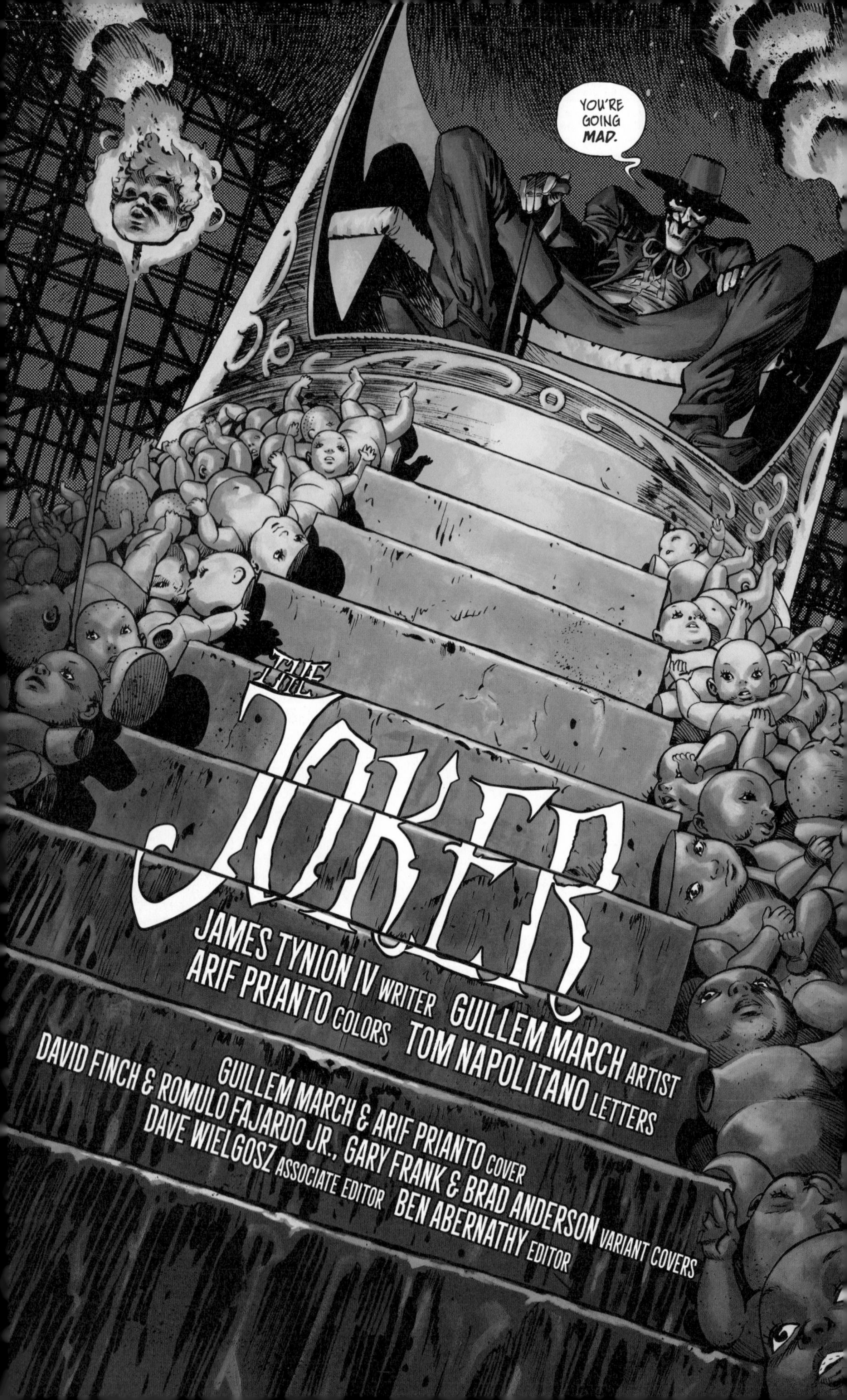
YOU'RE GOING MAD.
THE JOKER
JAMES TYNION IV WRITER GUILLEM MARCH ARTIST
ARIF PRIANTO COLORS TOM NAPOLITANO LETTERS
GUILLEM MARCH & ARIF PRIANTO COVER
DAVID FINCH & ROMULO FAJARDO JR., GARY FRANK & BRAD ANDERSON VARIANT COVERS
DAVE WIELGOSZ ASSOCIATE EDITOR BEN ABERNATHY EDITOR

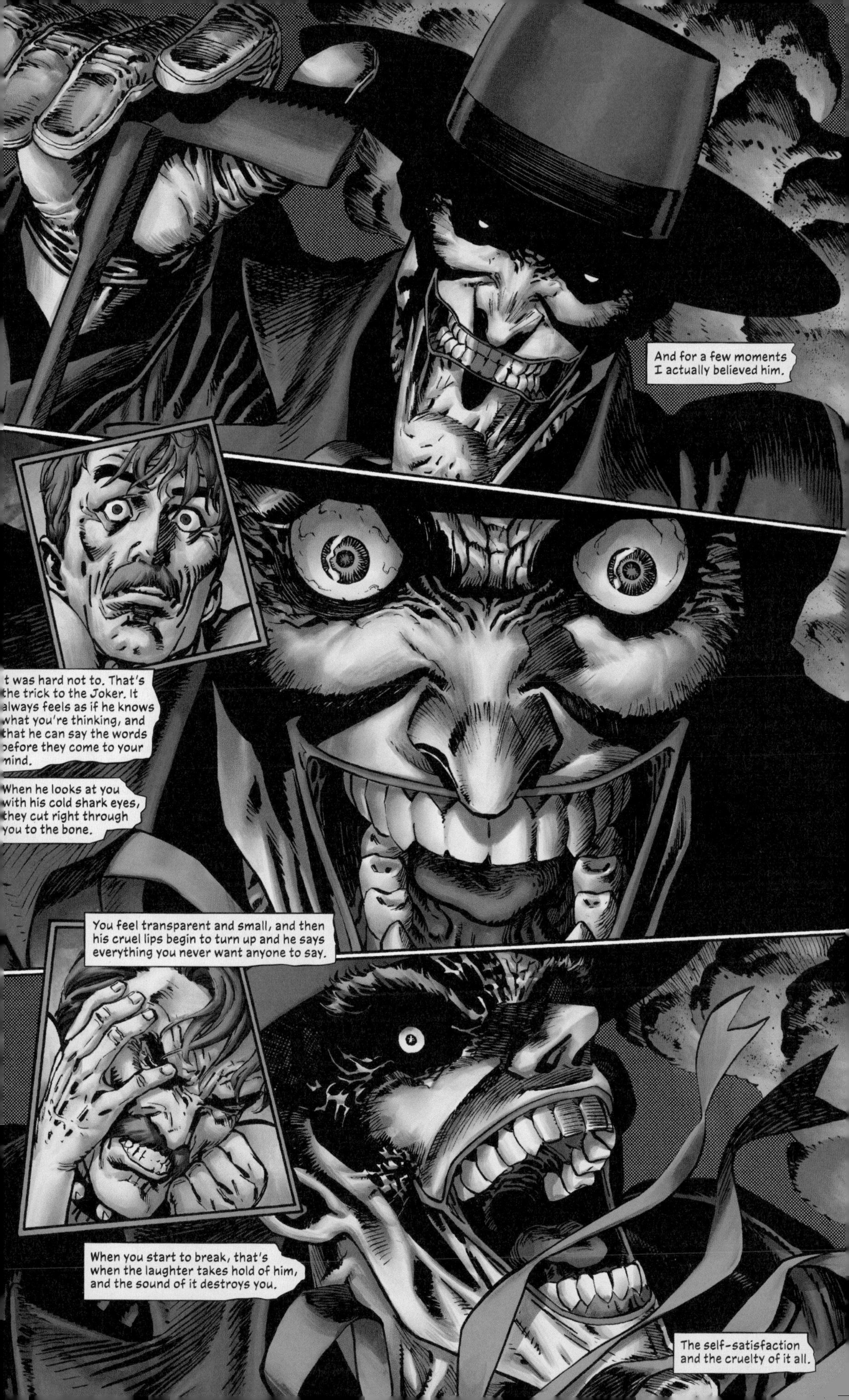
And for a few moments I actually believed him.
t was hard not to. That's the trick to the Joker. It always feels as if he knows what you're thinking, and that he can say the words before they come to your mind.
When he looks at you with his cold shark eyes, they cut right through you to the bone.
You feel transparent and small, and then his cruel lips begin to turn up and he says everything you never want anyone to say.
When you start to break, that's when the laughter takes hold of him, and the sound of it destroys you.
The self-satisfaction and the cruelty of it all.

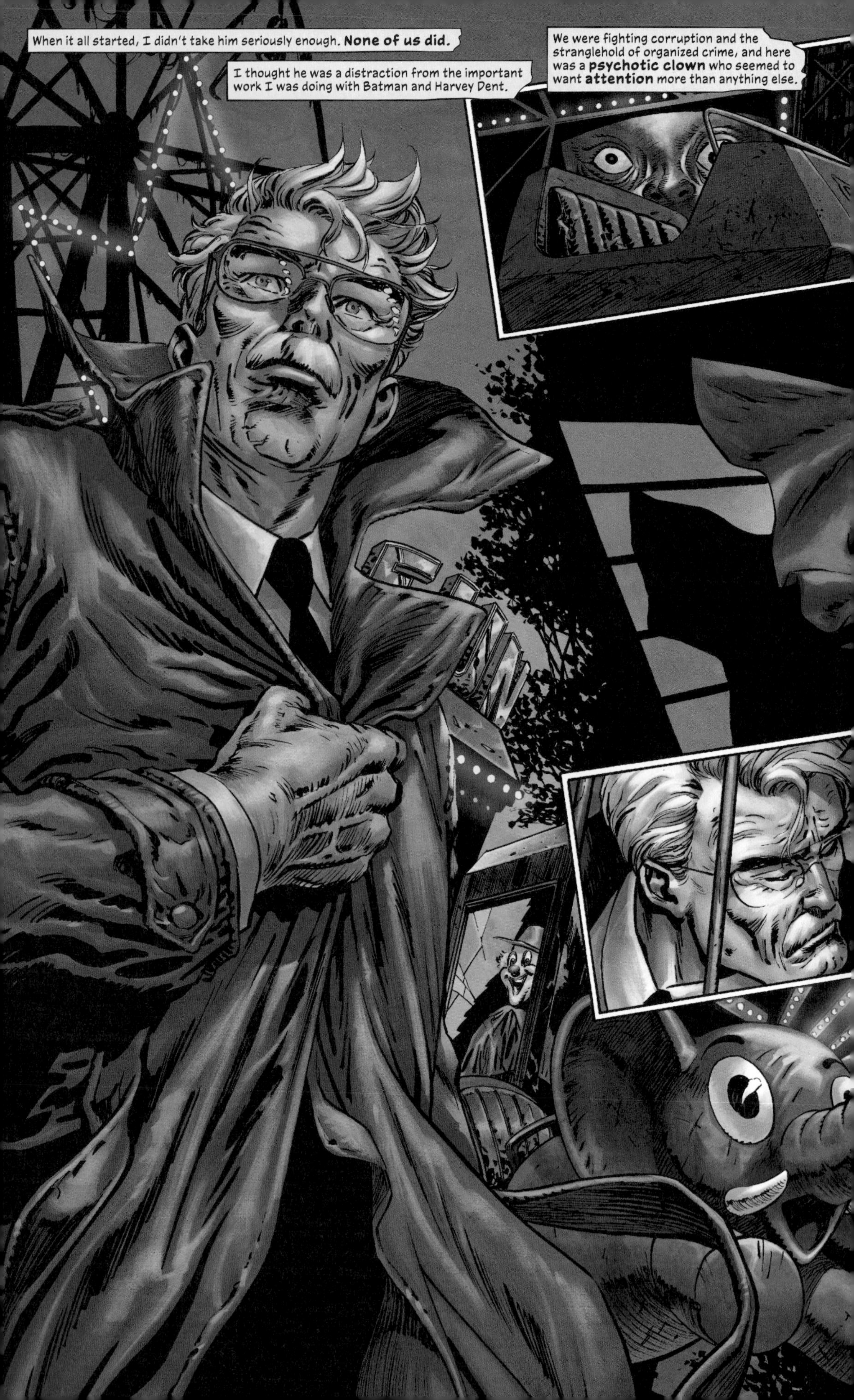

When it all started, I didn't take him seriously enough. **None of us did.**
I thought he was a distraction from the important work I was doing with Batman and Harvey Dent.
We were fighting corruption and the stranglehold of organized crime, and here was a **psychotic clown** who seemed to want **attention** more than anything else.

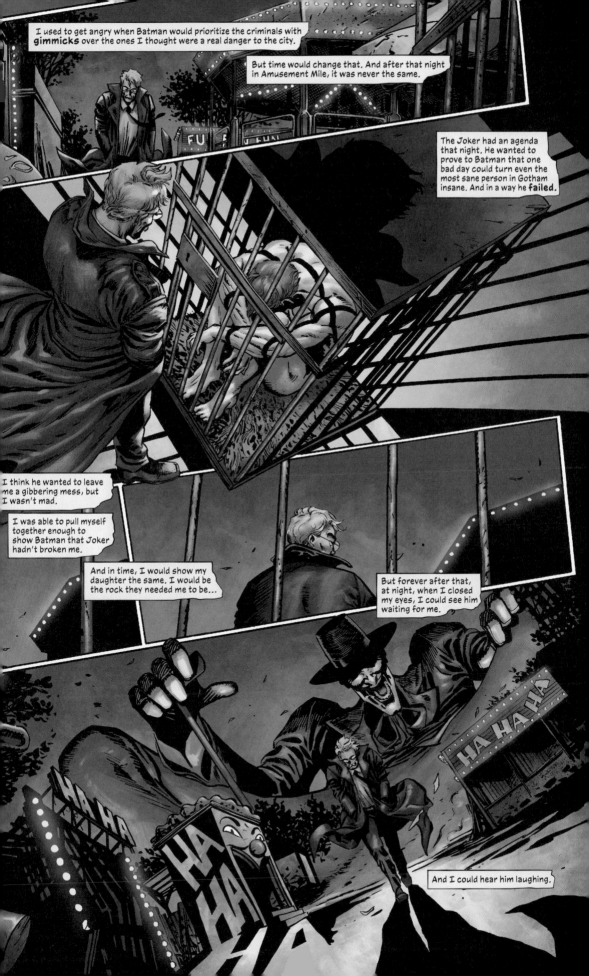

I used to get angry when Batman would prioritize the criminals with **gimmicks** over the ones I thought were a real danger to the city.

But time would change that. And after that night in Amusement Mile, it was never the same.

The Joker had an agenda that night. He wanted to prove to Batman that one bad day could turn even the most sane person in Gotham insane. And in a way he **failed**.

I think he wanted to leave me a gibbering mess, but I wasn't mad.

I was able to pull myself together enough to show Batman that Joker hadn't broken me.

And in time, I would show my daughter the same. I would be the rock they needed me to be...

But forever after that, at night, when I closed my eyes, I could see him waiting for me.

And I could hear him laughing.

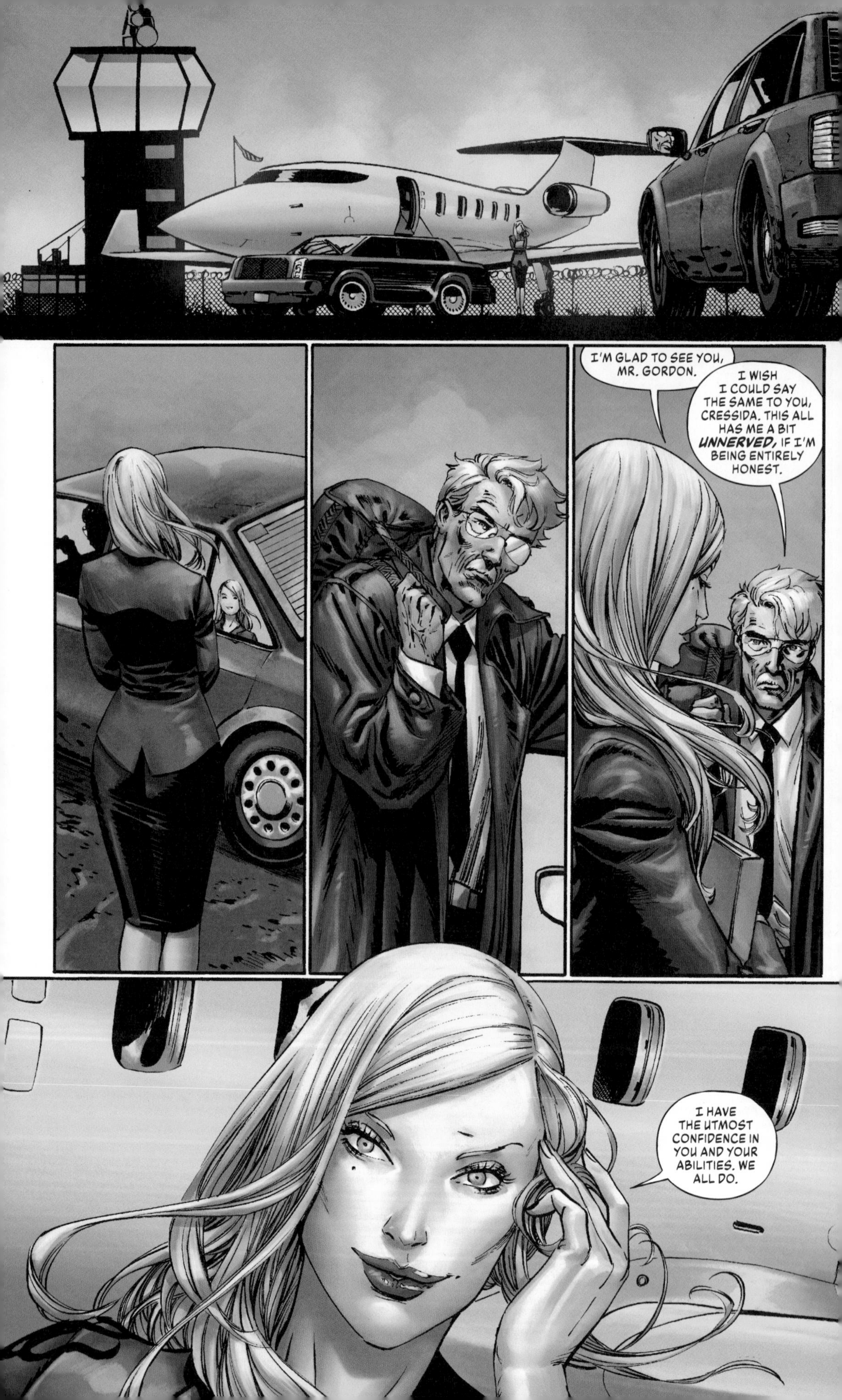

I'M GLAD TO SEE YOU, MR. GORDON.
I WISH I COULD SAY THE SAME TO YOU, CRESSIDA. THIS ALL HAS ME A BIT *UNNERVED,* IF I'M BEING ENTIRELY HONEST.
I HAVE THE UTMOST CONFIDENCE IN YOU AND YOUR ABILITIES. WE ALL DO.

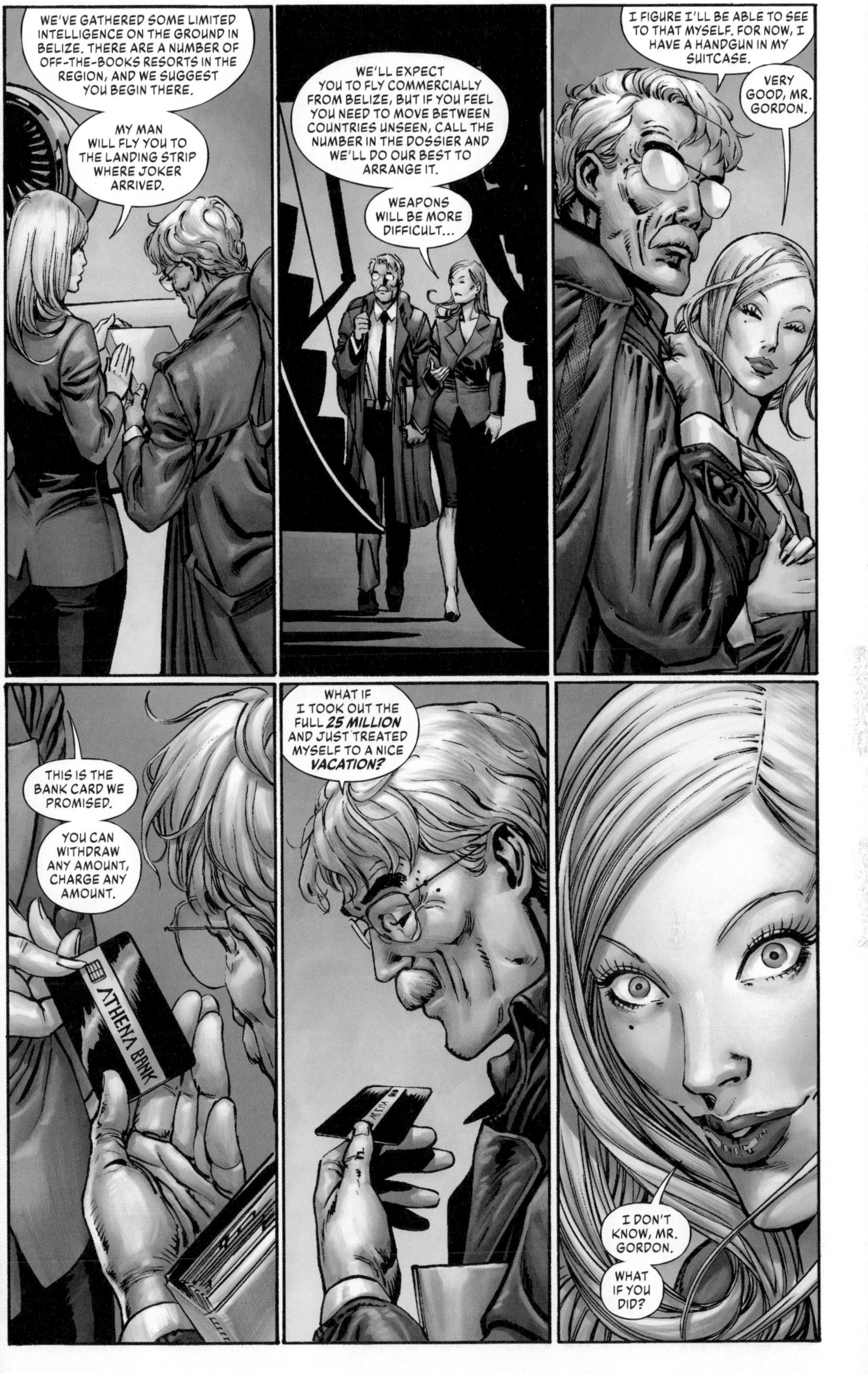
WE'VE GATHERED SOME LIMITED INTELLIGENCE ON THE GROUND IN BELIZE. THERE ARE A NUMBER OF OFF-THE-BOOKS RESORTS IN THE REGION, AND WE SUGGEST YOU BEGIN THERE.
MY MAN WILL FLY YOU TO THE LANDING STRIP WHERE JOKER ARRIVED.
WE'LL EXPECT YOU TO FLY COMMERCIALLY FROM BELIZE, BUT IF YOU FEEL YOU NEED TO MOVE BETWEEN COUNTRIES UNSEEN, CALL THE NUMBER IN THE DOSSIER AND WE'LL DO OUR BEST TO ARRANGE IT.
WEAPONS WILL BE MORE DIFFICULT...
I FIGURE I'LL BE ABLE TO SEE TO THAT MYSELF. FOR NOW, I HAVE A HANDGUN IN MY SUITCASE.
VERY GOOD, MR. GORDON.
THIS IS THE BANK CARD WE PROMISED.
YOU CAN WITHDRAW ANY AMOUNT, CHARGE ANY AMOUNT.
ATHENA BANK
WHAT IF I TOOK OUT THE FULL **25 MILLION** AND JUST TREATED MYSELF TO A NICE **VACATION?**
I DON'T KNOW, MR. GORDON.
WHAT IF YOU DID?

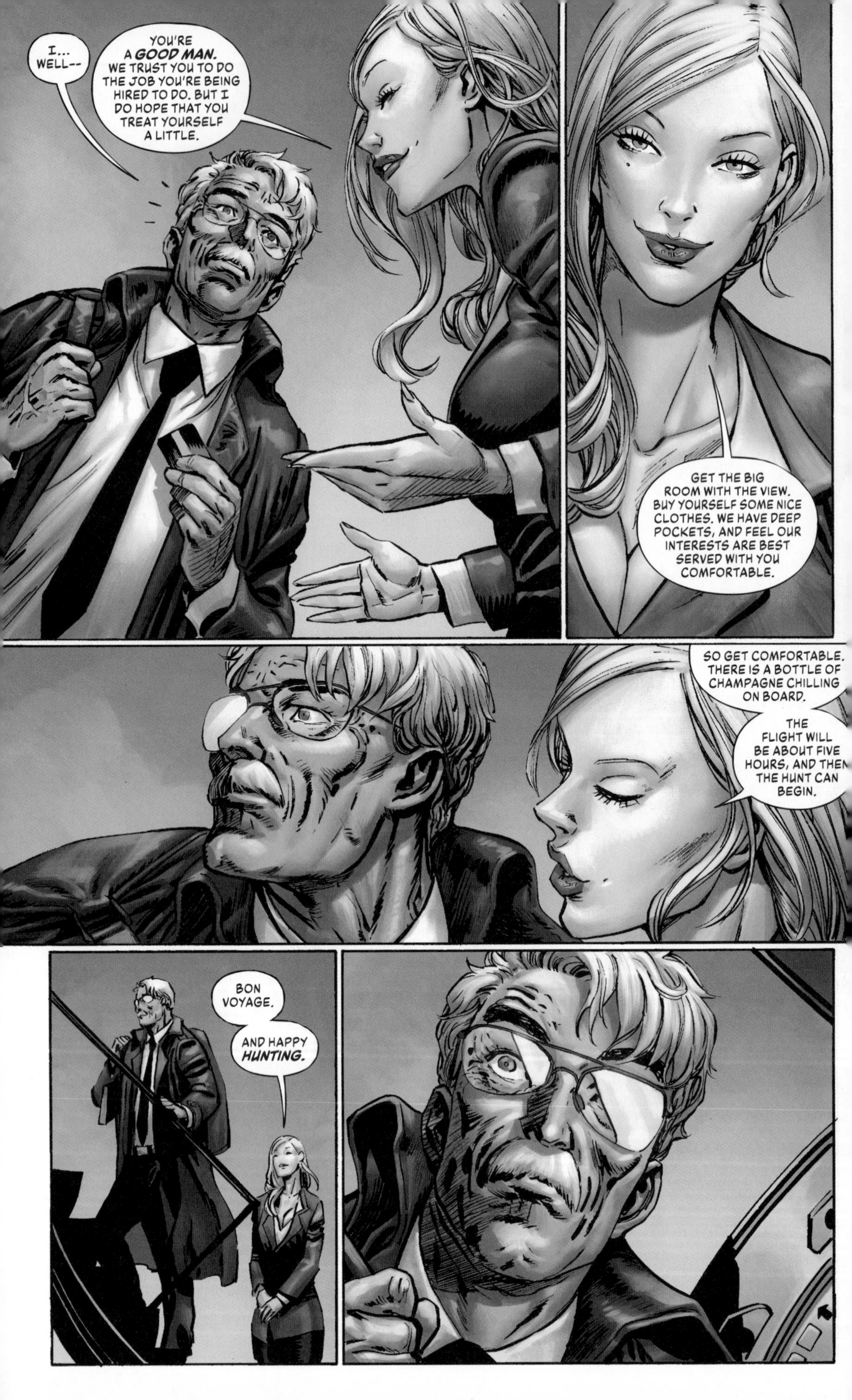

I... WELL--
YOU'RE A GOOD MAN. WE TRUST YOU TO DO THE JOB YOU'RE BEING HIRED TO DO. BUT I DO HOPE THAT YOU TREAT YOURSELF A LITTLE.
GET THE BIG ROOM WITH THE VIEW. BUY YOURSELF SOME NICE CLOTHES. WE HAVE DEEP POCKETS, AND FEEL OUR INTERESTS ARE BEST SERVED WITH YOU COMFORTABLE.
SO GET COMFORTABLE. THERE IS A BOTTLE OF CHAMPAGNE CHILLING ON BOARD.
THE FLIGHT WILL BE ABOUT FIVE HOURS, AND THEN THE HUNT CAN BEGIN.
BON VOYAGE.
AND HAPPY HUNTING.

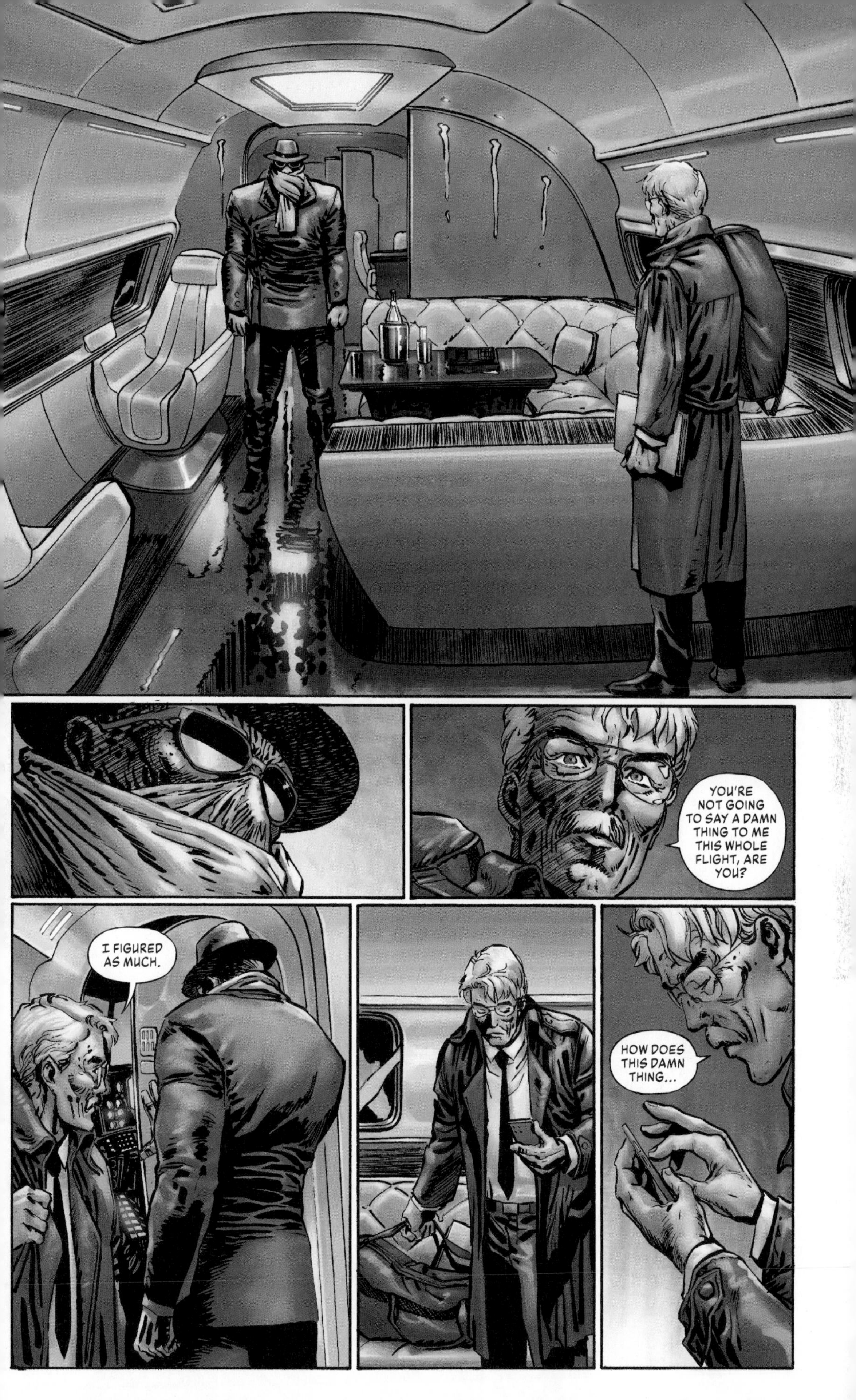

YOU'RE NOT GOING TO SAY A DAMN THING TO ME THIS WHOLE FLIGHT, ARE YOU?
I FIGURED AS MUCH.
HOW DOES THIS DAMN THING...

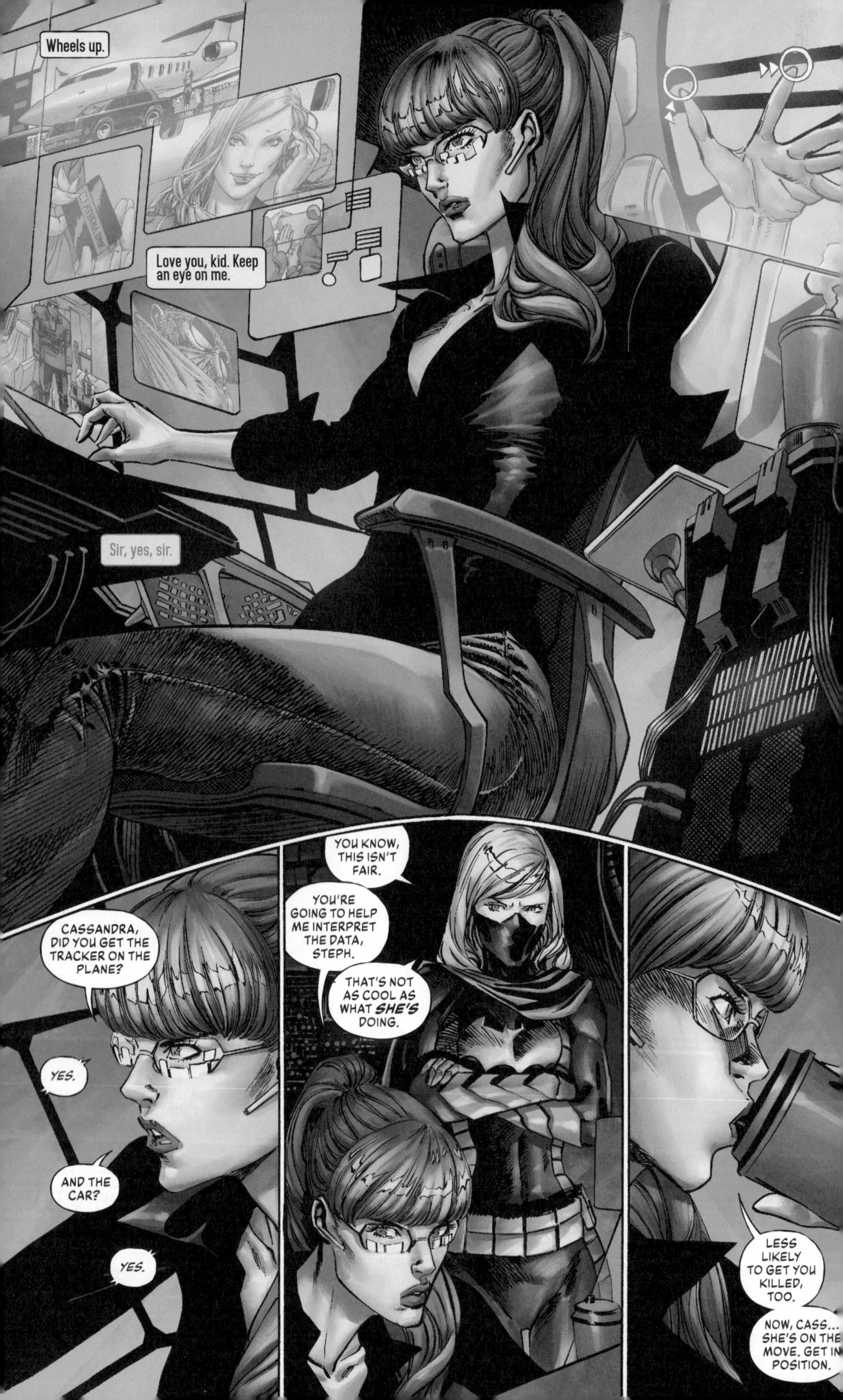

Wheels up.
Love you, kid. Keep an eye on me.
Sir, yes, sir.
CASSANDRA, DID YOU GET THE TRACKER ON THE PLANE?
YES.
AND THE CAR?
YES.
YOU KNOW, THIS ISN'T FAIR.
YOU'RE GOING TO HELP ME INTERPRET THE DATA, STEPH.
THAT'S NOT AS COOL AS WHAT SHE'S DOING.
LESS LIKELY TO GET YOU KILLED, TOO.
NOW, CASS... SHE'S ON THE MOVE. GET IN POSITION.

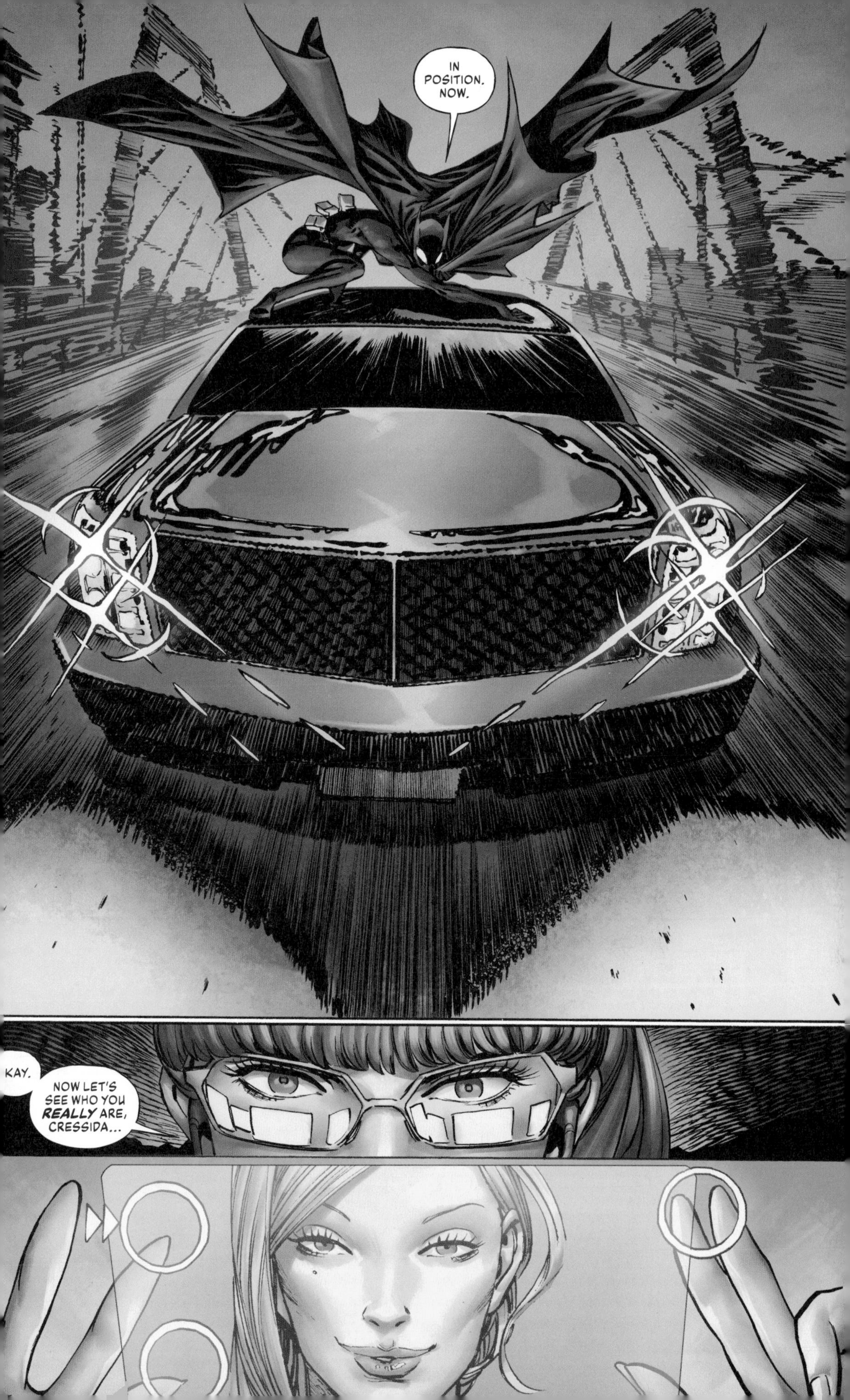
IN POSITION. NOW.
KAY.
NOW LET'S SEE WHO YOU *REALLY* ARE, CRESSIDA...

Chapter Eight: Gut Work

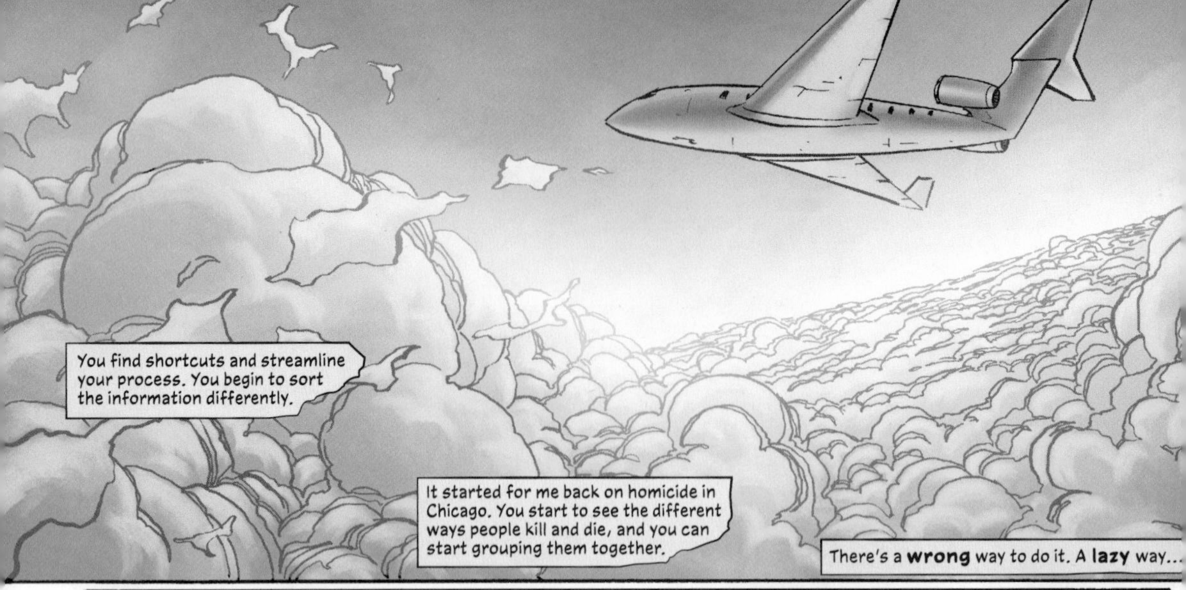
You find shortcuts and streamline your process. You begin to sort the information differently.
It started for me back on homicide in Chicago. You start to see the different ways people kill and die, and you can start grouping them together.
There's a **wrong** way to do it. A **lazy** way...

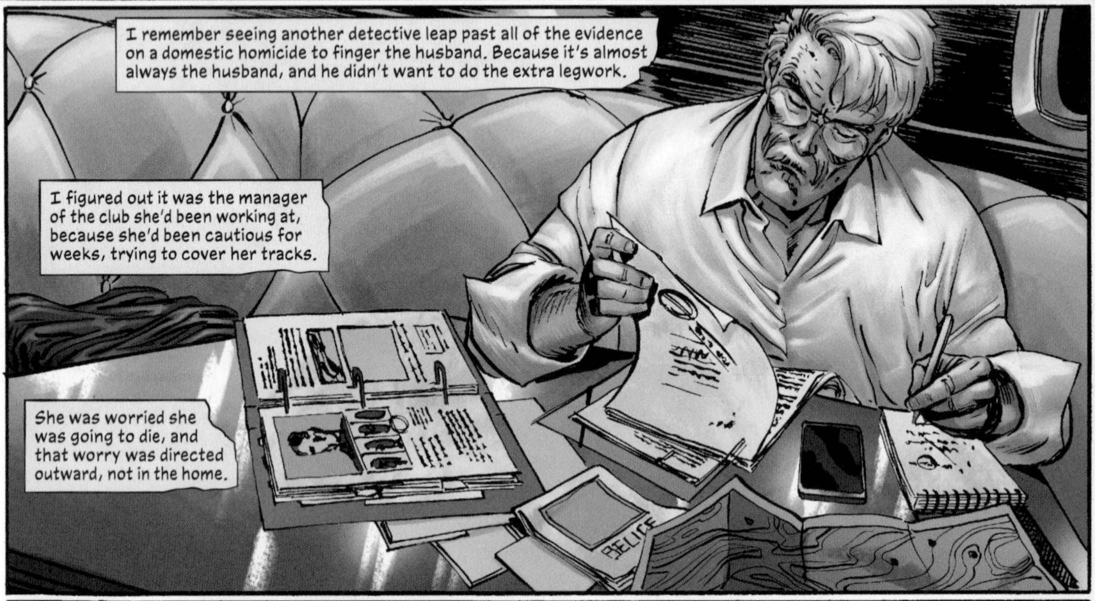
I remember seeing another detective leap past all of the evidence on a domestic homicide to finger the husband. Because it's almost always the husband, and he didn't want to do the extra legwork.
I figured out it was the manager of the club she'd been working at, because she'd been cautious for weeks, trying to cover her tracks.
She was worried she was going to die, and that worry was directed outward, not in the home.

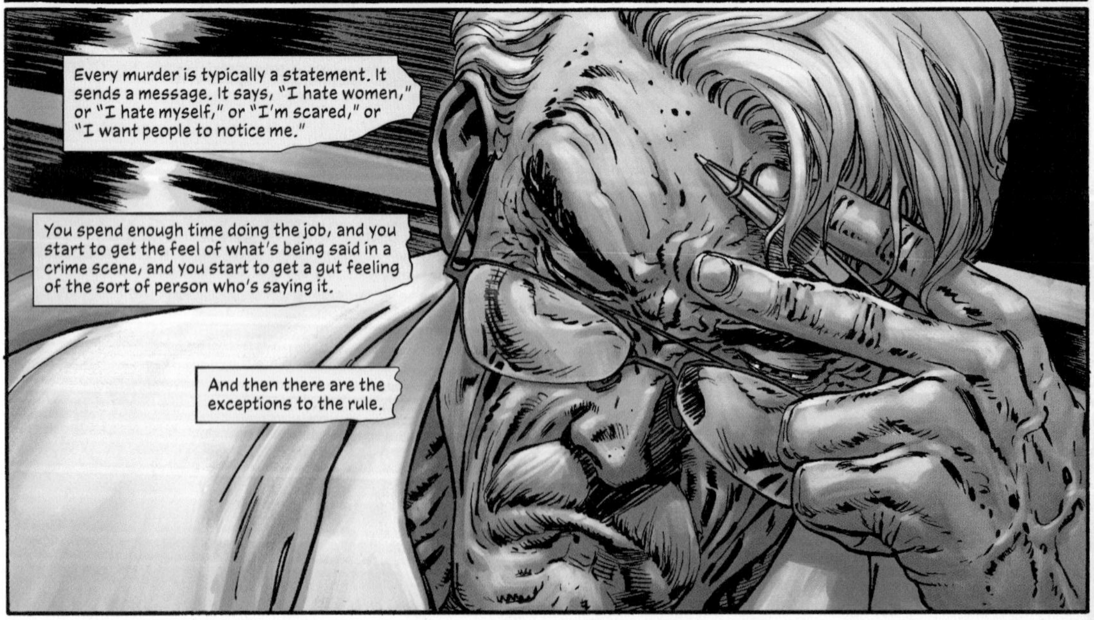
Every murder is typically a statement. It sends a message. It says, "I hate women," or "I hate myself," or "I'm scared," or "I want people to notice me."
You spend enough time doing the job, and you start to get the feel of what's being said in a crime scene, and you start to get a gut feeling of the sort of person who's saying it.
And then there are the exceptions to the rule.

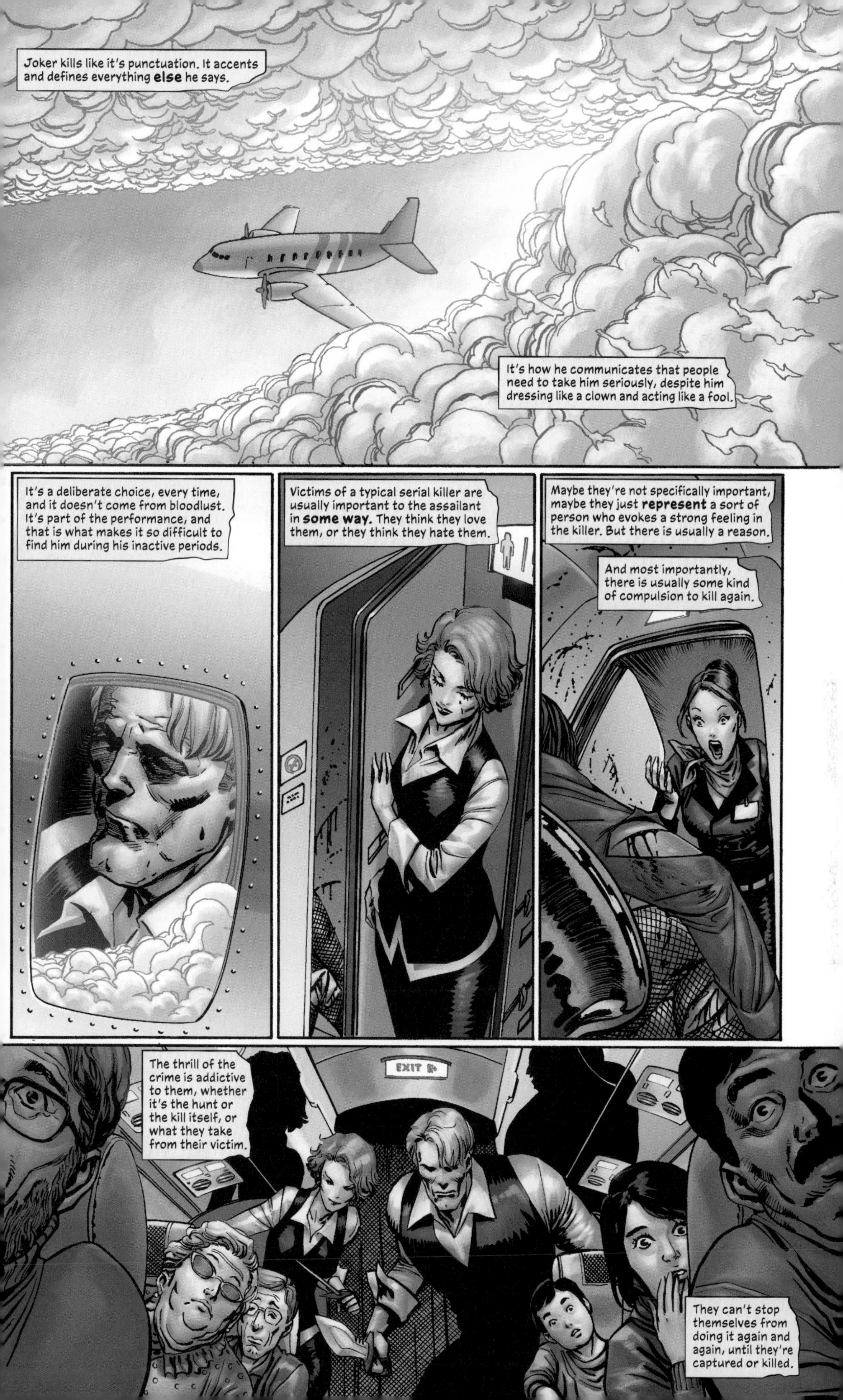
Joker kills like it's punctuation. It accents and defines everything else he says.
It's how he communicates that people need to take him seriously, despite him dressing like a clown and acting like a fool.
It's a deliberate choice, every time, and it doesn't come from bloodlust. It's part of the performance, and that is what makes it so difficult to find him during his inactive periods.
Victims of a typical serial killer are usually important to the assailant in some way. They think they love them, or they think they hate them.
Maybe they're not specifically important, maybe they just represent a sort of person who evokes a strong feeling in the killer. But there is usually a reason.
And most importantly, there is usually some kind of compulsion to kill again.
The thrill of the crime is addictive to them, whether it's the hunt or the kill itself, or what they take from their victim.
EXIT
They can't stop themselves from doing it again and again, until they're captured or killed.

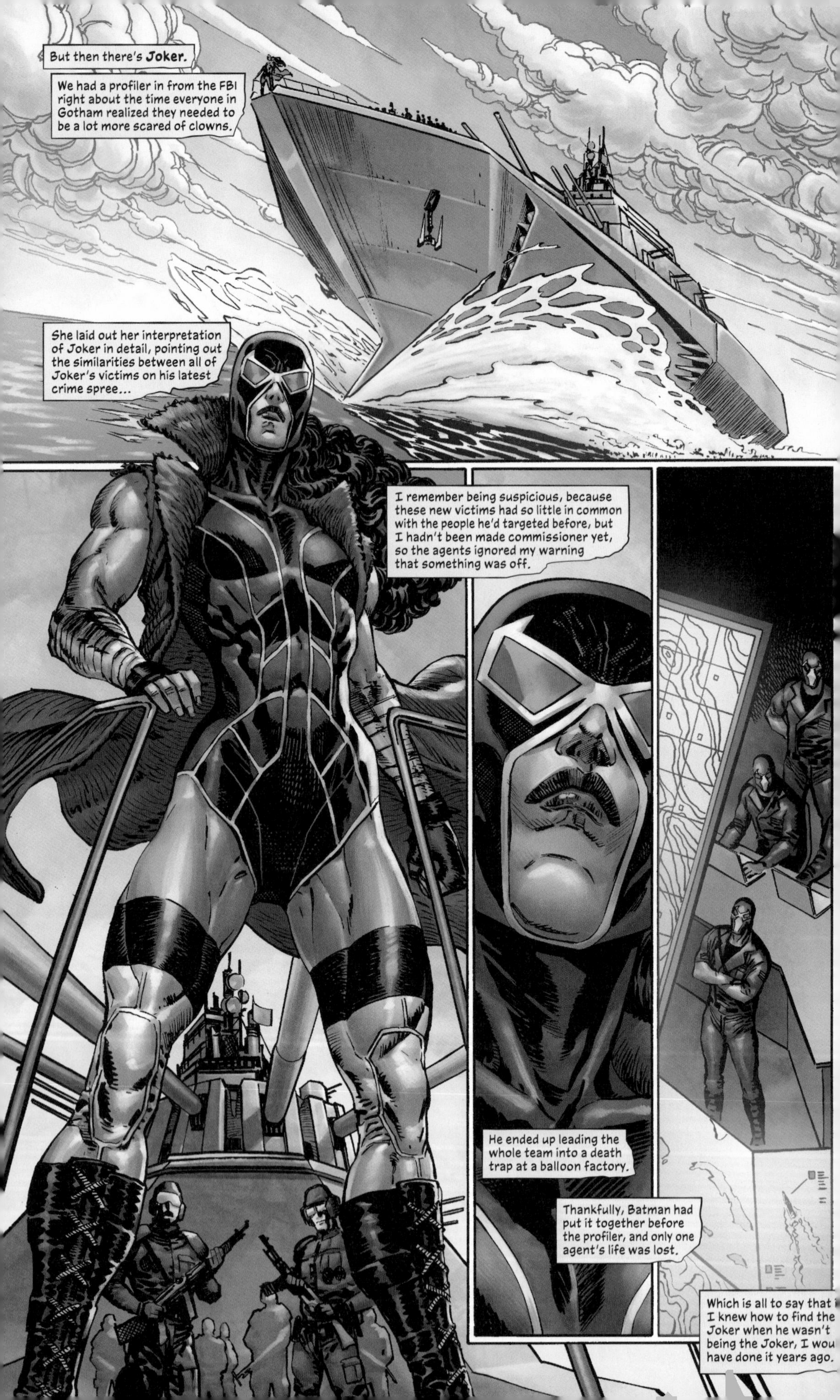

But then there's **Joker.**
We had a profiler in from the FBI right about the time everyone in Gotham realized they needed to be a lot more scared of clowns.
She laid out her interpretation of Joker in detail, pointing out the similarities between all of Joker's victims on his latest crime spree...
I remember being suspicious, because these new victims had so little in common with the people he'd targeted before, but I hadn't been made commissioner yet, so the agents ignored my warning that something was off.
He ended up leading the whole team into a death trap at a balloon factory.
Thankfully, Batman had put it together before the profiler, and only one agent's life was lost.
Which is all to say that I knew how to find the Joker when he wasn't being the Joker, I wou have done it years ago.

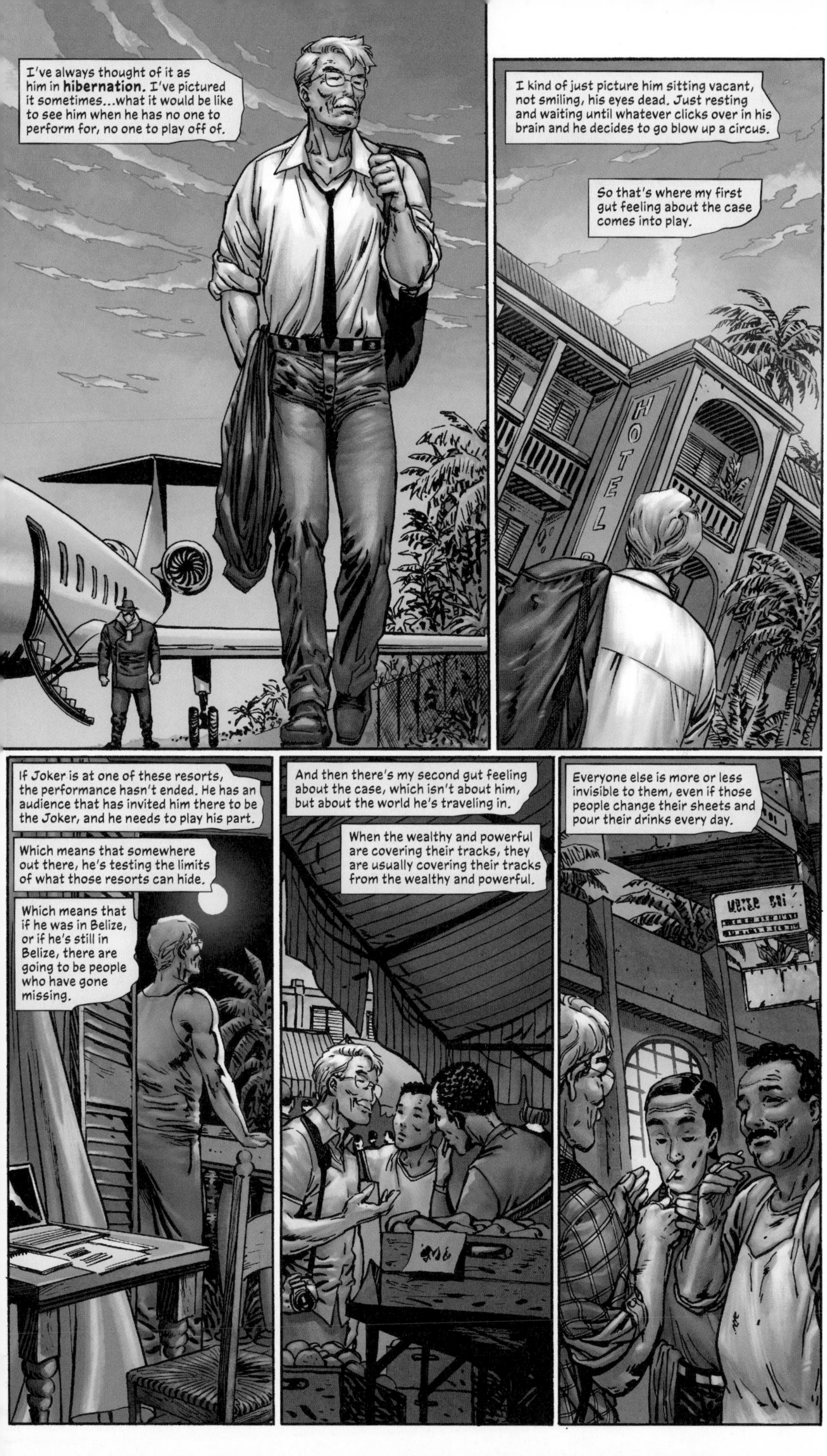
I've always thought of it as him in **hibernation.** I've pictured it sometimes...what it would be like to see him when he has no one to perform for, no one to play off of.
I kind of just picture him sitting vacant, not smiling, his eyes dead. Just resting and waiting until whatever clicks over in his brain and he decides to go blow up a circus.
So that's where my first gut feeling about the case comes into play.
HOTEL
If Joker is at one of these resorts, the performance hasn't ended. He has an audience that has invited him there to be the Joker, and he needs to play his part.
Which means that somewhere out there, he's testing the limits of what those resorts can hide.
Which means that if he was in Belize, or if he's still in Belize, there are going to be people who have gone missing.
And then there's my second gut feeling about the case, which isn't about him, but about the world he's traveling in.
When the wealthy and powerful are covering their tracks, they are usually covering their tracks from the wealthy and powerful.
Everyone else is more or less invisible to them, even if those people change their sheets and pour their drinks every day.

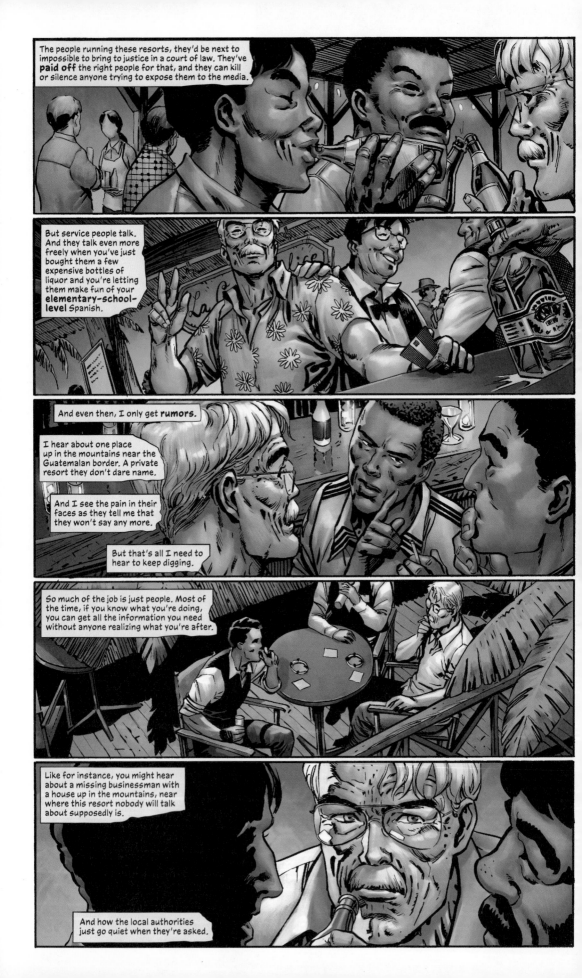

The people running these resorts, they'd be next to impossible to bring to justice in a court of law. They've **paid off** the right people for that, and they can kill or silence anyone trying to expose them to the media.

But service people talk. And they talk even more freely when you've just bought them a few expensive bottles of liquor and you're letting them make fun of your **elementary-school-level** Spanish.

And even then, I only get **rumors**.

I hear about one place up in the mountains near the Guatemalan border. A private resort they don't dare name.

And I see the pain in their faces as they tell me that they won't say any more.

But that's all I need to hear to keep digging.

So much of the job is just people. Most of the time, if you know what you're doing, you can get all the information you need without anyone realizing what you're after.

Like for instance, you might hear about a missing businessman with a house up in the mountains, near where this resort nobody will talk about supposedly is.

And how the local authorities just go quiet when they're asked.

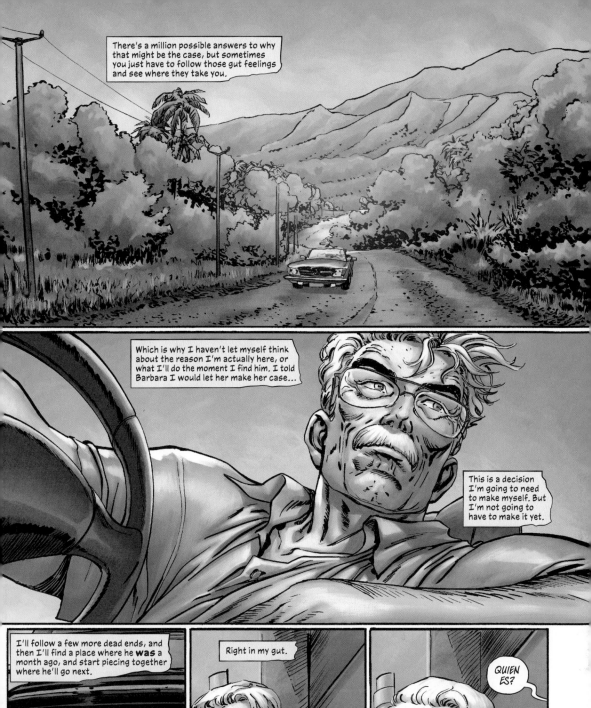

There's a million possible answers to why that might be the case, but sometimes you just have to follow those gut feelings and see where they take you.

Which is why I haven't let myself think about the reason I'm actually here, or what I'll do the moment I find him. I told Barbara I would let her make her case...

This is a decision I'm going to need to make myself. But I'm not going to have to make it yet.

I'll follow a few more dead ends, and then I'll find a place where he **was** a month ago, and start piecing together where he'll go next.

I'm not going to have to make a decision for a while yet. I feel that one too.

Right in my gut.

QUIEN ES?

SORRY... MY SPANISH ISN'T TOO STRONG. I WAS JUST HOPING TO ASK A FEW QUESTIONS. I'M LOOKING FOR AN OLD FRIEND OF MINE.

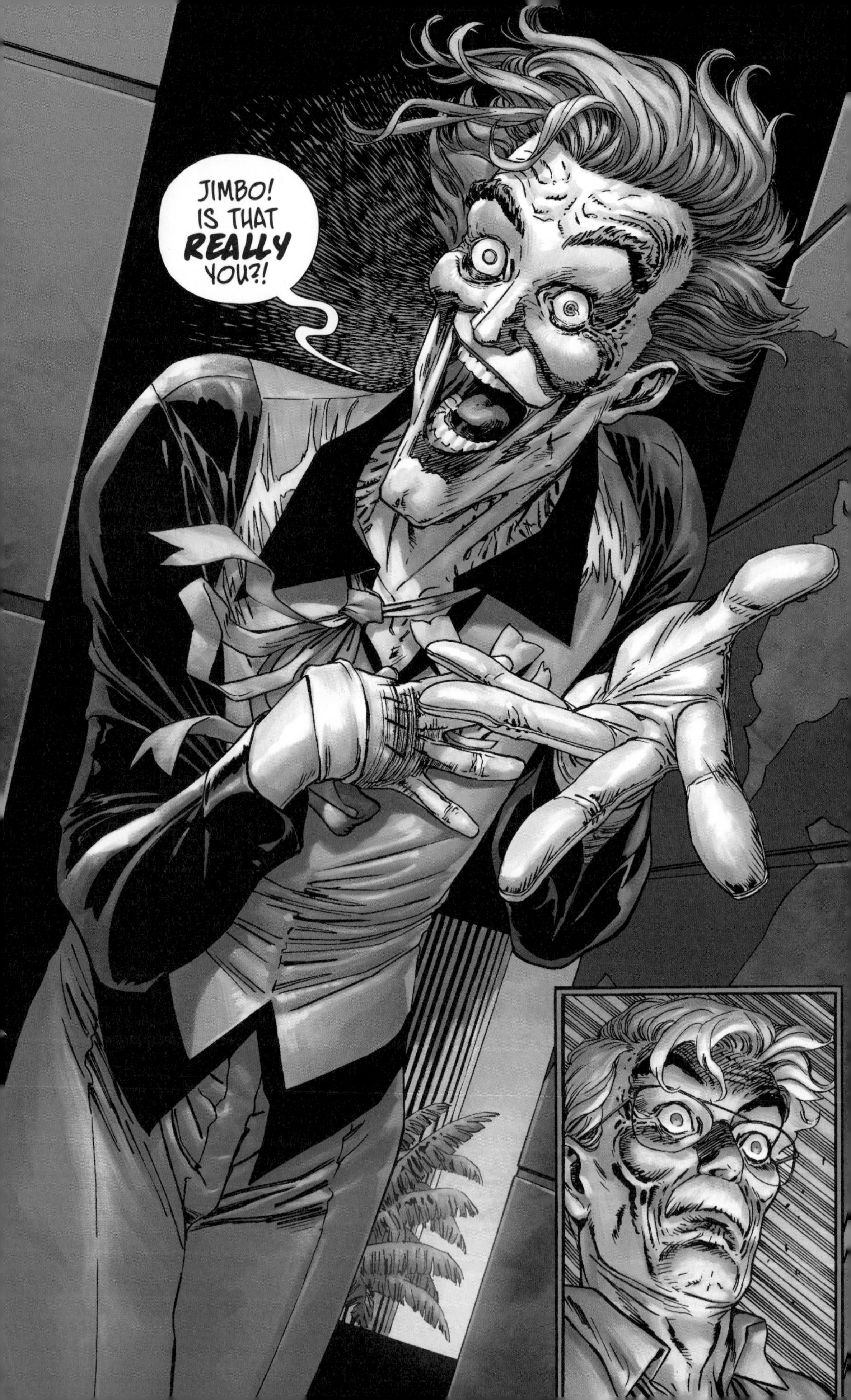
JIMBO! IS THAT **REALLY** YOU?!

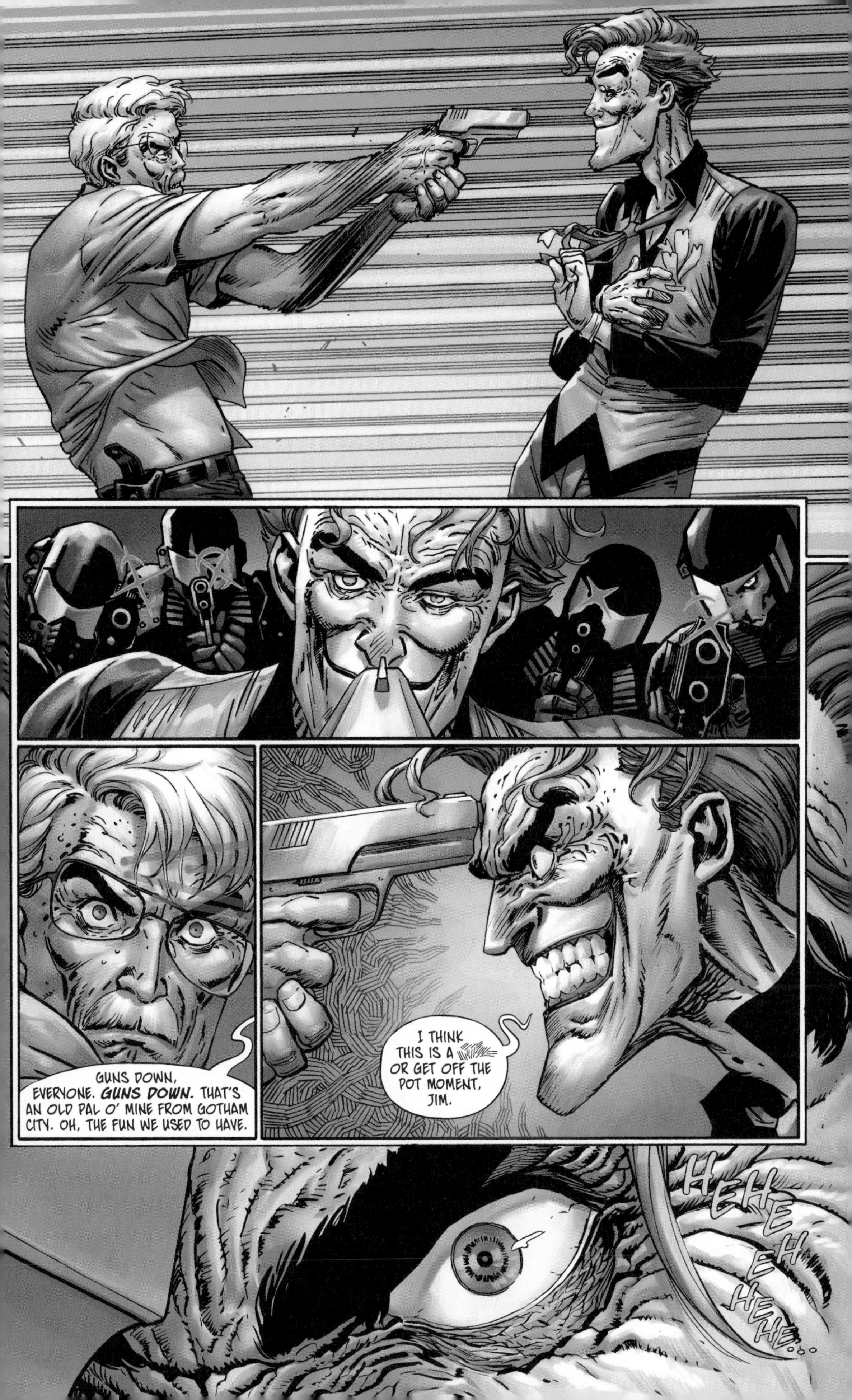
GUNS DOWN, EVERYONE. **GUNS DOWN.** THAT'S AN OLD PAL O' MINE FROM GOTHAM CITY. OH, THE FUN WE USED TO HAVE.
I THINK THIS IS A OR GET OFF THE POT MOMENT, JIM.
HEHEHEHEHEHEHE...

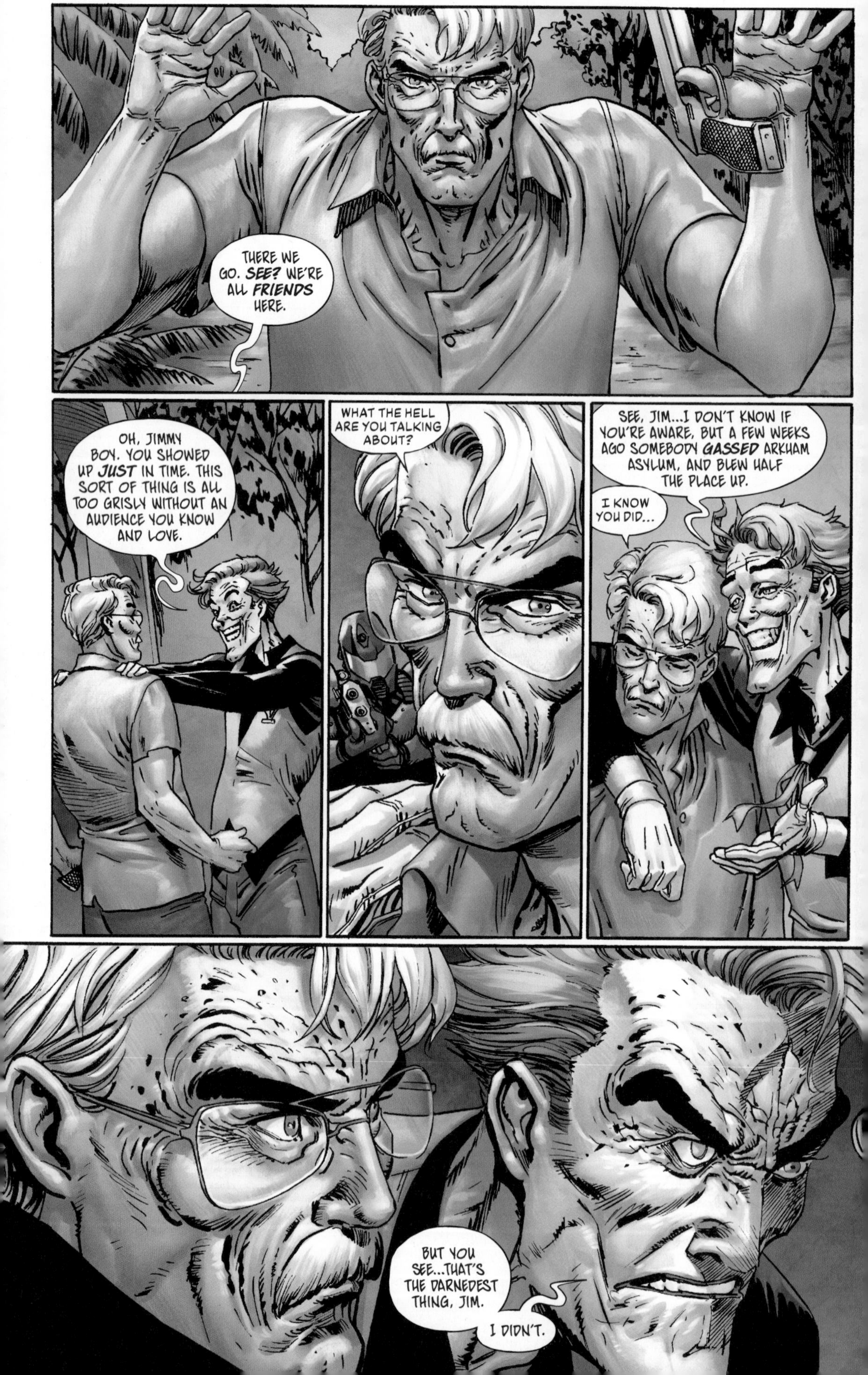
THERE WE GO. SEE? WE'RE ALL FRIENDS HERE.
OH, JIMMY BOY. YOU SHOWED UP JUST IN TIME. THIS SORT OF THING IS ALL TOO GRISLY WITHOUT AN AUDIENCE YOU KNOW AND LOVE.
WHAT THE HELL ARE YOU TALKING ABOUT?
SEE, JIM...I DON'T KNOW IF YOU'RE AWARE, BUT A FEW WEEKS AGO SOMEBODY GASSED ARKHAM ASYLUM, AND BLEW HALF THE PLACE UP.
I KNOW YOU DID...
BUT YOU SEE...THAT'S THE DARNEDEST THING, JIM.
I DIDN'T.

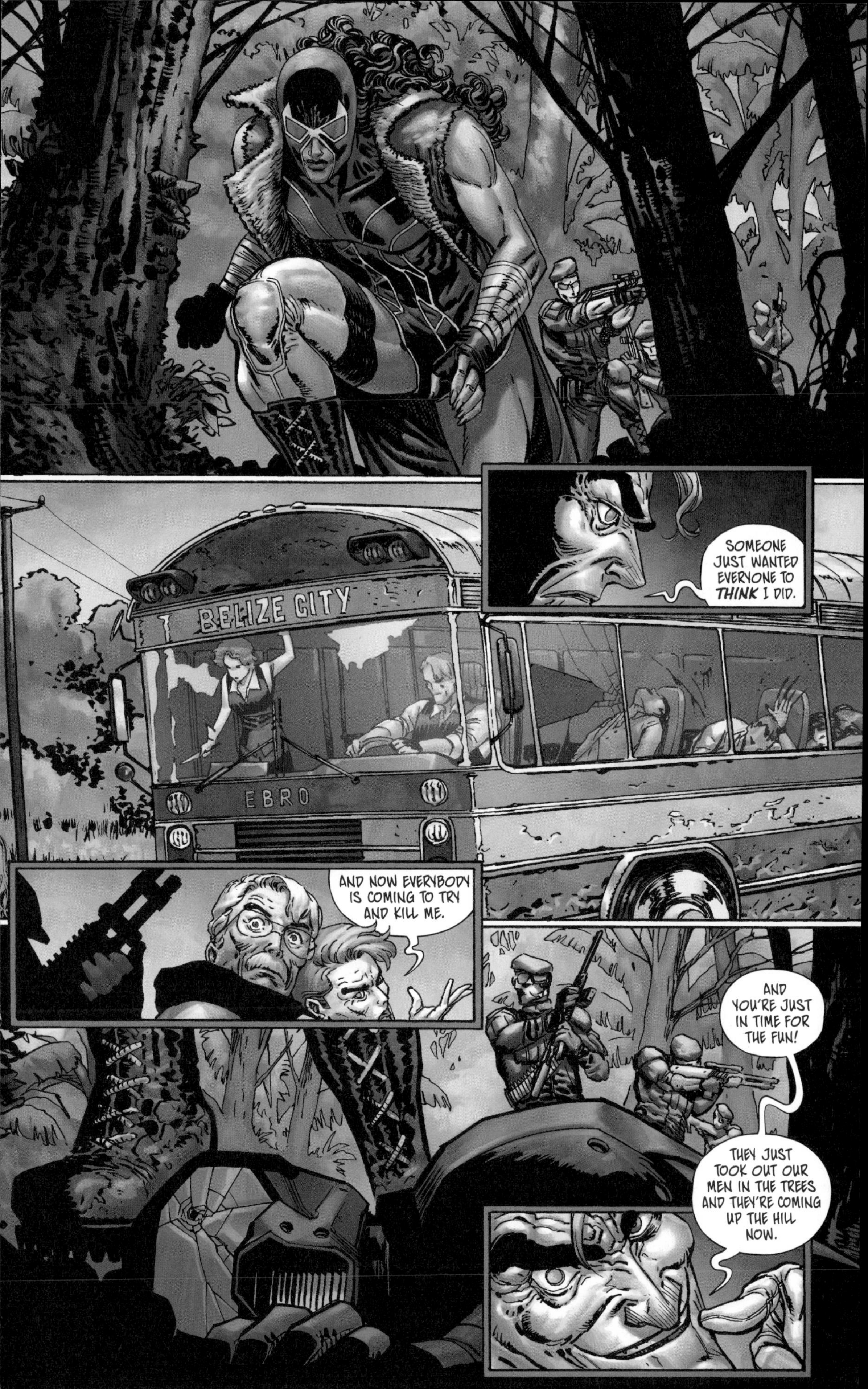
BELIZE CITY
EBRO
SOMEONE JUST WANTED EVERYONE TO *THINK* I DID.
AND NOW EVERYBODY IS COMING TO TRY AND KILL ME.
AND YOU'RE JUST IN TIME FOR THE FUN!
THEY JUST TOOK OUT OUR MEN IN THE TREES AND THEY'RE COMING UP THE HILL NOW.

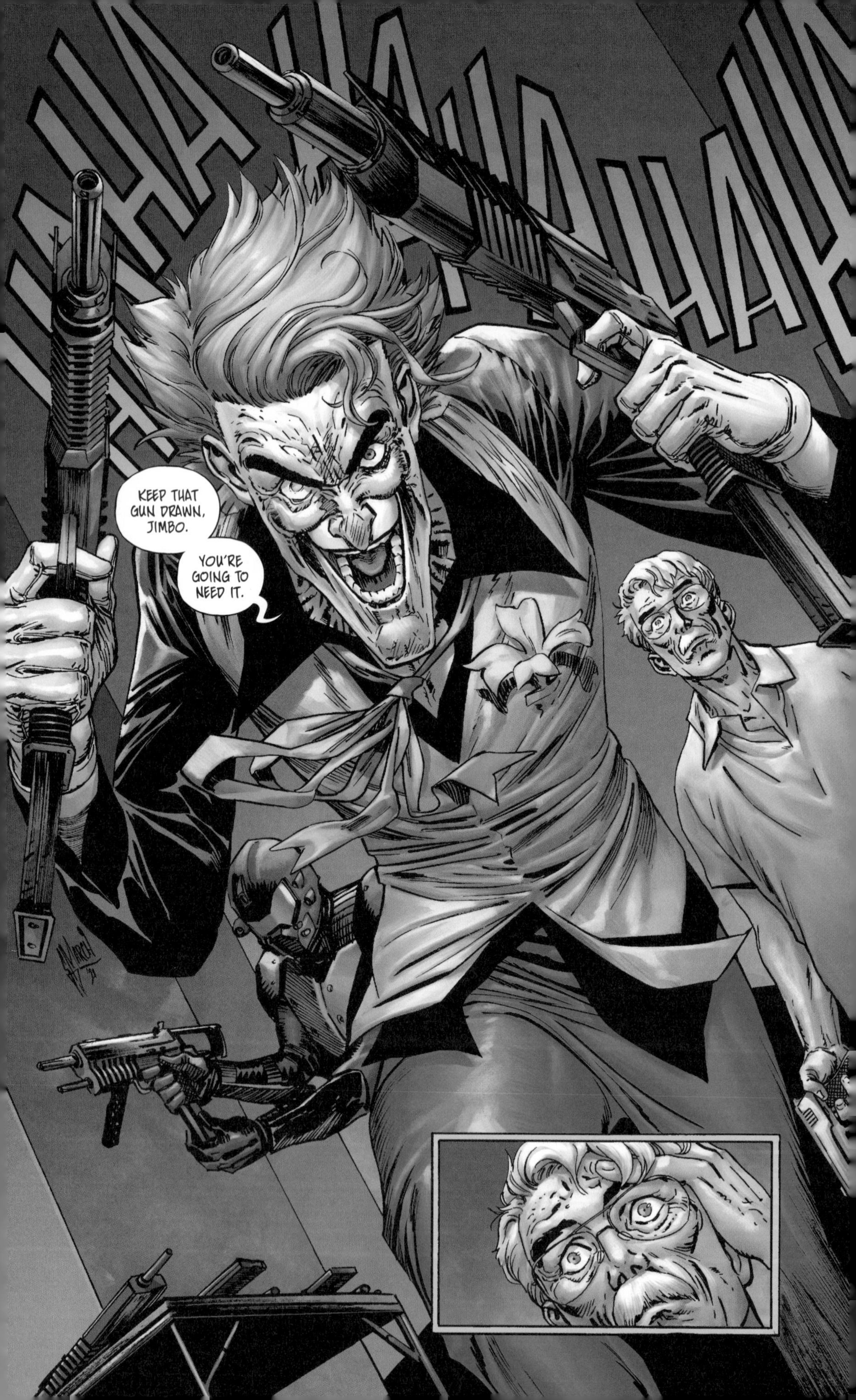
KEEP THAT GUN DRAWN, JIMBO.
YOU'RE GOING TO NEED IT.

The Joker #4
Cover Art by Guillem March
Colors by Arif Prianto

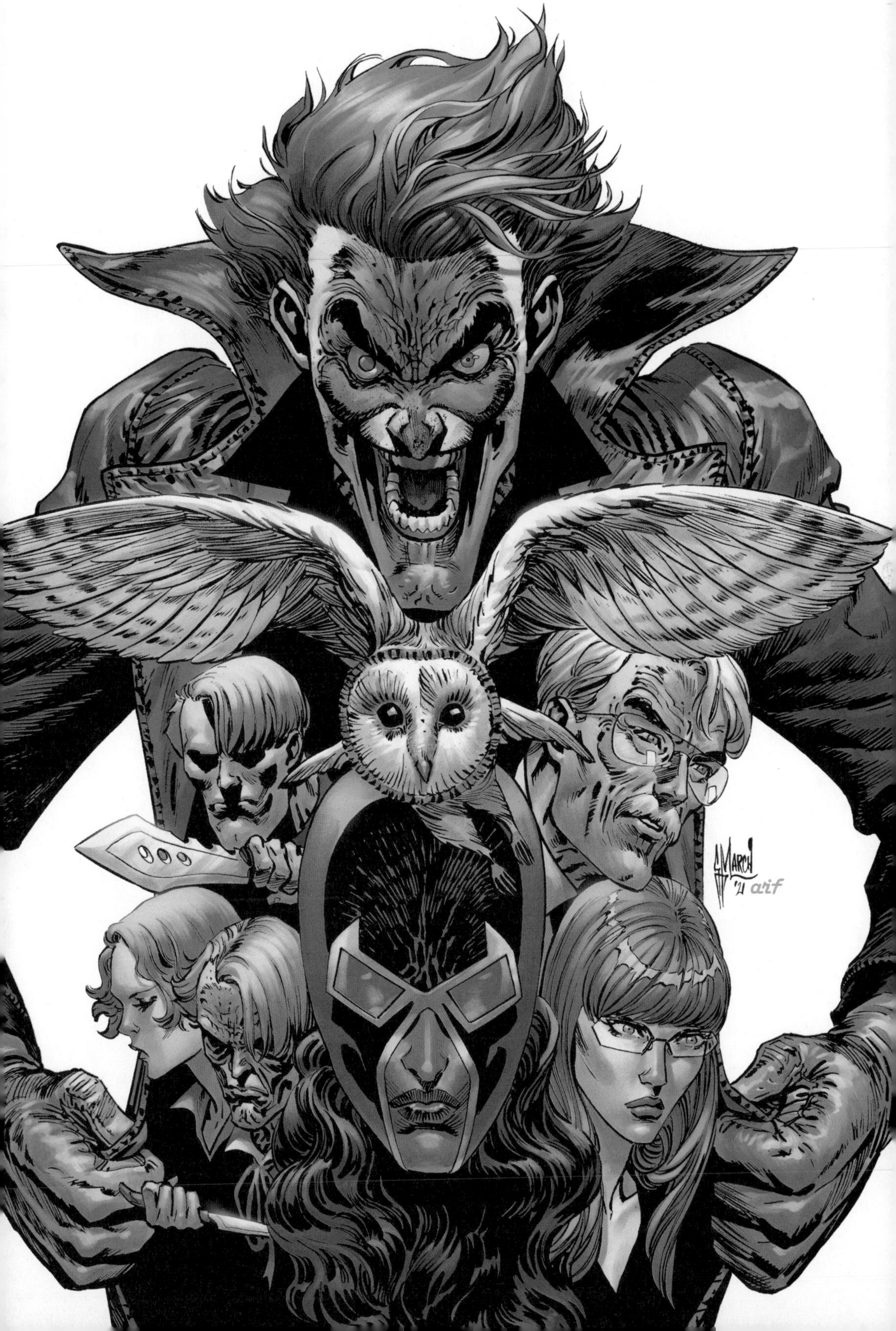

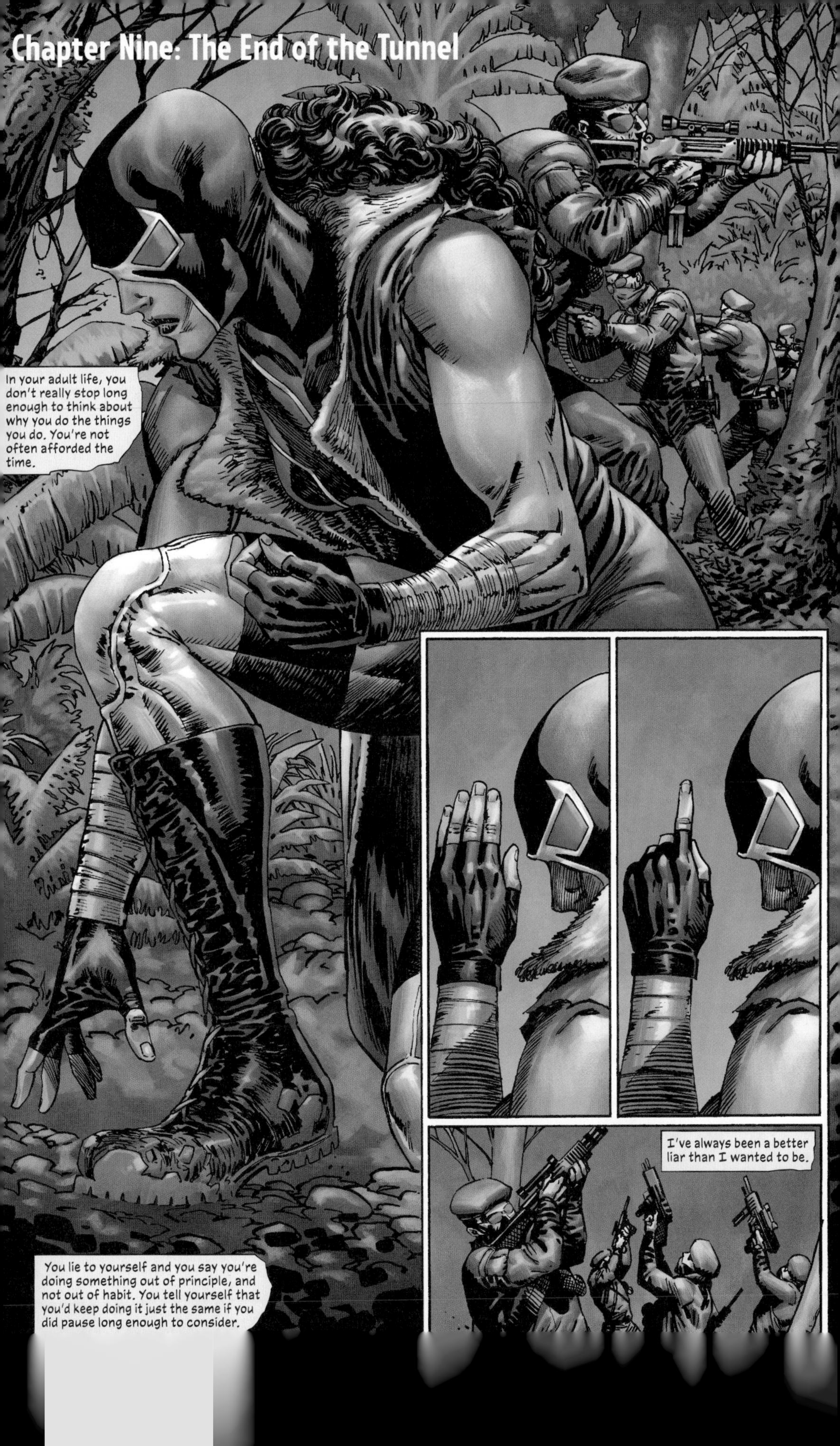

Chapter Nine: The End of the Tunnel
In your adult life, you don't really stop long enough to think about why you do the things you do. You're not often afforded the time.
I've always been a better liar than I wanted to be.
You lie to yourself and you say you're doing something out of principle, and not out of habit. You tell yourself that you'd keep doing it just the same if you did pause long enough to consider.

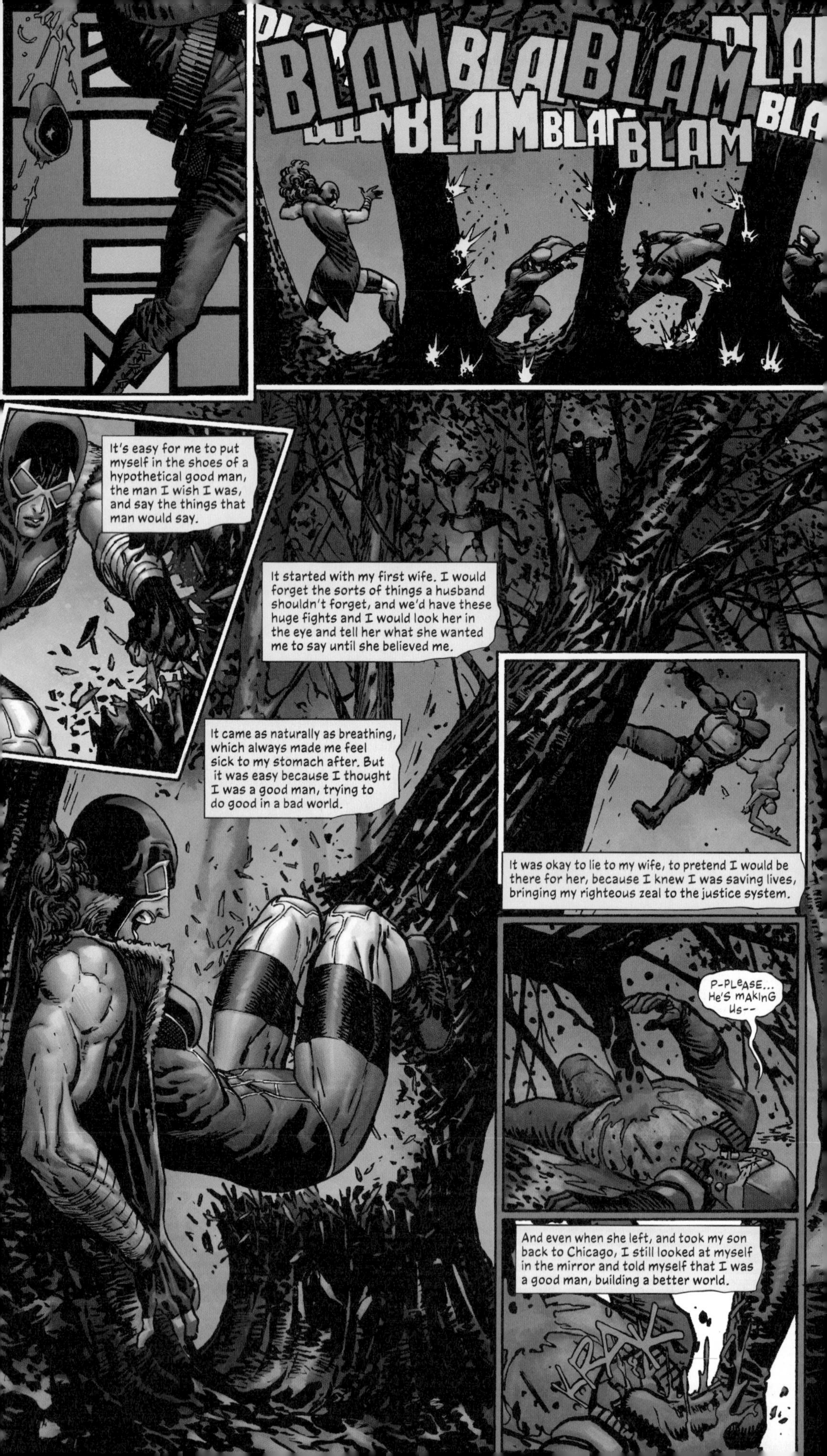
BLAM BLAM BLAM
BLAM BLAM BLAM
It's easy for me to put myself in the shoes of a hypothetical good man, the man I wish I was, and say the things that man would say.
It started with my first wife. I would forget the sorts of things a husband shouldn't forget, and we'd have these huge fights and I would look her in the eye and tell her what she wanted me to say until she believed me.
It came as naturally as breathing, which always made me feel sick to my stomach after. But it was easy because I thought I was a good man, trying to do good in a bad world.
It was okay to lie to my wife, to pretend I would be there for her, because I knew I was saving lives, bringing my righteous zeal to the justice system.
P-PLEASE... HE'S MAKING US--
And even when she left, and took my son back to Chicago, I still looked at myself in the mirror and told myself that I was a good man, building a better world.

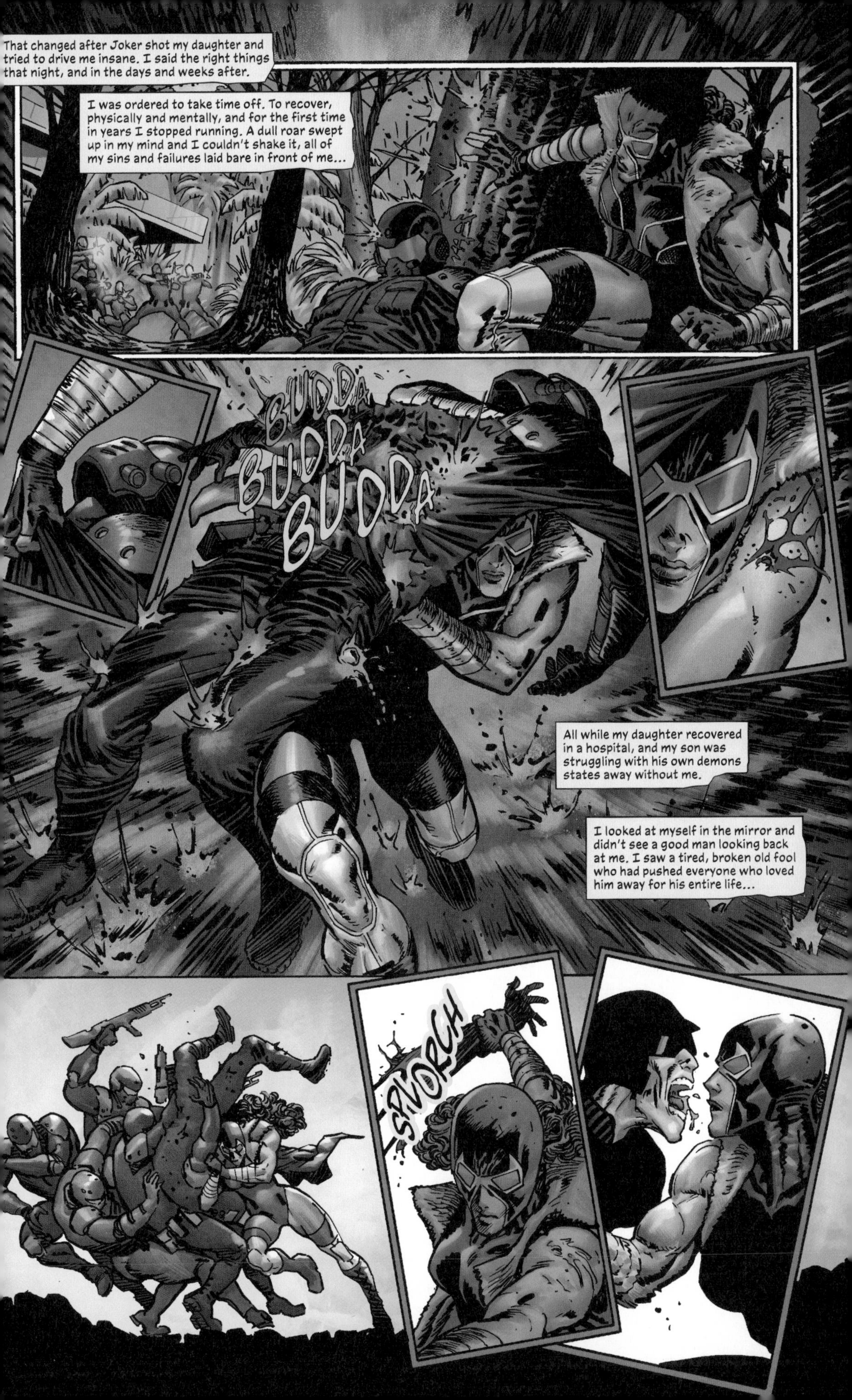
That changed after Joker shot my daughter and tried to drive me insane. I said the right things that night, and in the days and weeks after.
I was ordered to take time off. To recover, physically and mentally, and for the first time in years I stopped running. A dull roar swept up in my mind and I couldn't shake it, all of my sins and failures laid bare in front of me...
BUDDA BUDDA BUDDA
All while my daughter recovered in a hospital, and my son was struggling with his own demons states away without me.
I looked at myself in the mirror and didn't see a good man looking back at me. I saw a tired, broken old fool who had pushed everyone who loved him away for his entire life...
SPLORCH

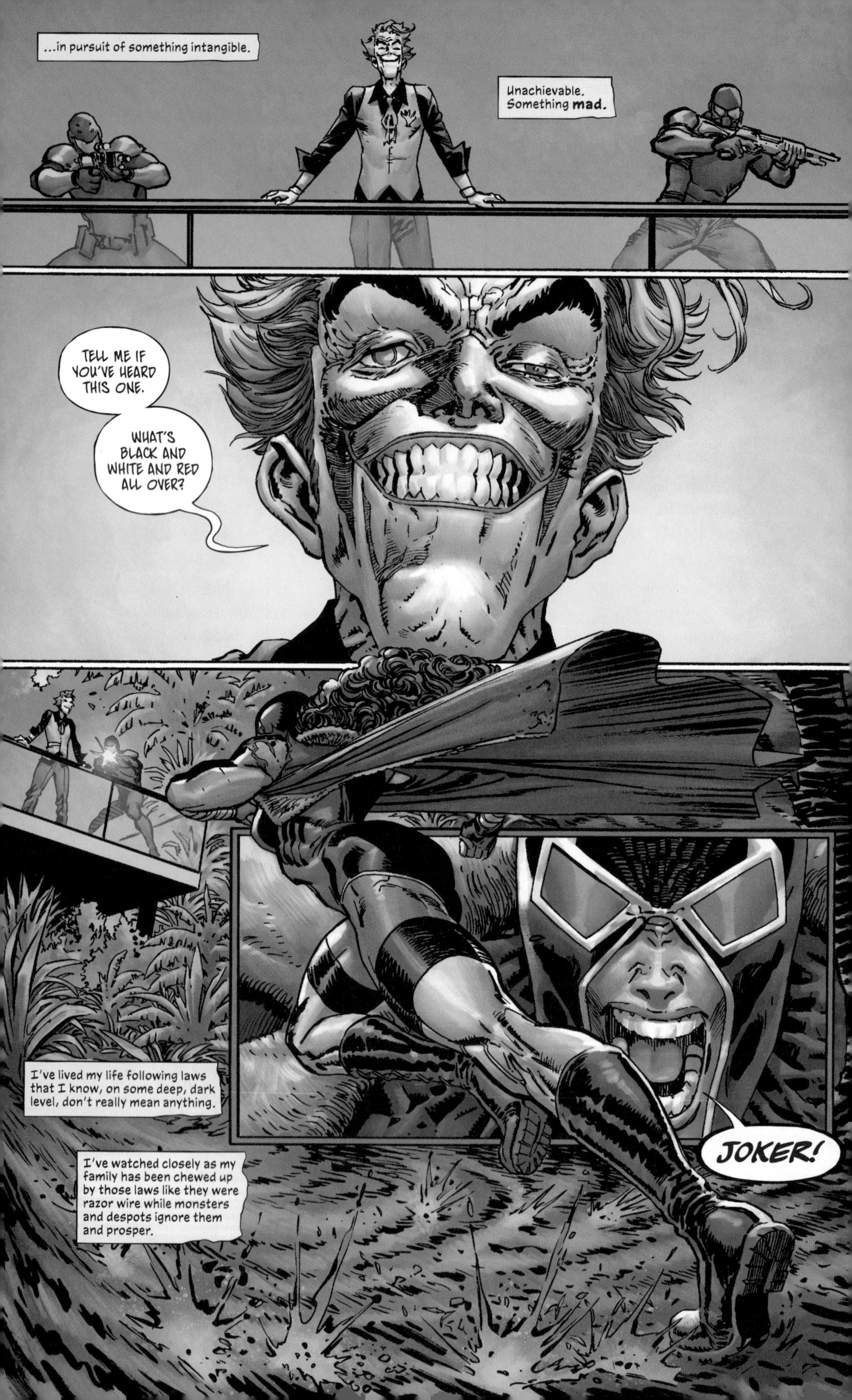
...in pursuit of something intangible.
Unachievable. Something **mad.**
TELL ME IF YOU'VE HEARD THIS ONE.
WHAT'S BLACK AND WHITE AND RED ALL OVER?
I've lived my life following laws that I know, on some deep, dark level, don't really mean anything.
I've watched closely as my family has been chewed up by those laws like they were razor wire while monsters and despots ignore them and prosper.
JOKER!

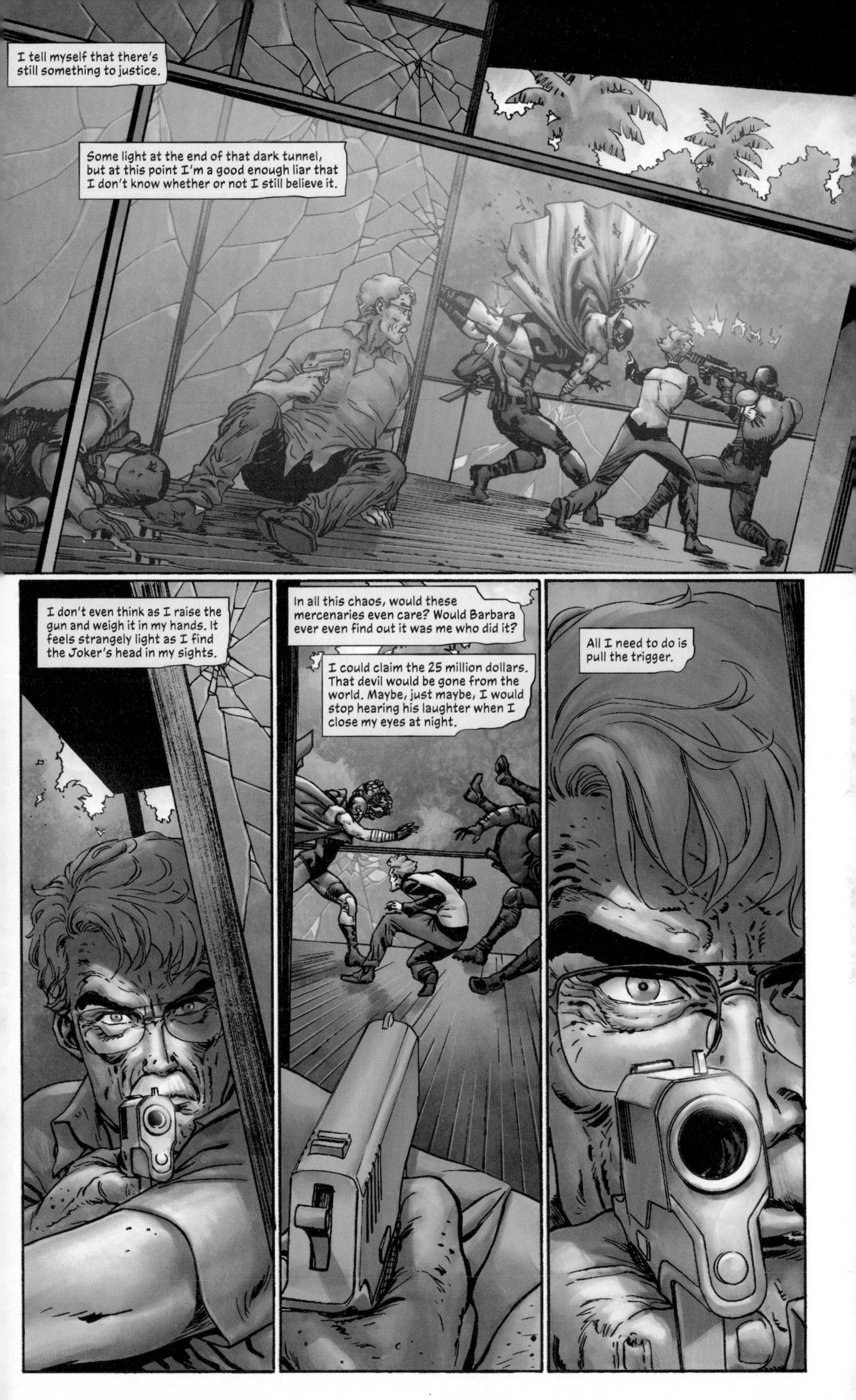
I tell myself that there's still something to justice.
Some light at the end of that dark tunnel, but at this point I'm a good enough liar that I don't know whether or not I still believe it.
I don't even think as I raise the gun and weigh it in my hands. It feels strangely light as I find the Joker's head in my sights.
In all this chaos, would these mercenaries even care? Would Barbara ever even find out it was me who did it?
I could claim the 25 million dollars. That devil would be gone from the world. Maybe, just maybe, I would stop hearing his laughter when I close my eyes at night.
All I need to do is pull the trigger.

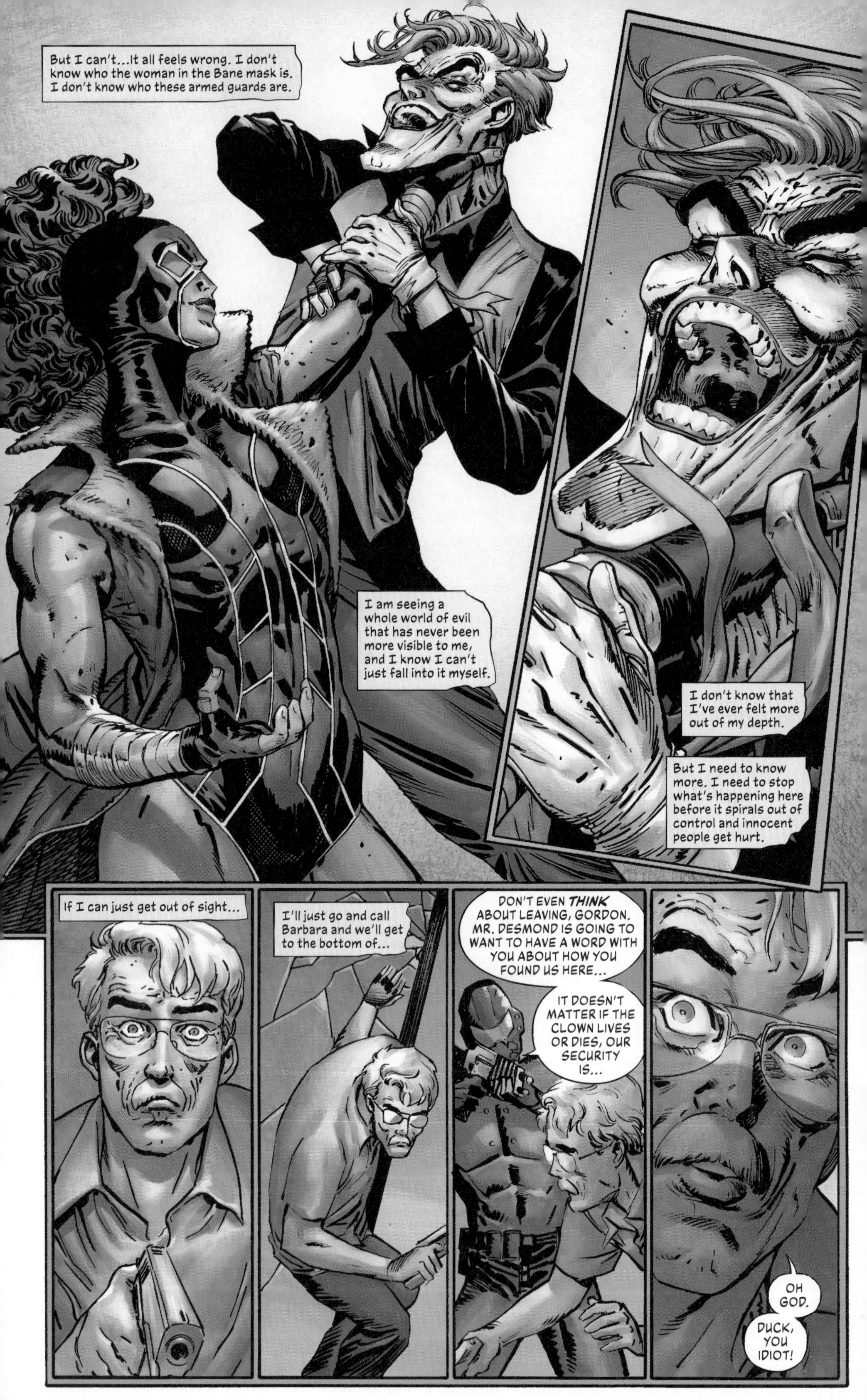

But I can't...It all feels wrong. I don't know who the woman in the Bane mask is. I don't know who these armed guards are.
I am seeing a whole world of evil that has never been more visible to me, and I know I can't just fall into it myself.
I don't know that I've ever felt more out of my depth.
But I need to know more. I need to stop what's happening here before it spirals out of control and innocent people get hurt.
If I can just get out of sight...
I'll just go and call Barbara and we'll get to the bottom of...
DON'T EVEN THINK ABOUT LEAVING, GORDON. MR. DESMOND IS GOING TO WANT TO HAVE A WORD WITH YOU ABOUT HOW YOU FOUND US HERE...
IT DOESN'T MATTER IF THE CLOWN LIVES OR DIES, OUR SECURITY IS...
OH GOD.
DUCK, YOU IDIOT!

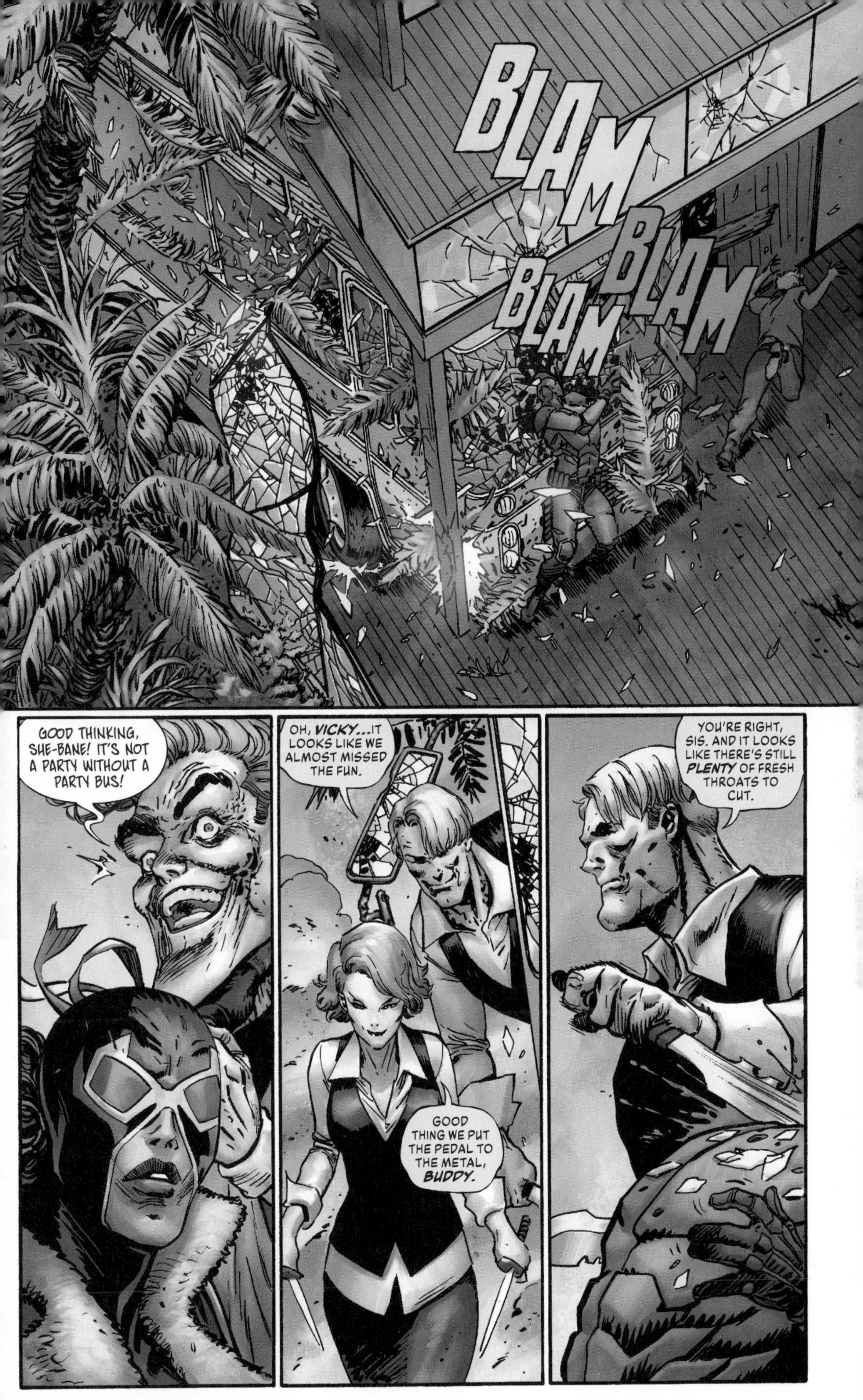
BLAM
BLAM
BLAM
GOOD THINKING, SHE-BANE! IT'S NOT A PARTY WITHOUT A PARTY BUS!
OH, VICKY...IT LOOKS LIKE WE ALMOST MISSED THE FUN.
GOOD THING WE PUT THE PEDAL TO THE METAL, BUDDY.
YOU'RE RIGHT, SIS. AND IT LOOKS LIKE THERE'S STILL PLENTY OF FRESH THROATS TO CUT.

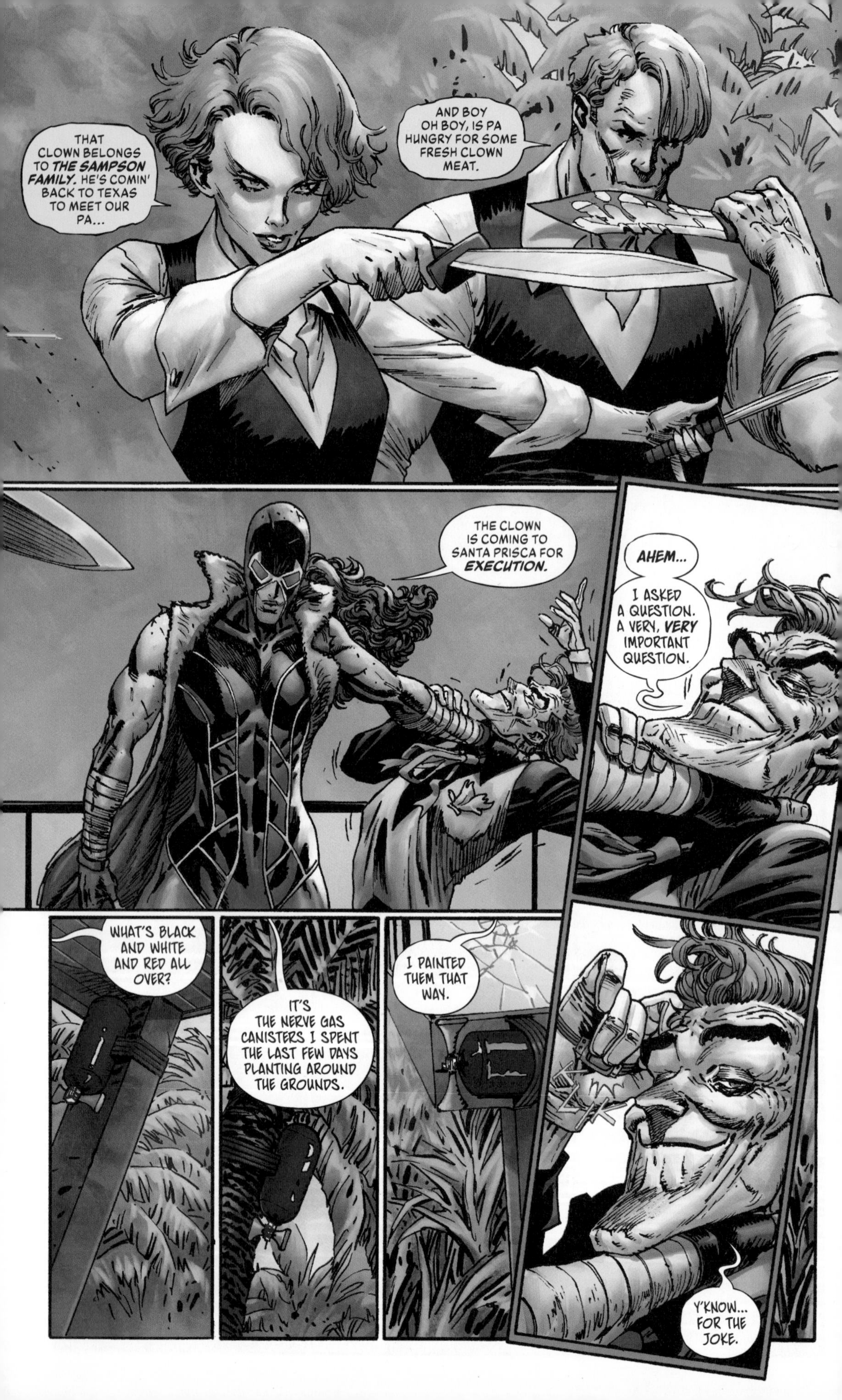

THAT CLOWN BELONGS TO **THE SAMPSON FAMILY.** HE'S COMIN' BACK TO TEXAS TO MEET OUR PA...
AND BOY OH BOY, IS PA HUNGRY FOR SOME FRESH CLOWN MEAT.
THE CLOWN IS COMING TO SANTA PRISCA FOR **EXECUTION.**
AHEM...
I ASKED A QUESTION. A VERY, **VERY** IMPORTANT QUESTION.
WHAT'S BLACK AND WHITE AND RED ALL OVER?
IT'S THE NERVE GAS CANISTERS I SPENT THE LAST FEW DAYS PLANTING AROUND THE GROUNDS.
I PAINTED THEM THAT WAY.
Y'KNOW... FOR THE JOKE.

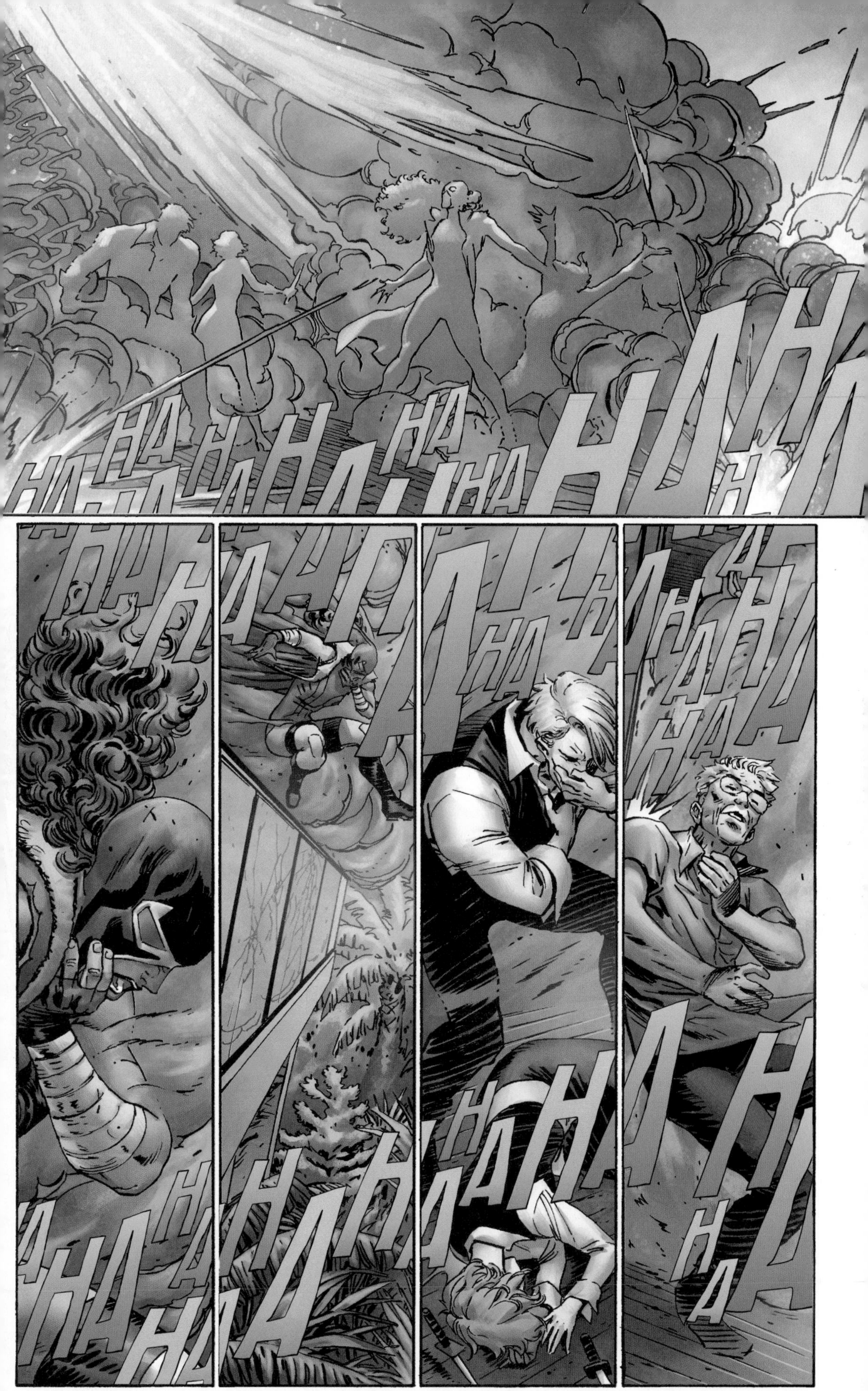
SSSSSS
HA HA HA HA HA HA HA HA HA
HA HA HA HA
HA HA HA HA
HA HA HA HA
HA HA HA HA
HA HA HA HA

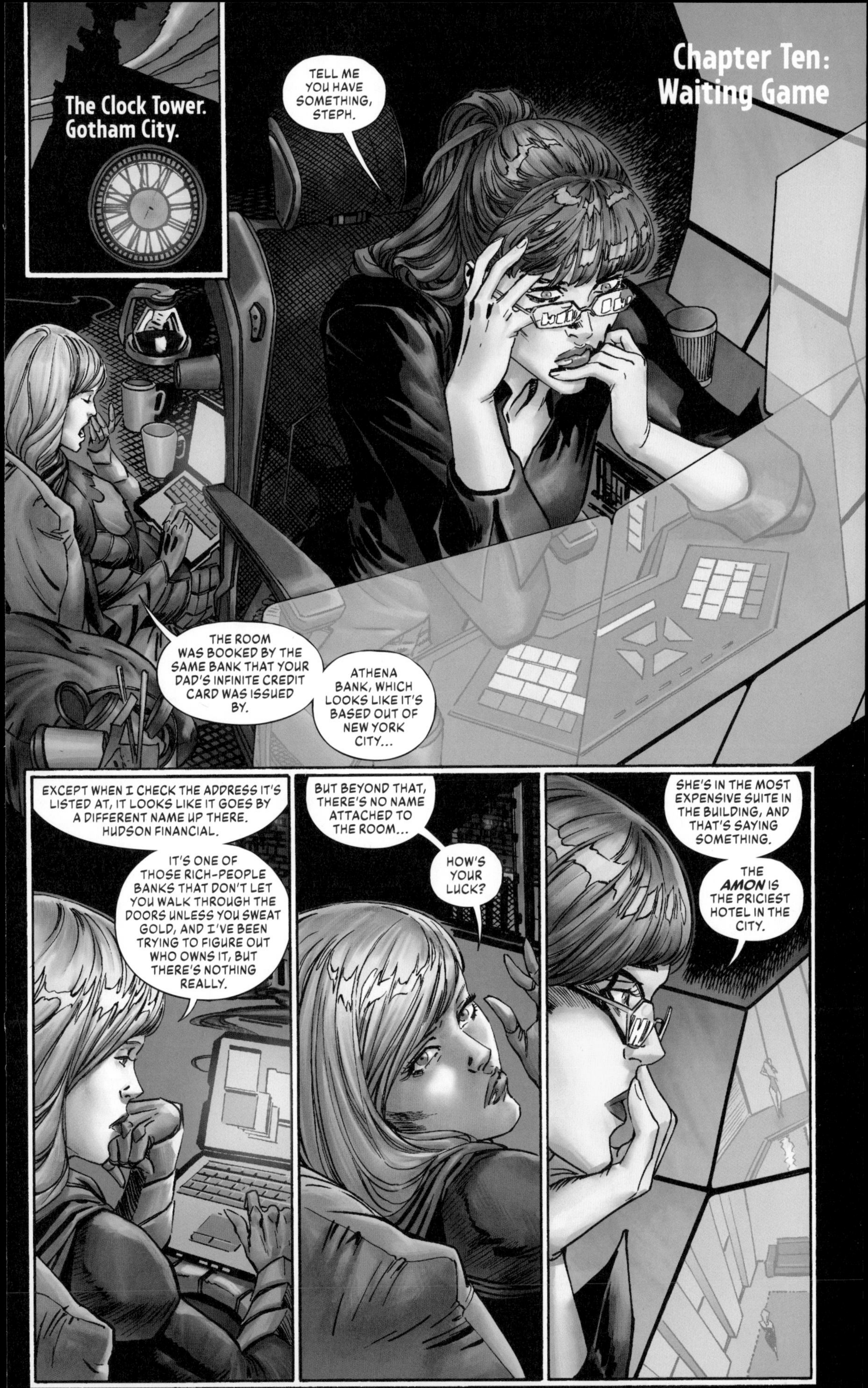

The Clock Tower. Gotham City.
Chapter Ten: Waiting Game
TELL ME YOU HAVE SOMETHING, STEPH.
THE ROOM WAS BOOKED BY THE SAME BANK THAT YOUR DAD'S INFINITE CREDIT CARD WAS ISSUED BY.
ATHENA BANK, WHICH LOOKS LIKE IT'S BASED OUT OF NEW YORK CITY...
EXCEPT WHEN I CHECK THE ADDRESS IT'S LISTED AT, IT LOOKS LIKE IT GOES BY A DIFFERENT NAME UP THERE. HUDSON FINANCIAL.
IT'S ONE OF THOSE RICH-PEOPLE BANKS THAT DON'T LET YOU WALK THROUGH THE DOORS UNLESS YOU SWEAT GOLD, AND I'VE BEEN TRYING TO FIGURE OUT WHO OWNS IT, BUT THERE'S NOTHING REALLY.
BUT BEYOND THAT, THERE'S NO NAME ATTACHED TO THE ROOM...
HOW'S YOUR LUCK?
SHE'S IN THE MOST EXPENSIVE SUITE IN THE BUILDING, AND THAT'S SAYING SOMETHING.
THE AMON IS THE PRICIEST HOTEL IN THE CITY.

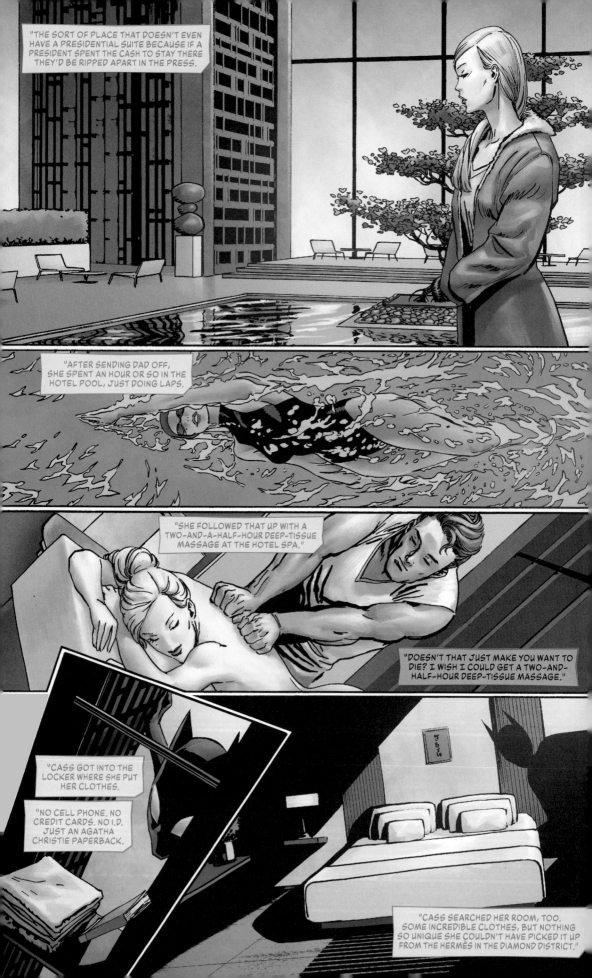

"THE SORT OF PLACE THAT DOESN'T EVEN HAVE A PRESIDENTIAL SUITE BECAUSE IF A PRESIDENT SPENT THE CASH TO STAY THERE THEY'D BE RIPPED APART IN THE PRESS.

"AFTER SENDING DAD OFF, SHE SPENT AN HOUR OR SO IN THE HOTEL POOL, JUST DOING LAPS.

"SHE FOLLOWED THAT UP WITH A TWO-AND-A-HALF-HOUR DEEP-TISSUE MASSAGE AT THE HOTEL SPA."

"DOESN'T THAT JUST MAKE YOU WANT TO DIE? I WISH I COULD GET A TWO-AND-HALF-HOUR DEEP-TISSUE MASSAGE."

"CASS GOT INTO THE LOCKER WHERE SHE PUT HER CLOTHES.

"NO CELL PHONE. NO CREDIT CARDS. NO I.D. JUST AN AGATHA CHRISTIE PAPERBACK.

"CASS SEARCHED HER ROOM, TOO. SOME INCREDIBLE CLOTHES, BUT NOTHING SO UNIQUE SHE COULDN'T HAVE PICKED IT UP FROM THE HERMÈS IN THE DIAMOND DISTRICT."

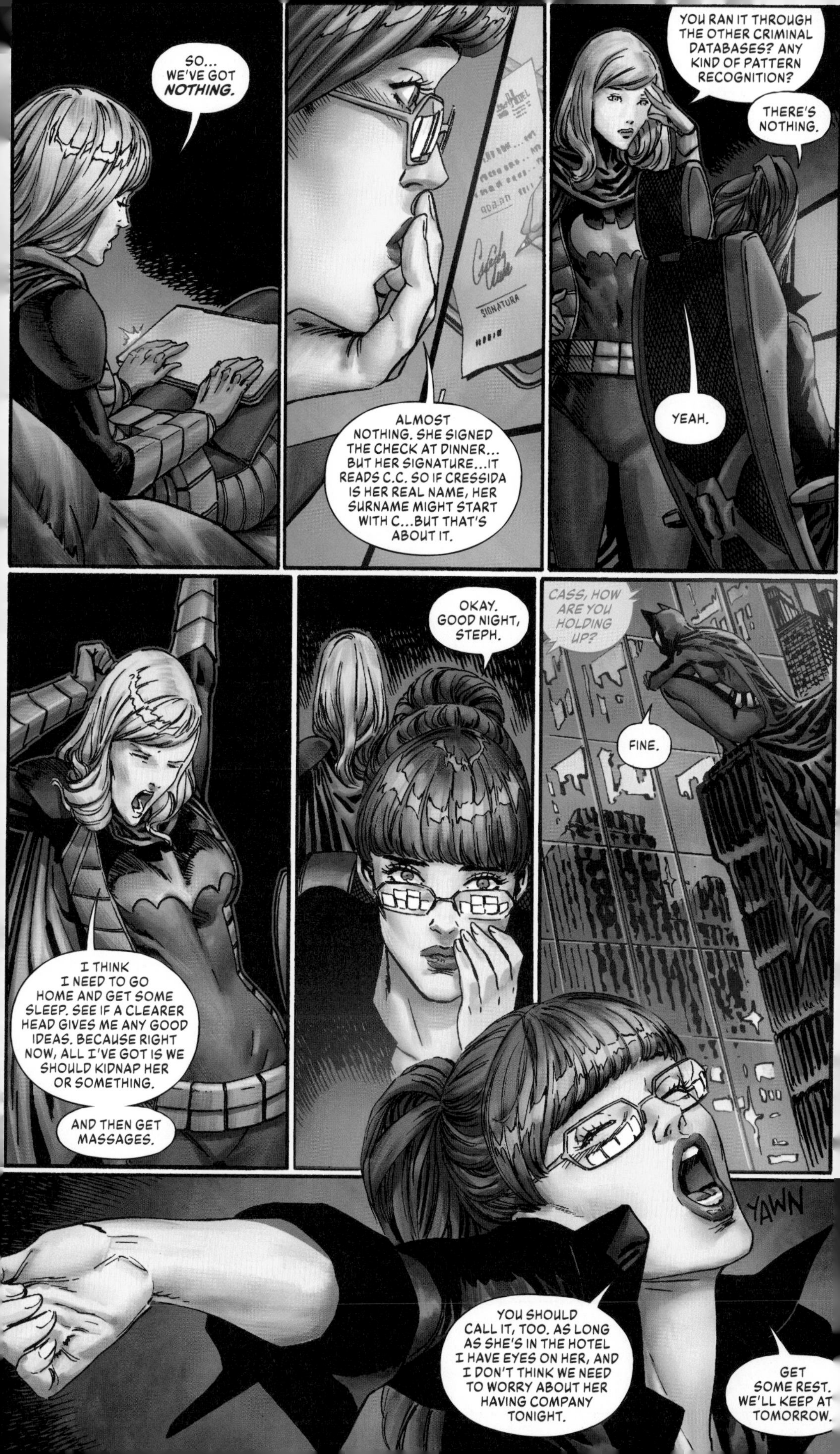
SO... WE'VE GOT *NOTHING.*
ALMOST NOTHING. SHE SIGNED THE CHECK AT DINNER... BUT HER SIGNATURE...IT READS C.C. SO IF CRESSIDA IS HER REAL NAME, HER SURNAME MIGHT START WITH C...BUT THAT'S ABOUT IT.
SIGNATURA
YOU RAN IT THROUGH THE OTHER CRIMINAL DATABASES? ANY KIND OF PATTERN RECOGNITION?
THERE'S NOTHING.
YEAH.
I THINK I NEED TO GO HOME AND GET SOME SLEEP. SEE IF A CLEARER HEAD GIVES ME ANY GOOD IDEAS. BECAUSE RIGHT NOW, ALL I'VE GOT IS WE SHOULD KIDNAP HER OR SOMETHING.
AND THEN GET MASSAGES.
OKAY. GOOD NIGHT, STEPH.
CASS, HOW ARE YOU HOLDING UP?
FINE.
YAWN
YOU SHOULD CALL IT, TOO. AS LONG AS SHE'S IN THE HOTEL I HAVE EYES ON HER, AND I DON'T THINK WE NEED TO WORRY ABOUT HER HAVING COMPANY TONIGHT.
GET SOME REST. WE'LL KEEP AT TOMORROW.

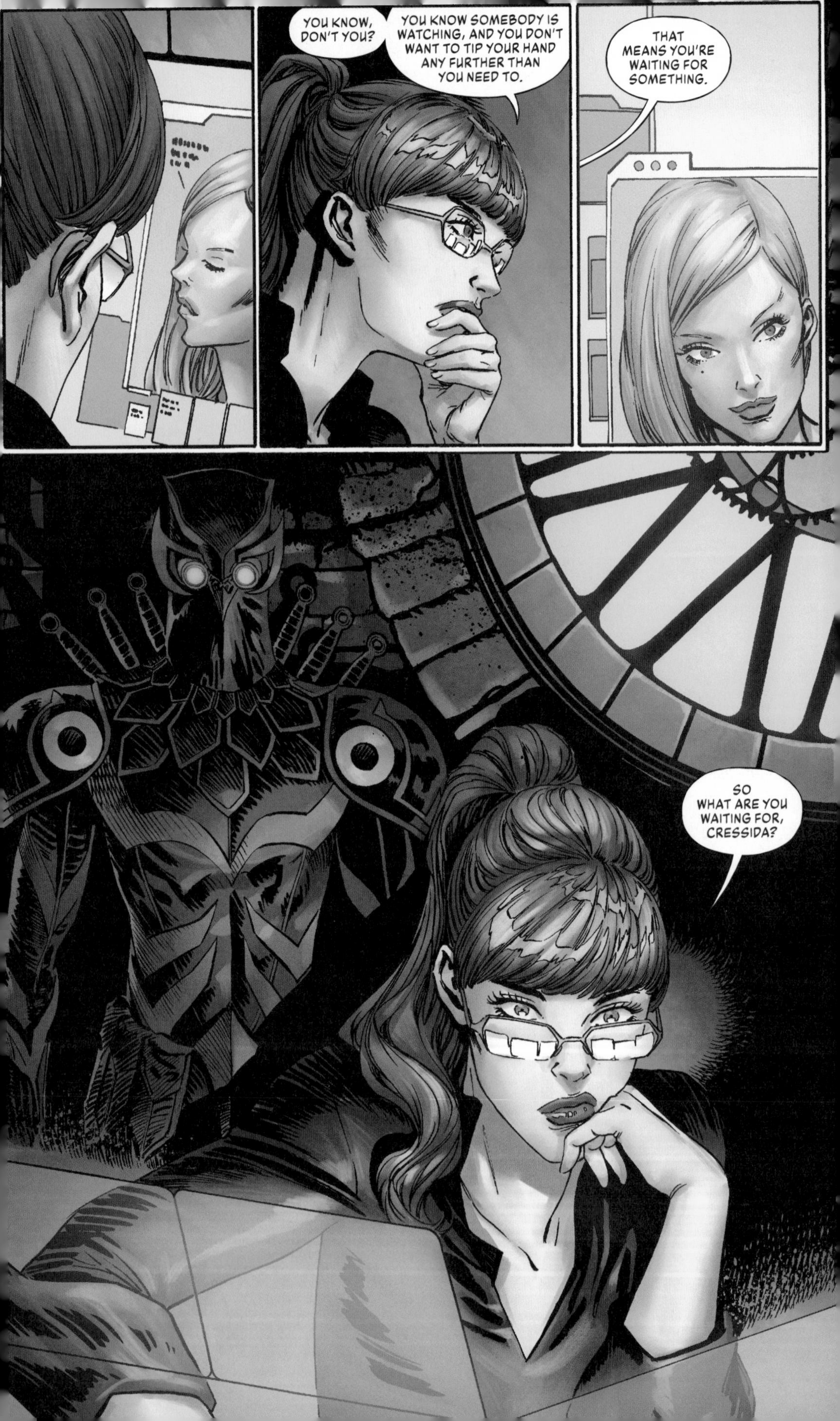

YOU KNOW, DON'T YOU?
YOU KNOW SOMEBODY IS WATCHING, AND YOU DON'T WANT TO TIP YOUR HAND ANY FURTHER THAN YOU NEED TO.
THAT MEANS YOU'RE WAITING FOR SOMETHING.
SO WHAT ARE YOU WAITING FOR, CRESSIDA?

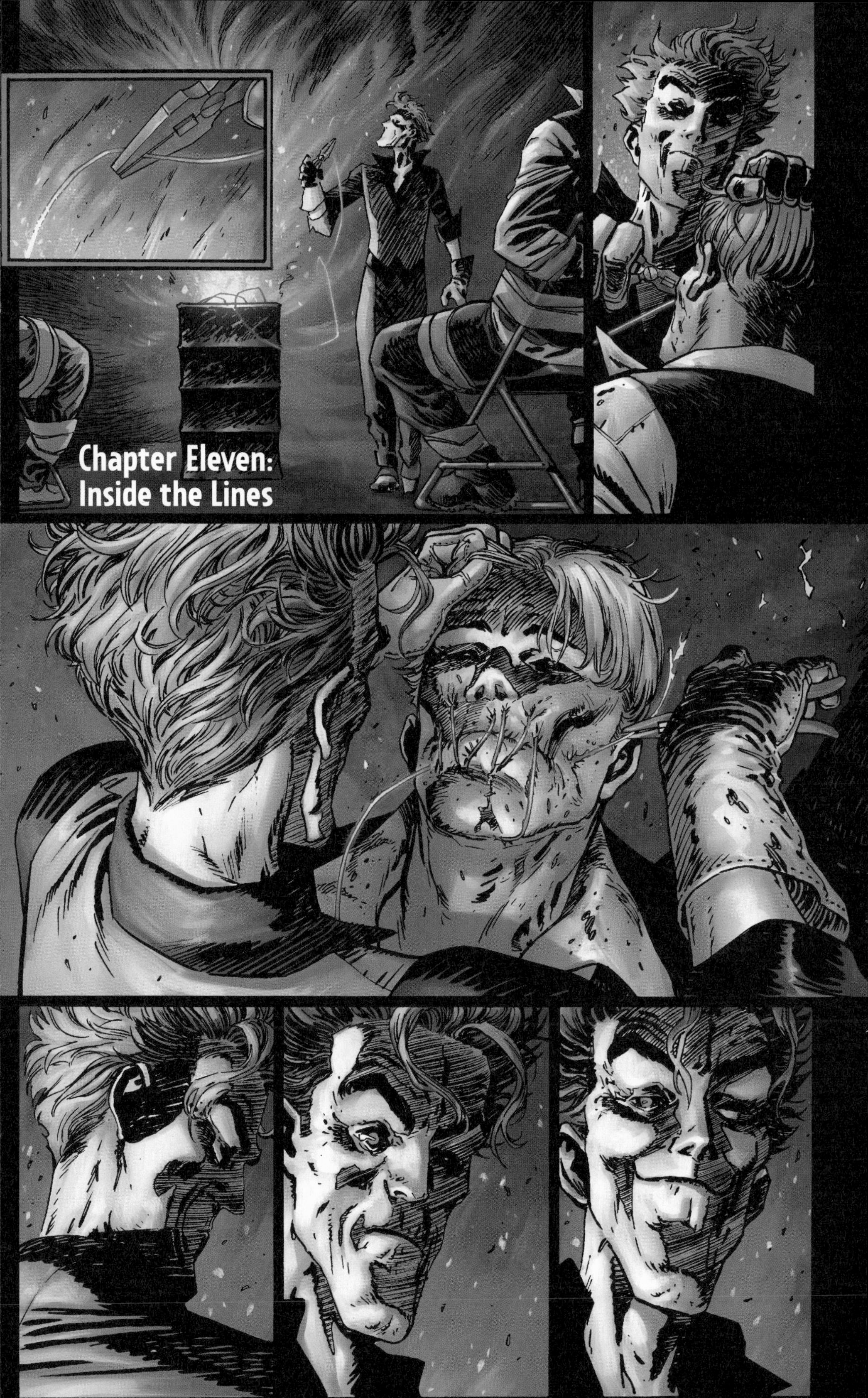
Chapter Eleven:
Inside the Lines

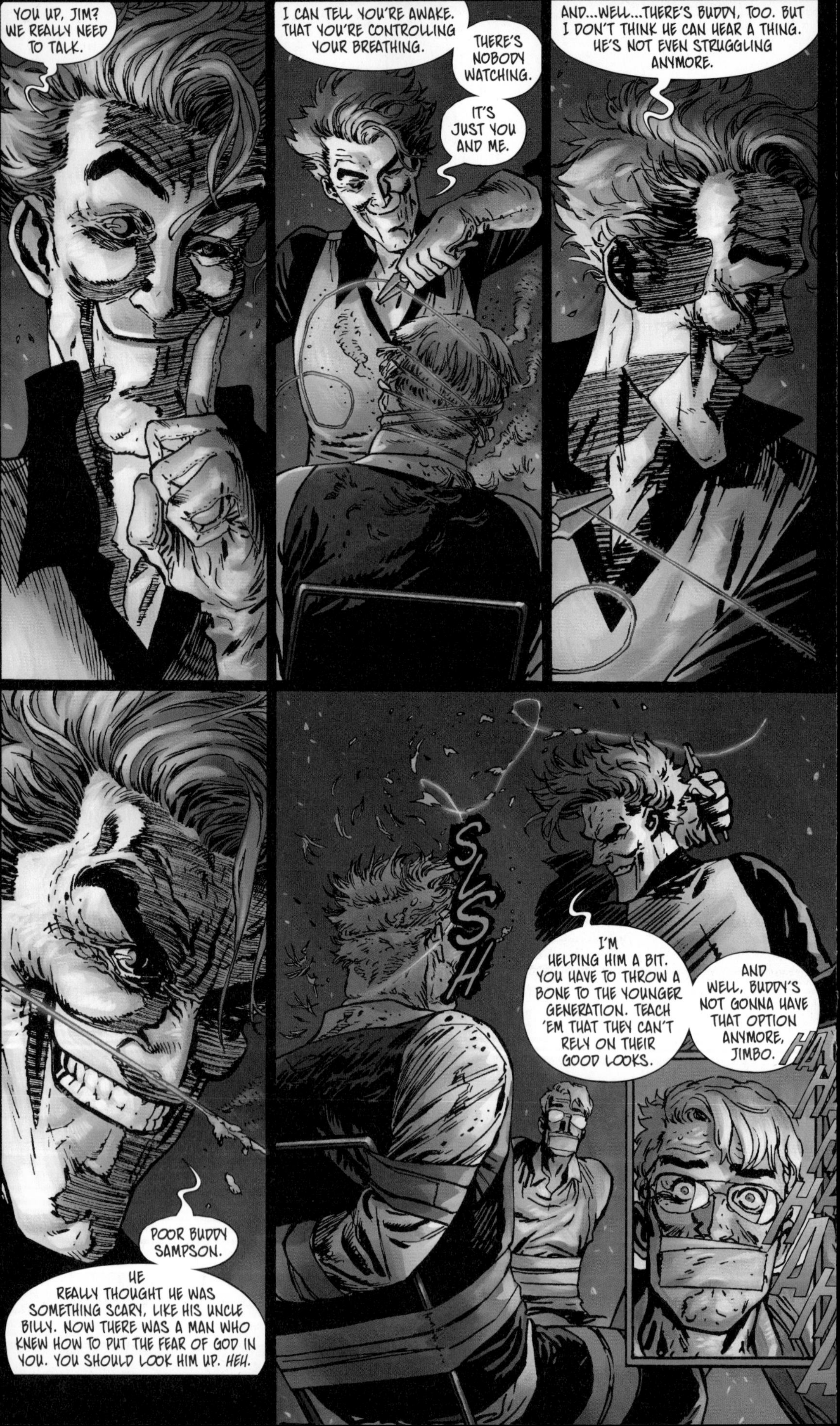

YOU UP, JIM? WE REALLY NEED TO TALK.
I CAN TELL YOU'RE AWAKE. THAT YOU'RE CONTROLLING YOUR BREATHING.
THERE'S NOBODY WATCHING.
IT'S JUST YOU AND ME.
AND...WELL...THERE'S BUDDY, TOO. BUT I DON'T THINK HE CAN HEAR A THING. HE'S NOT EVEN STRUGGLING ANYMORE.
POOR BUDDY SAMPSON.
HE REALLY THOUGHT HE WAS SOMETHING SCARY, LIKE HIS UNCLE BILLY. NOW THERE WAS A MAN WHO KNEW HOW TO PUT THE FEAR OF GOD IN YOU. YOU SHOULD LOOK HIM UP. HEH.
SLSH
I'M HELPING HIM A BIT. YOU HAVE TO THROW A BONE TO THE YOUNGER GENERATION. TEACH 'EM THAT THEY CAN'T RELY ON THEIR GOOD LOOKS.
AND WELL, BUDDY'S NOT GONNA HAVE THAT OPTION ANYMORE, JIMBO.

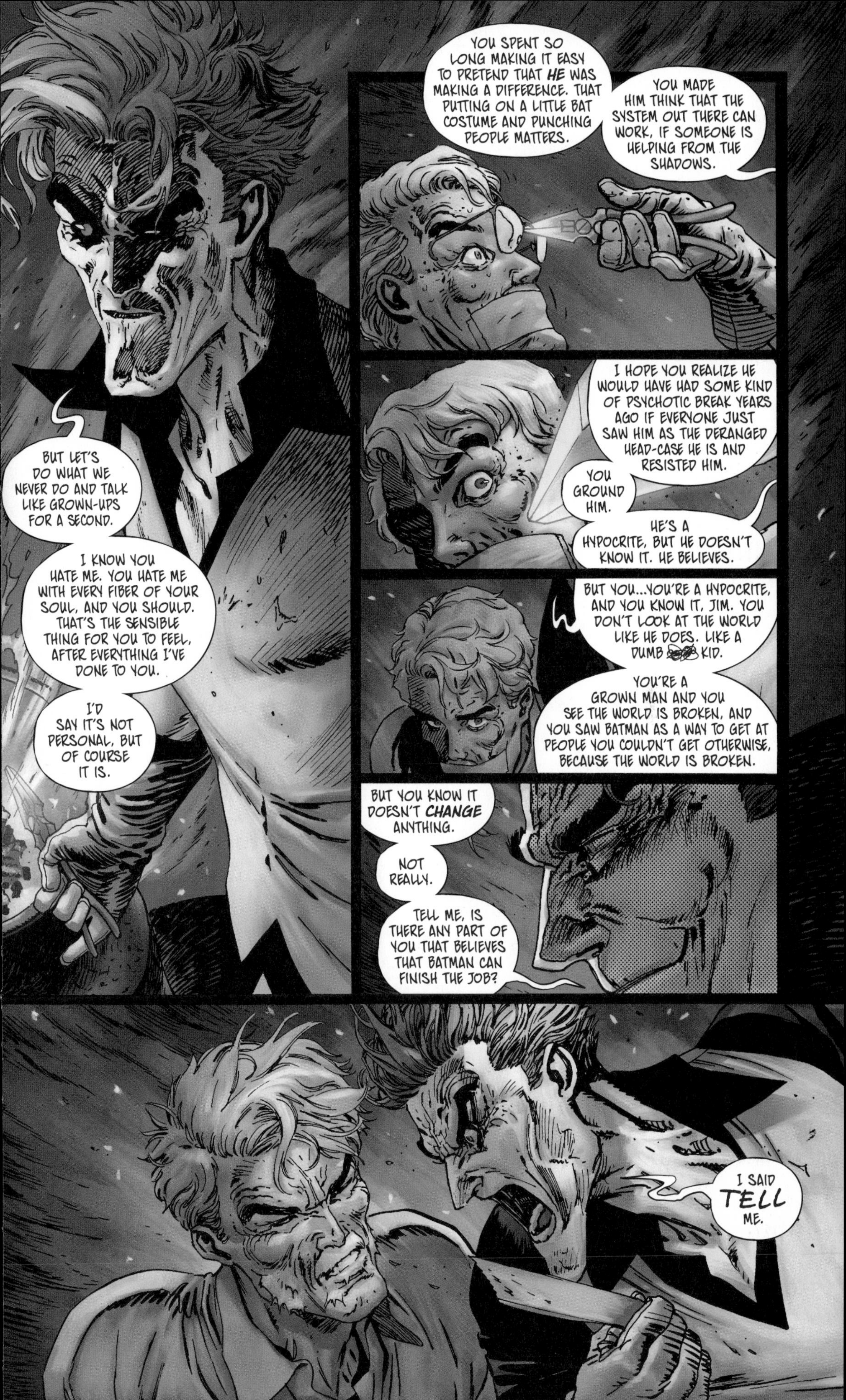
BUT LET'S DO WHAT WE NEVER DO AND TALK LIKE GROWN-UPS FOR A SECOND.
I KNOW YOU HATE ME. YOU HATE ME WITH EVERY FIBER OF YOUR SOUL, AND YOU SHOULD. THAT'S THE SENSIBLE THING FOR YOU TO FEEL, AFTER EVERYTHING I'VE DONE TO YOU.
I'D SAY IT'S NOT PERSONAL, BUT OF COURSE IT IS.
YOU SPENT SO LONG MAKING IT EASY TO PRETEND THAT *HE* WAS MAKING A DIFFERENCE. THAT PUTTING ON A LITTLE BAT COSTUME AND PUNCHING PEOPLE MATTERS.
YOU MADE HIM THINK THAT THE SYSTEM OUT THERE CAN WORK, IF SOMEONE IS HELPING FROM THE SHADOWS.
I HOPE YOU REALIZE HE WOULD HAVE HAD SOME KIND OF PSYCHOTIC BREAK YEARS AGO IF EVERYONE JUST SAW HIM AS THE DERANGED HEAD-CASE HE IS AND RESISTED HIM.
YOU GROUND HIM.
HE'S A HYPOCRITE, BUT HE DOESN'T KNOW IT. HE BELIEVES.
BUT YOU...YOU'RE A HYPOCRITE, AND YOU KNOW IT, JIM. YOU DON'T LOOK AT THE WORLD LIKE HE DOES. LIKE A DUMB KID.
YOU'RE A GROWN MAN AND YOU SEE THE WORLD IS BROKEN, AND YOU SAW BATMAN AS A WAY TO GET AT PEOPLE YOU COULDN'T GET OTHERWISE, BECAUSE THE WORLD IS BROKEN.
BUT YOU KNOW IT DOESN'T **CHANGE** ANYTHING.
NOT REALLY.
TELL ME, IS THERE ANY PART OF YOU THAT BELIEVES THAT BATMAN CAN FINISH THE JOB?
I SAID **TELL** ME.

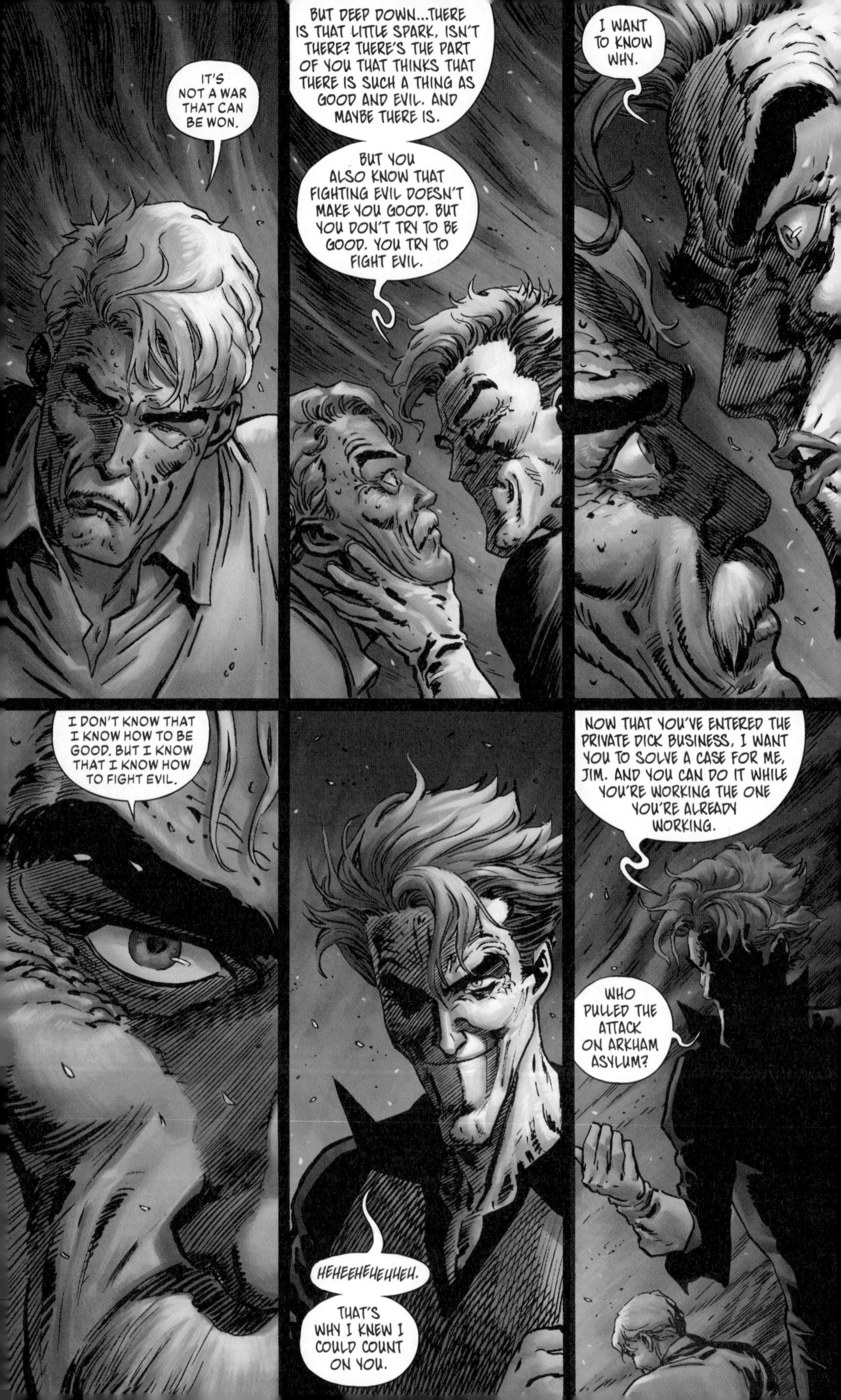
IT'S NOT A WAR THAT CAN BE WON.
BUT DEEP DOWN...THERE IS THAT LITTLE SPARK, ISN'T THERE? THERE'S THE PART OF YOU THAT THINKS THAT THERE IS SUCH A THING AS GOOD AND EVIL. AND MAYBE THERE IS.
BUT YOU ALSO KNOW THAT FIGHTING EVIL DOESN'T MAKE YOU GOOD. BUT YOU DON'T TRY TO BE GOOD. YOU TRY TO FIGHT EVIL.
I WANT TO KNOW WHY.
I DON'T KNOW THAT I KNOW HOW TO BE GOOD. BUT I KNOW THAT I KNOW HOW TO FIGHT EVIL.
HEHEEHEHEHHEH.
THAT'S WHY I KNEW I COULD COUNT ON YOU.
NOW THAT YOU'VE ENTERED THE PRIVATE DICK BUSINESS, I WANT YOU TO SOLVE A CASE FOR ME, JIM. AND YOU CAN DO IT WHILE YOU'RE WORKING THE ONE YOU'RE ALREADY WORKING.
WHO PULLED THE ATTACK ON ARKHAM ASYLUM?

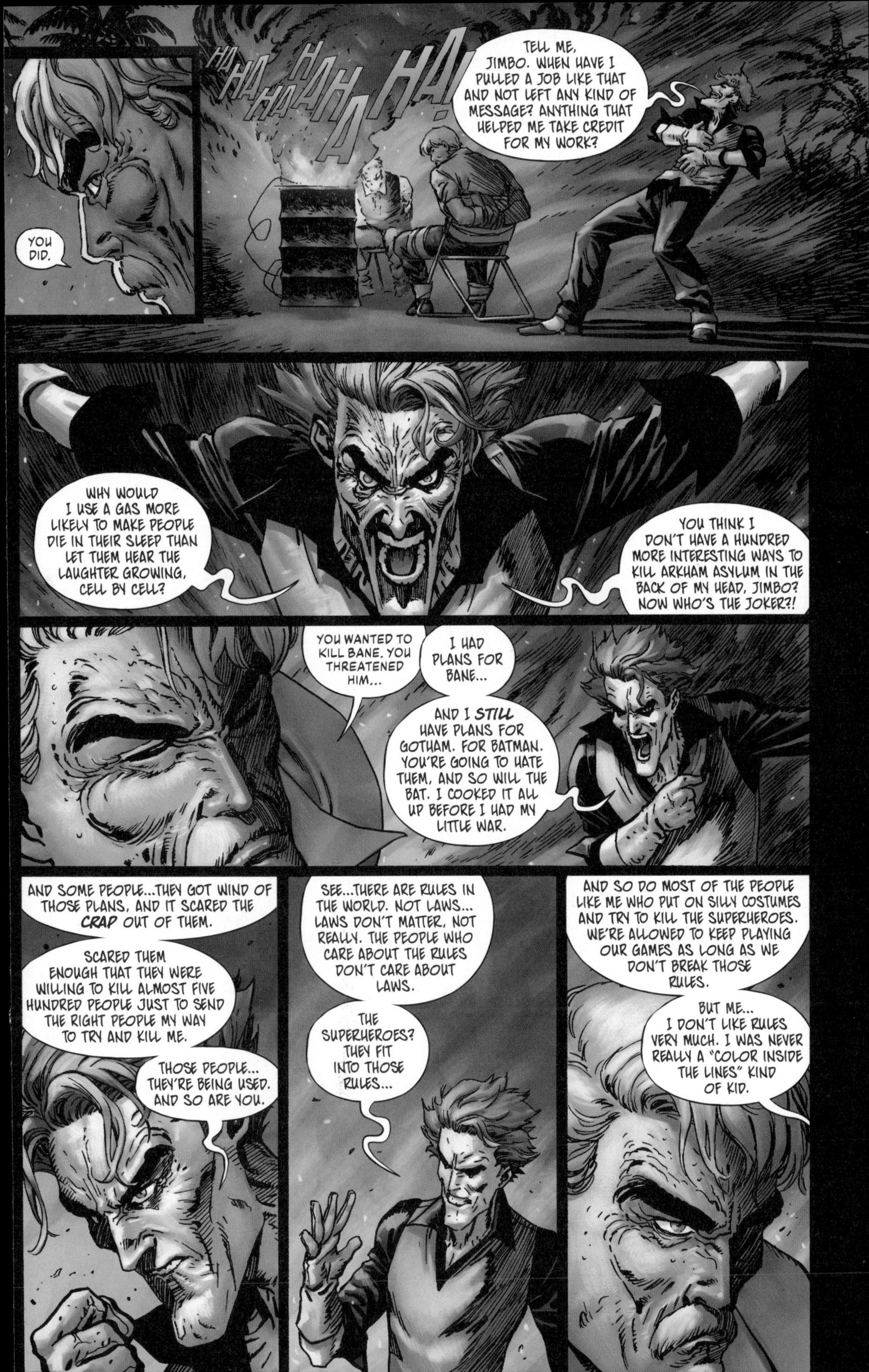
HA HA HA HA HAHAHA HA!
TELL ME, JIMBO. WHEN HAVE I PULLED A JOB LIKE THAT AND NOT LEFT ANY KIND OF MESSAGE? ANYTHING THAT HELPED ME TAKE CREDIT FOR MY WORK?
YOU DID.
WHY WOULD I USE A GAS MORE LIKELY TO MAKE PEOPLE DIE IN THEIR SLEEP THAN LET THEM HEAR THE LAUGHTER GROWING, CELL BY CELL?
YOU THINK I DON'T HAVE A HUNDRED MORE INTERESTING WAYS TO KILL ARKHAM ASYLUM IN THE BACK OF MY HEAD, JIMBO? NOW WHO'S THE JOKER?!
YOU WANTED TO KILL BANE. YOU THREATENED HIM...
I HAD PLANS FOR BANE...
AND I STILL HAVE PLANS FOR GOTHAM. FOR BATMAN. YOU'RE GOING TO HATE THEM, AND SO WILL THE BAT. I COOKED IT ALL UP BEFORE I HAD MY LITTLE WAR.
AND SOME PEOPLE...THEY GOT WIND OF THOSE PLANS, AND IT SCARED THE CRAP OUT OF THEM.
SCARED THEM ENOUGH THAT THEY WERE WILLING TO KILL ALMOST FIVE HUNDRED PEOPLE JUST TO SEND THE RIGHT PEOPLE MY WAY TO TRY AND KILL ME.
THOSE PEOPLE... THEY'RE BEING USED. AND SO ARE YOU.
SEE...THERE ARE RULES IN THE WORLD. NOT LAWS... LAWS DON'T MATTER, NOT REALLY. THE PEOPLE WHO CARE ABOUT THE RULES DON'T CARE ABOUT LAWS.
THE SUPERHEROES? THEY FIT INTO THOSE RULES...
AND SO DO MOST OF THE PEOPLE LIKE ME WHO PUT ON SILLY COSTUMES AND TRY TO KILL THE SUPERHEROES. WE'RE ALLOWED TO KEEP PLAYING OUR GAMES AS LONG AS WE DON'T BREAK THOSE RULES.
BUT ME... I DON'T LIKE RULES VERY MUCH. I WAS NEVER REALLY A "COLOR INSIDE THE LINES" KIND OF KID.

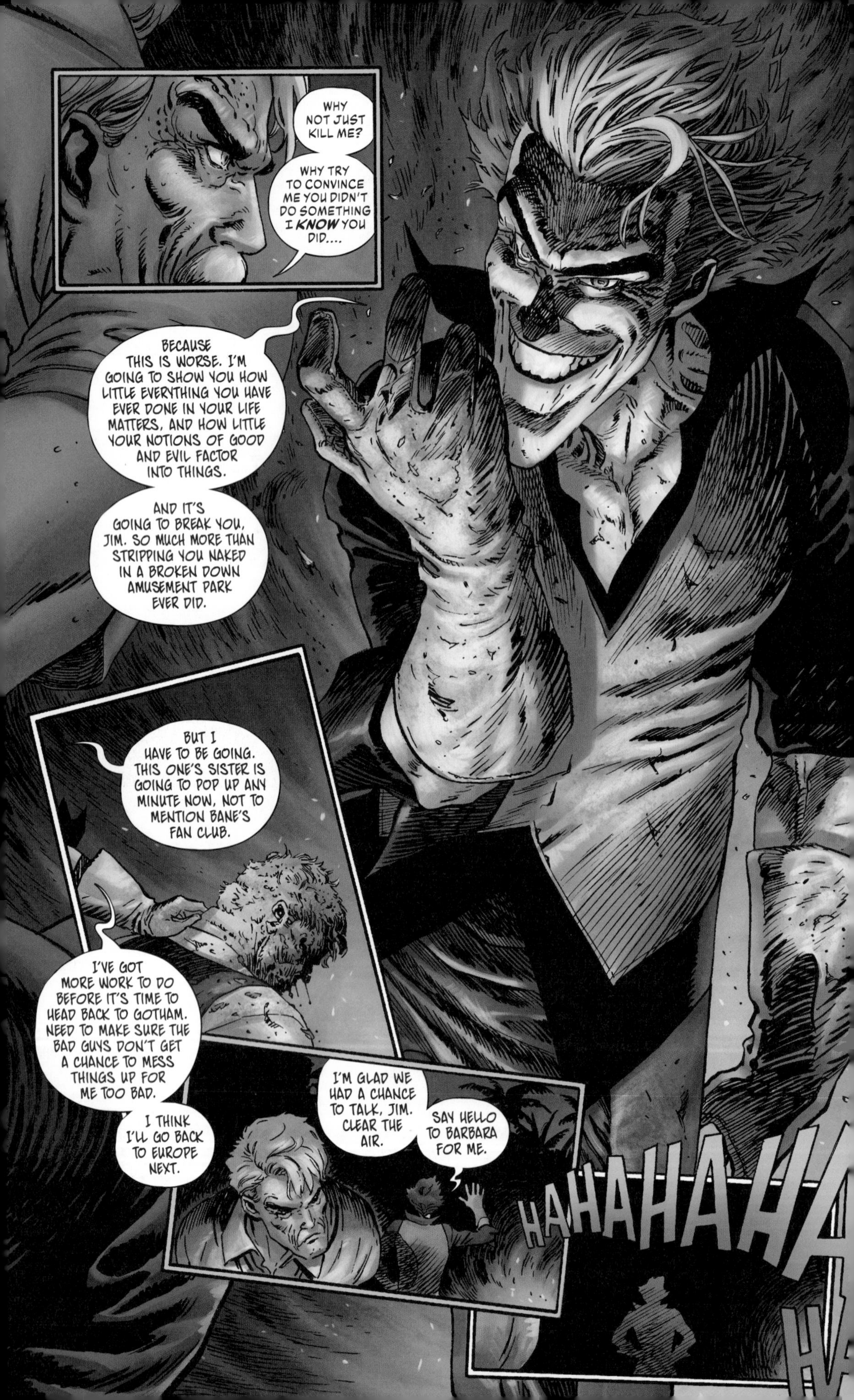
WHY NOT JUST KILL ME?
WHY TRY TO CONVINCE ME YOU DIDN'T DO SOMETHING I KNOW YOU DID....
BECAUSE THIS IS WORSE. I'M GOING TO SHOW YOU HOW LITTLE EVERYTHING YOU HAVE EVER DONE IN YOUR LIFE MATTERS, AND HOW LITTLE YOUR NOTIONS OF GOOD AND EVIL FACTOR INTO THINGS.
AND IT'S GOING TO BREAK YOU, JIM. SO MUCH MORE THAN STRIPPING YOU NAKED IN A BROKEN DOWN AMUSEMENT PARK EVER DID.
BUT I HAVE TO BE GOING. THIS ONE'S SISTER IS GOING TO POP UP ANY MINUTE NOW, NOT TO MENTION BANE'S FAN CLUB.
I'VE GOT MORE WORK TO DO BEFORE IT'S TIME TO HEAD BACK TO GOTHAM. NEED TO MAKE SURE THE BAD GUYS DON'T GET A CHANCE TO MESS THINGS UP FOR ME TOO BAD.
I THINK I'LL GO BACK TO EUROPE NEXT.
I'M GLAD WE HAD A CHANCE TO TALK, JIM. CLEAR THE AIR.
SAY HELLO TO BARBARA FOR ME.
HAHAHAHAHA
HA

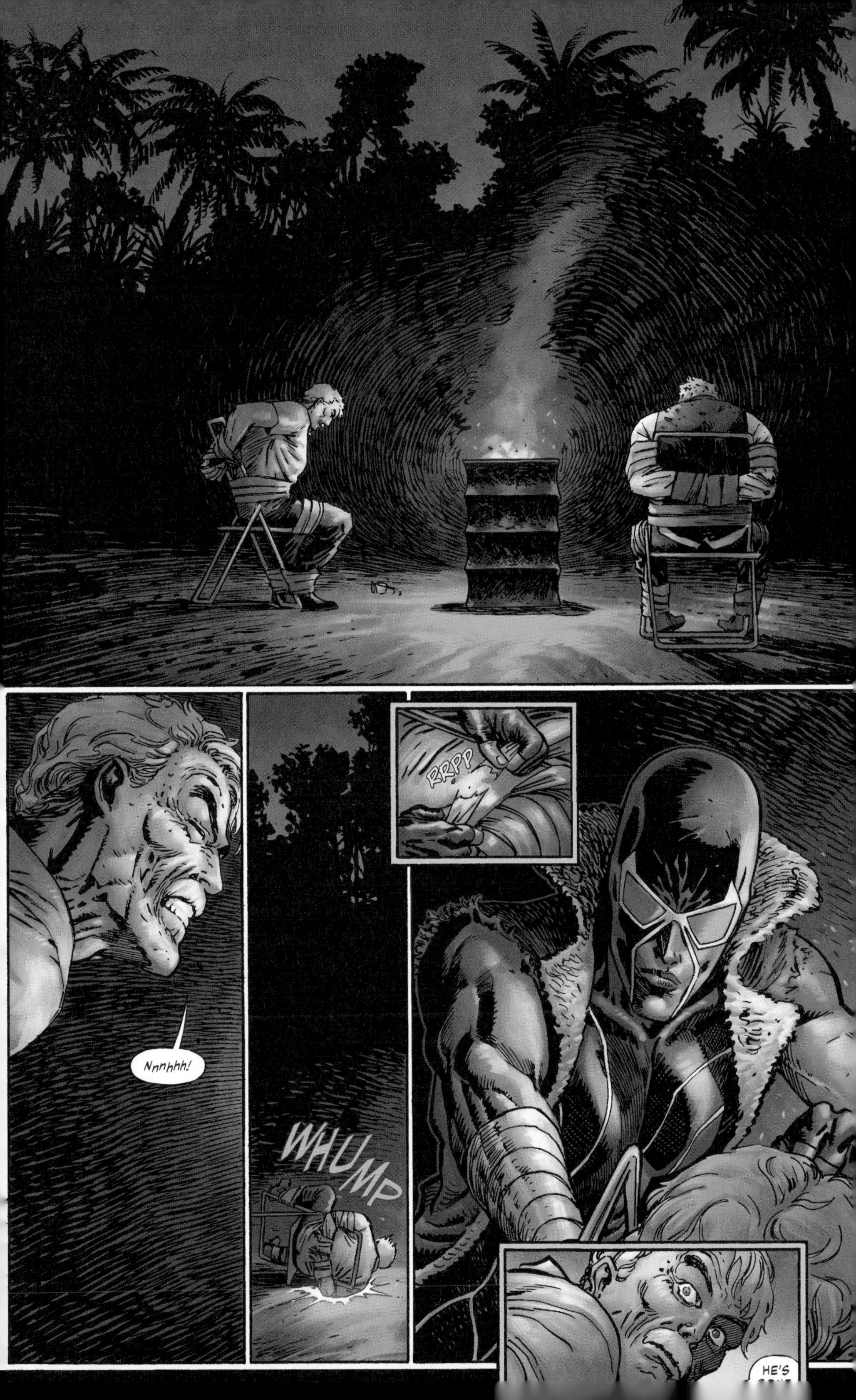
Nnnhhh!
WHUMP
RRPP
HE'S

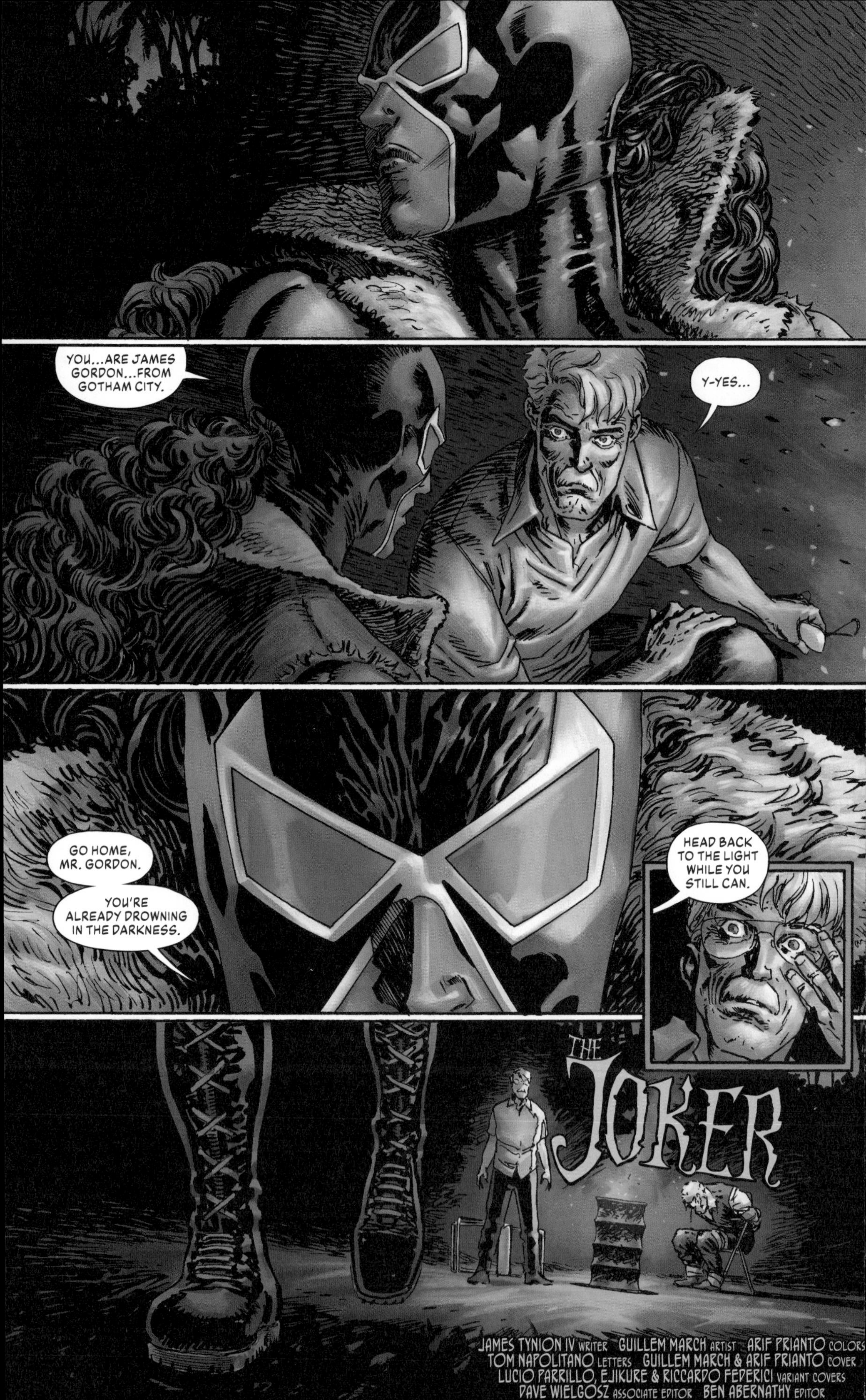
YOU...ARE JAMES GORDON...FROM GOTHAM CITY.
Y-YES...
GO HOME, MR. GORDON.
YOU'RE ALREADY DROWNING IN THE DARKNESS.
HEAD BACK TO THE LIGHT WHILE YOU STILL CAN.
THE JOKER
JAMES TYNION IV WRITER GUILLEM MARCH ARTIST ARIF PRIANTO COLORS
TOM NAPOLITANO LETTERS GUILLEM MARCH & ARIF PRIANTO COVER
LUCIO PARRILLO, EJIKURE & RICCARDO FEDERICI VARIANT COVERS
DAVE WIELGOSZ ASSOCIATE EDITOR BEN ABERNATHY EDITOR

The Joker #5
Cover Art by Guillem March
Colors by Arif Prianto

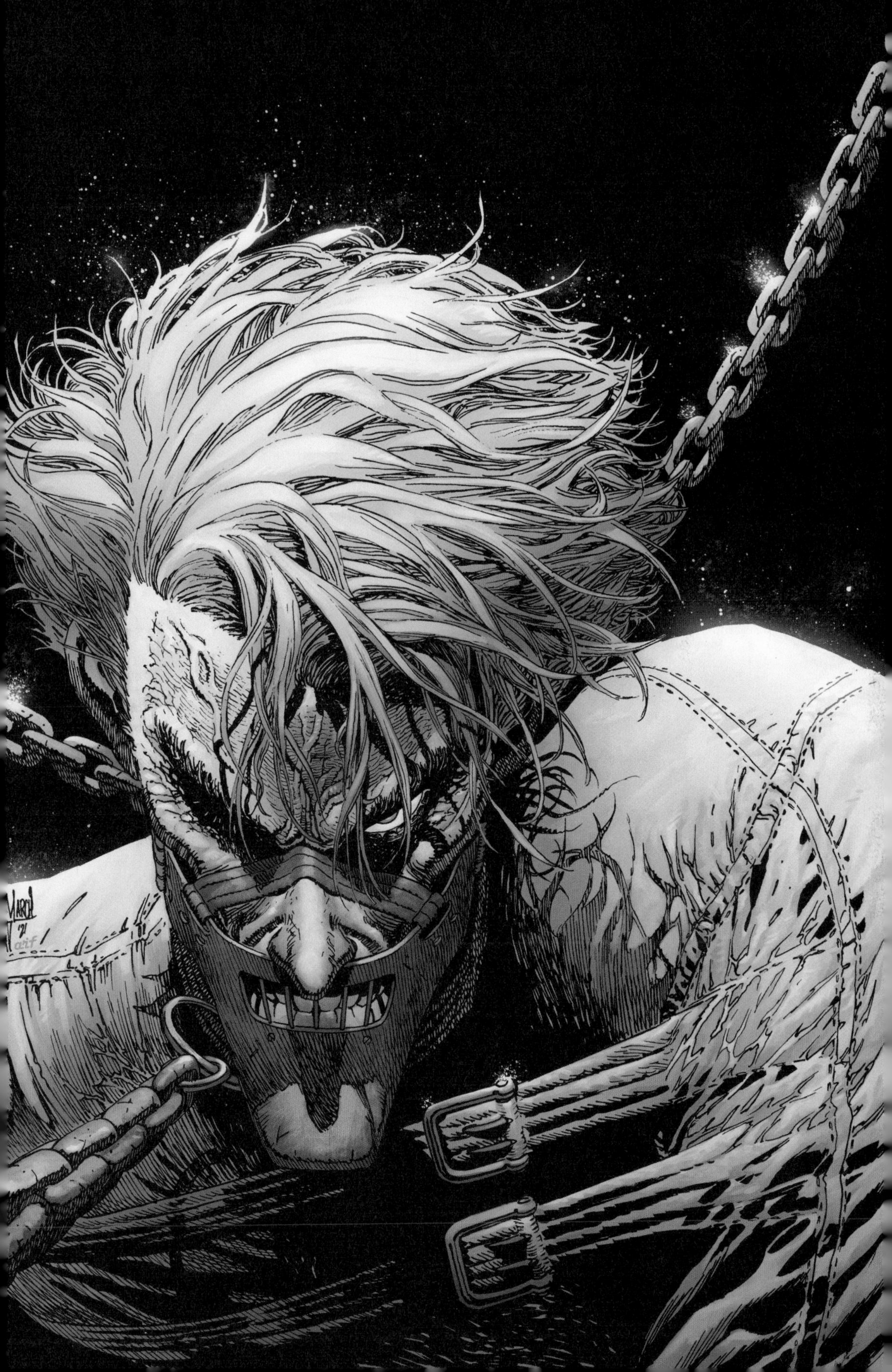

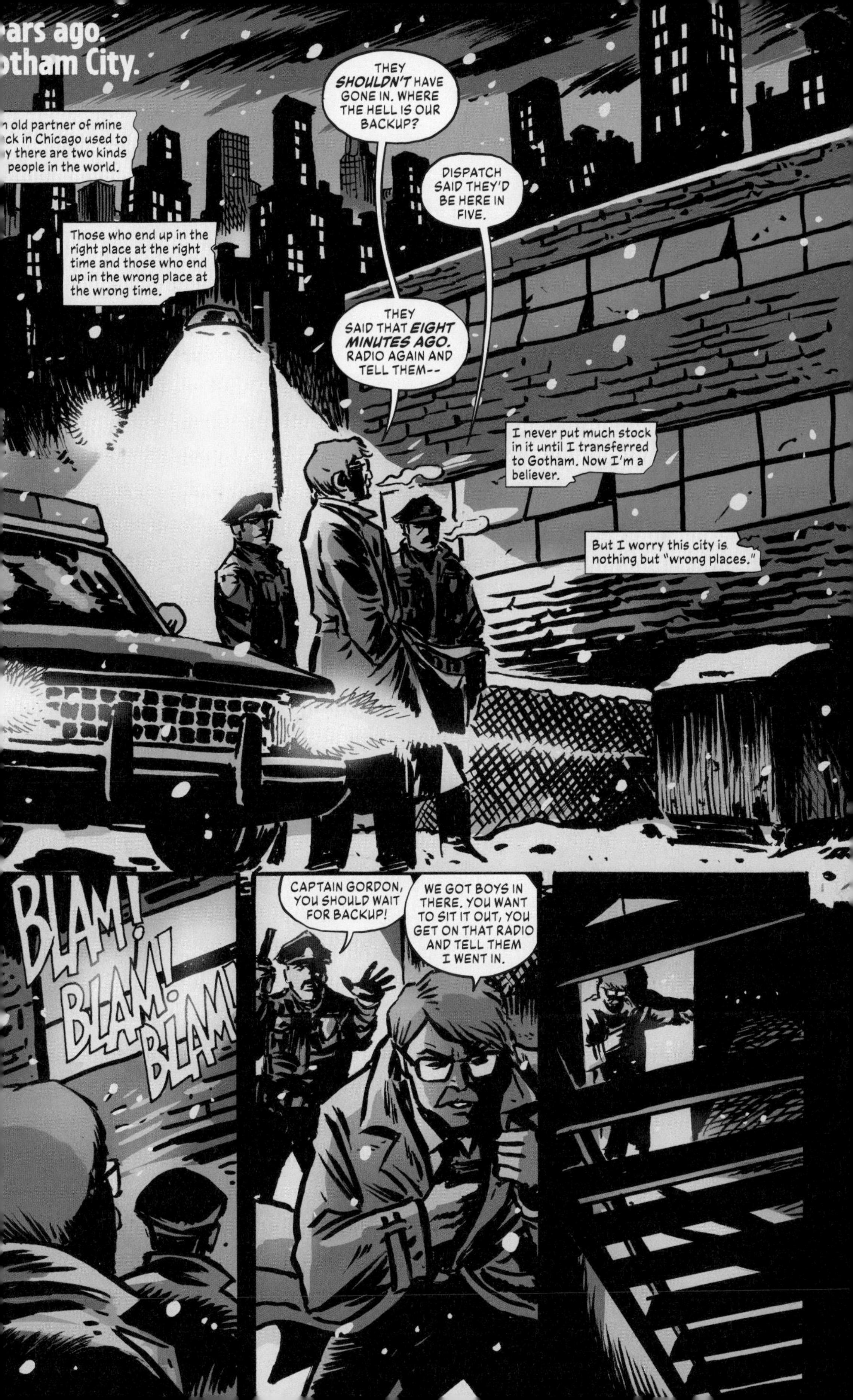

ars ago.
otham City.
n old partner of mine ck in Chicago used to y there are two kinds people in the world.
Those who end up in the right place at the right time and those who end up in the wrong place at the wrong time.
THEY SHOULDN'T HAVE GONE IN. WHERE THE HELL IS OUR BACKUP?
DISPATCH SAID THEY'D BE HERE IN FIVE.
THEY SAID THAT EIGHT MINUTES AGO. RADIO AGAIN AND TELL THEM--
I never put much stock in it until I transferred to Gotham. Now I'm a believer.
But I worry this city is nothing but "wrong places."
BLAM! BLAM! BLAM!
CAPTAIN GORDON, YOU SHOULD WAIT FOR BACKUP!
WE GOT BOYS IN THERE. YOU WANT TO SIT IT OUT, YOU GET ON THAT RADIO AND TELL THEM I WENT IN.

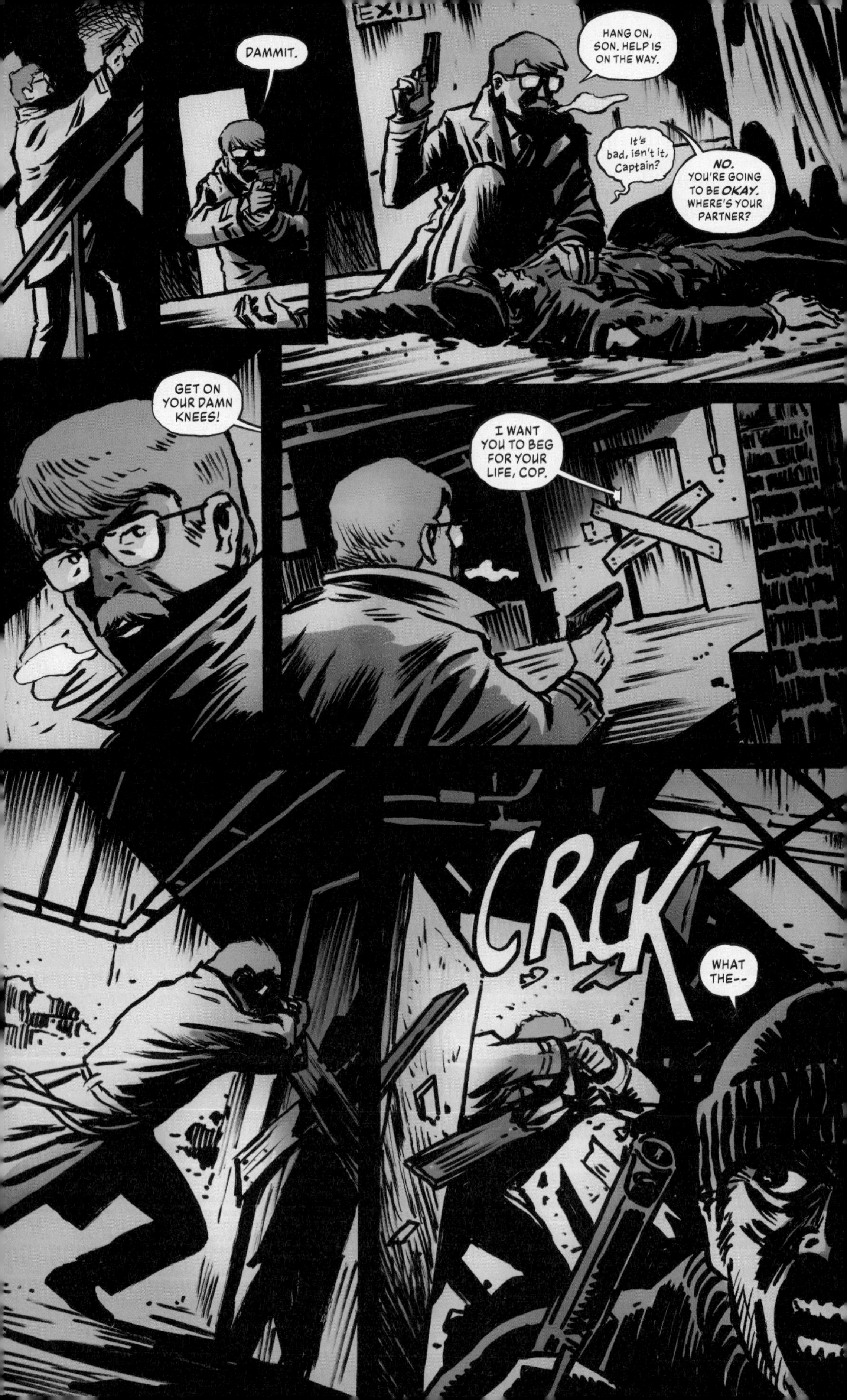
DAMMIT.
HANG ON, SON. HELP IS ON THE WAY.
It's bad, isn't it, Captain?
NO. YOU'RE GOING TO BE OKAY. WHERE'S YOUR PARTNER?
GET ON YOUR DAMN KNEES!
I WANT YOU TO BEG FOR YOUR LIFE, COP.
CRCK
WHAT THE--

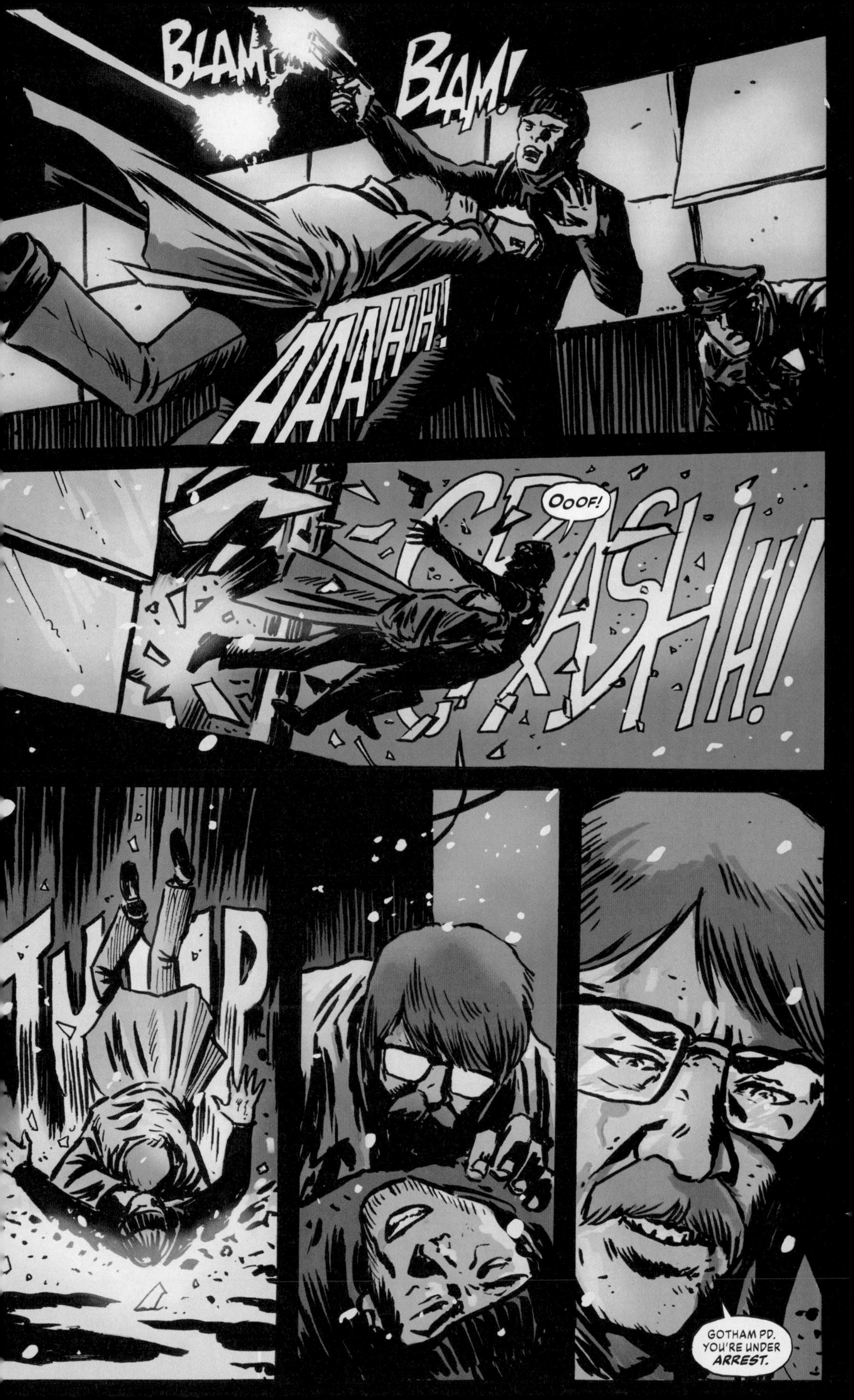
BLAM!
BLAM!
AAAHHH!
OOOF!
CRASHH!
THUMP
GOTHAM PD. YOU'RE UNDER ARREST.

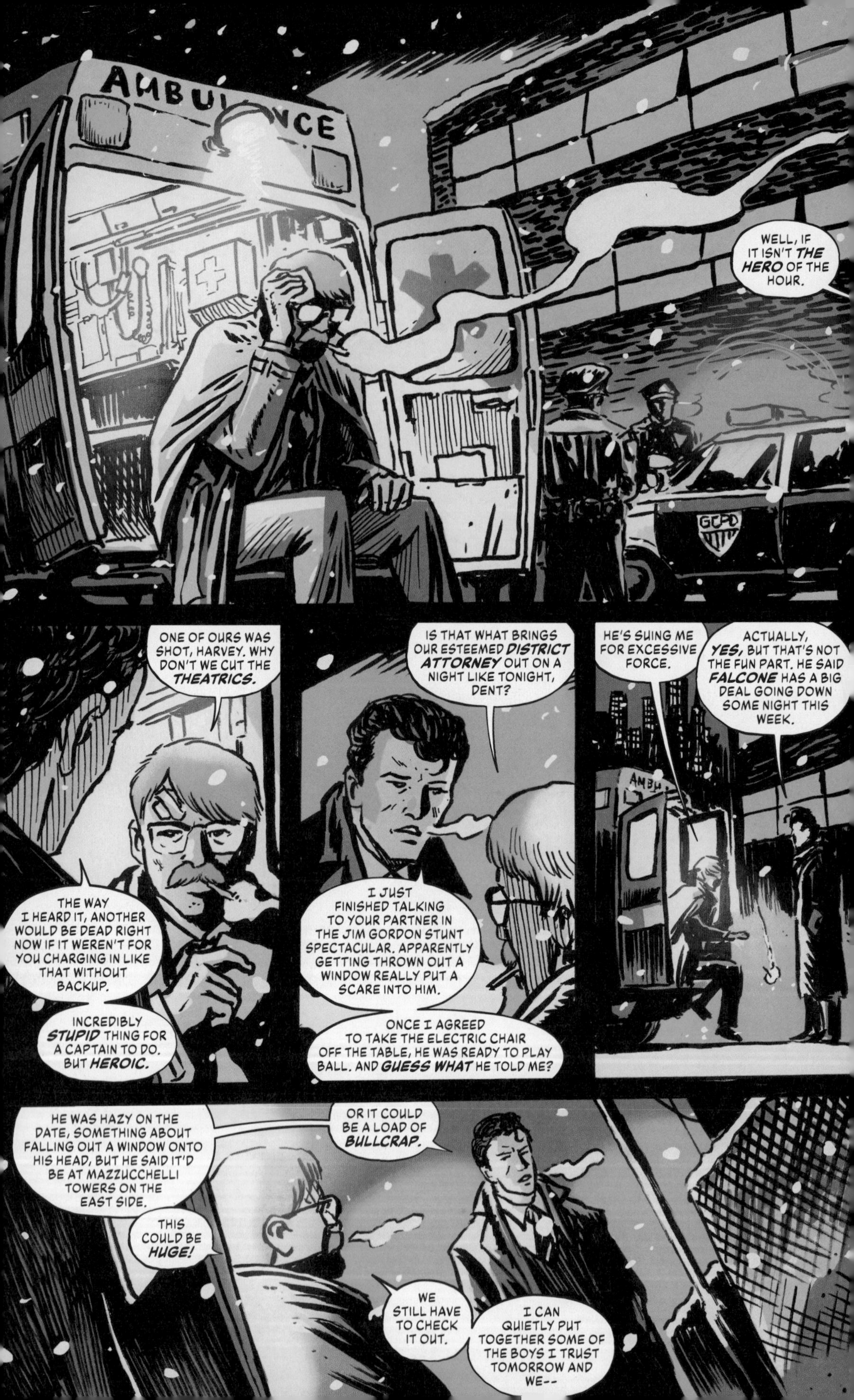
AMBU NCE
WELL, IF IT ISN'T THE HERO OF THE HOUR.
GCPD
ONE OF OURS WAS SHOT, HARVEY. WHY DON'T WE CUT THE THEATRICS.
THE WAY I HEARD IT, ANOTHER WOULD BE DEAD RIGHT NOW IF IT WEREN'T FOR YOU CHARGING IN LIKE THAT WITHOUT BACKUP.
INCREDIBLY STUPID THING FOR A CAPTAIN TO DO. BUT HEROIC.
IS THAT WHAT BRINGS OUR ESTEEMED DISTRICT ATTORNEY OUT ON A NIGHT LIKE TONIGHT, DENT?
I JUST FINISHED TALKING TO YOUR PARTNER IN THE JIM GORDON STUNT SPECTACULAR. APPARENTLY GETTING THROWN OUT A WINDOW REALLY PUT A SCARE INTO HIM.
ONCE I AGREED TO TAKE THE ELECTRIC CHAIR OFF THE TABLE, HE WAS READY TO PLAY BALL. AND GUESS WHAT HE TOLD ME?
HE'S SUING ME FOR EXCESSIVE FORCE.
ACTUALLY, YES, BUT THAT'S NOT THE FUN PART. HE SAID FALCONE HAS A BIG DEAL GOING DOWN SOME NIGHT THIS WEEK.
HE WAS HAZY ON THE DATE, SOMETHING ABOUT FALLING OUT A WINDOW ONTO HIS HEAD, BUT HE SAID IT'D BE AT MAZZUCCHELLI TOWERS ON THE EAST SIDE.
THIS COULD BE HUGE!
OR IT COULD BE A LOAD OF BULLCRAP.
WE STILL HAVE TO CHECK IT OUT.
I CAN QUIETLY PUT TOGETHER SOME OF THE BOYS I TRUST TOMORROW AND WE--

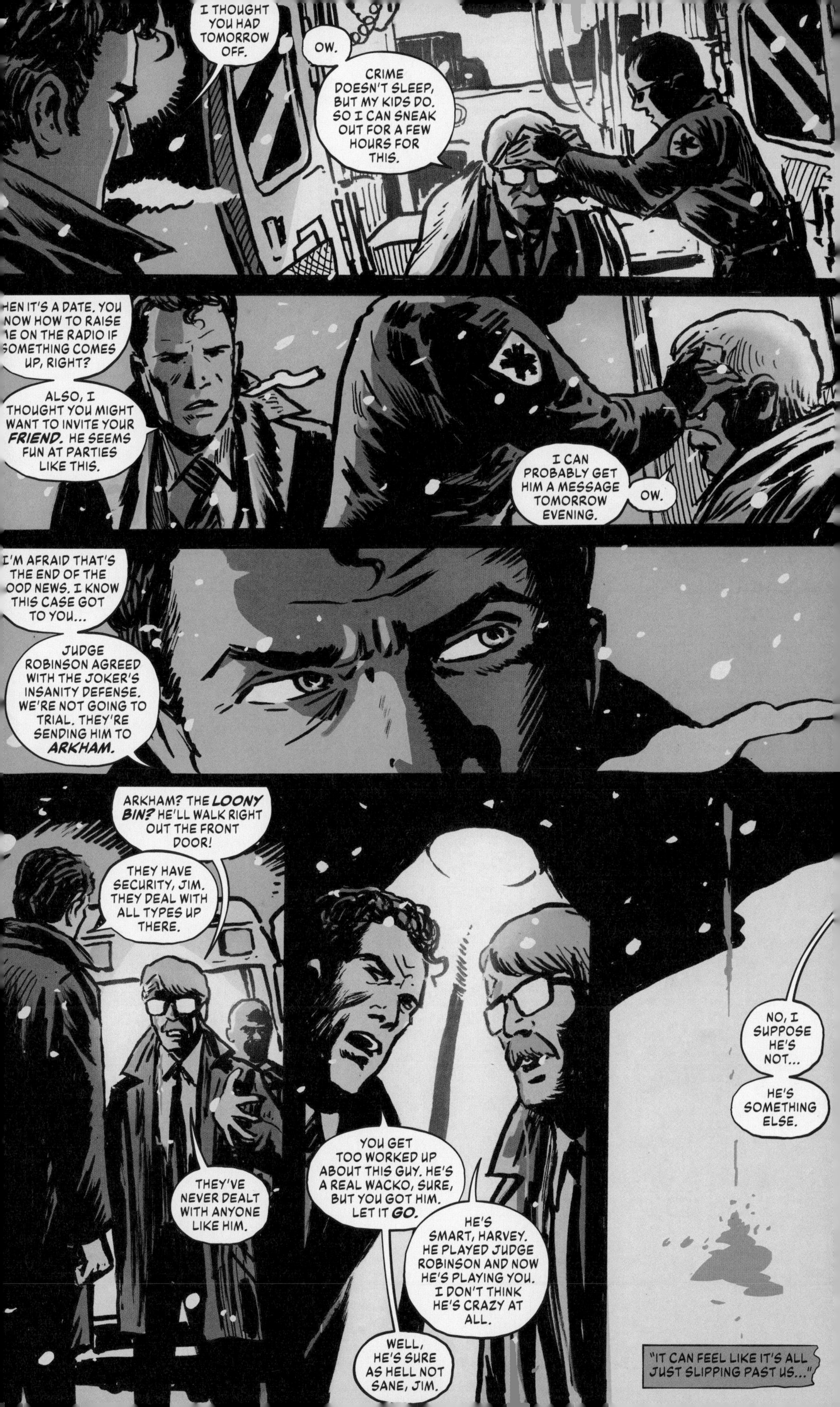
I THOUGHT YOU HAD TOMORROW OFF.
OW.
CRIME DOESN'T SLEEP, BUT MY KIDS DO. SO I CAN SNEAK OUT FOR A FEW HOURS FOR THIS.
HEN IT'S A DATE. YOU NOW HOW TO RAISE ME ON THE RADIO IF SOMETHING COMES UP, RIGHT?
ALSO, I THOUGHT YOU MIGHT WANT TO INVITE YOUR FRIEND. HE SEEMS FUN AT PARTIES LIKE THIS.
I CAN PROBABLY GET HIM A MESSAGE TOMORROW EVENING.
OW.
I'M AFRAID THAT'S THE END OF THE OOD NEWS. I KNOW THIS CASE GOT TO YOU...
JUDGE ROBINSON AGREED WITH THE JOKER'S INSANITY DEFENSE. WE'RE NOT GOING TO TRIAL. THEY'RE SENDING HIM TO ARKHAM.
ARKHAM? THE LOONY BIN? HE'LL WALK RIGHT OUT THE FRONT DOOR!
THEY HAVE SECURITY, JIM. THEY DEAL WITH ALL TYPES UP THERE.
THEY'VE NEVER DEALT WITH ANYONE LIKE HIM.
YOU GET TOO WORKED UP ABOUT THIS GUY. HE'S A REAL WACKO, SURE, BUT YOU GOT HIM. LET IT GO.
HE'S SMART, HARVEY. HE PLAYED JUDGE ROBINSON AND NOW HE'S PLAYING YOU. I DON'T THINK HE'S CRAZY AT ALL.
WELL, HE'S SURE AS HELL NOT SANE, JIM.
NO, I SUPPOSE HE'S NOT...
HE'S SOMETHING ELSE.
"IT CAN FEEL LIKE IT'S ALL JUST SLIPPING PAST US..."

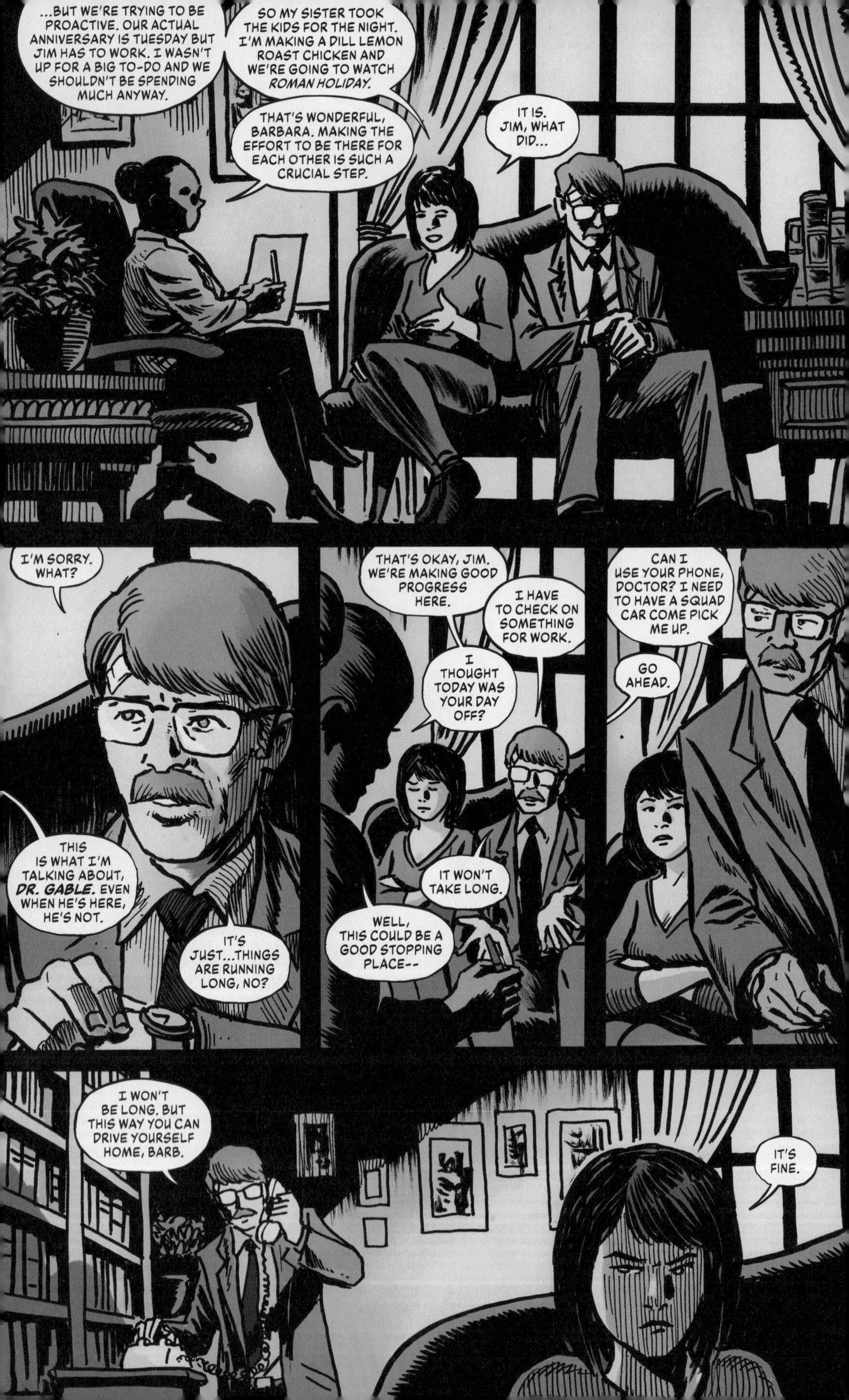
...BUT WE'RE TRYING TO BE PROACTIVE. OUR ACTUAL ANNIVERSARY IS TUESDAY BUT JIM HAS TO WORK. I WASN'T UP FOR A BIG TO-DO AND WE SHOULDN'T BE SPENDING MUCH ANYWAY.
SO MY SISTER TOOK THE KIDS FOR THE NIGHT. I'M MAKING A DILL LEMON ROAST CHICKEN AND WE'RE GOING TO WATCH *ROMAN HOLIDAY.*
THAT'S WONDERFUL, BARBARA. MAKING THE EFFORT TO BE THERE FOR EACH OTHER IS SUCH A CRUCIAL STEP.
IT IS. JIM, WHAT DID...
I'M SORRY. WHAT?
THIS IS WHAT I'M TALKING ABOUT, **DR. GABLE.** EVEN WHEN HE'S HERE, HE'S NOT.
IT'S JUST...THINGS ARE RUNNING LONG, NO?
THAT'S OKAY, JIM. WE'RE MAKING GOOD PROGRESS HERE.
I HAVE TO CHECK ON SOMETHING FOR WORK.
I THOUGHT TODAY WAS YOUR DAY OFF?
IT WON'T TAKE LONG.
WELL, THIS COULD BE A GOOD STOPPING PLACE--
CAN I USE YOUR PHONE, DOCTOR? I NEED TO HAVE A SQUAD CAR COME PICK ME UP.
GO AHEAD.
I WON'T BE LONG. BUT THIS WAY YOU CAN DRIVE YOURSELF HOME, BARB.
IT'S FINE.

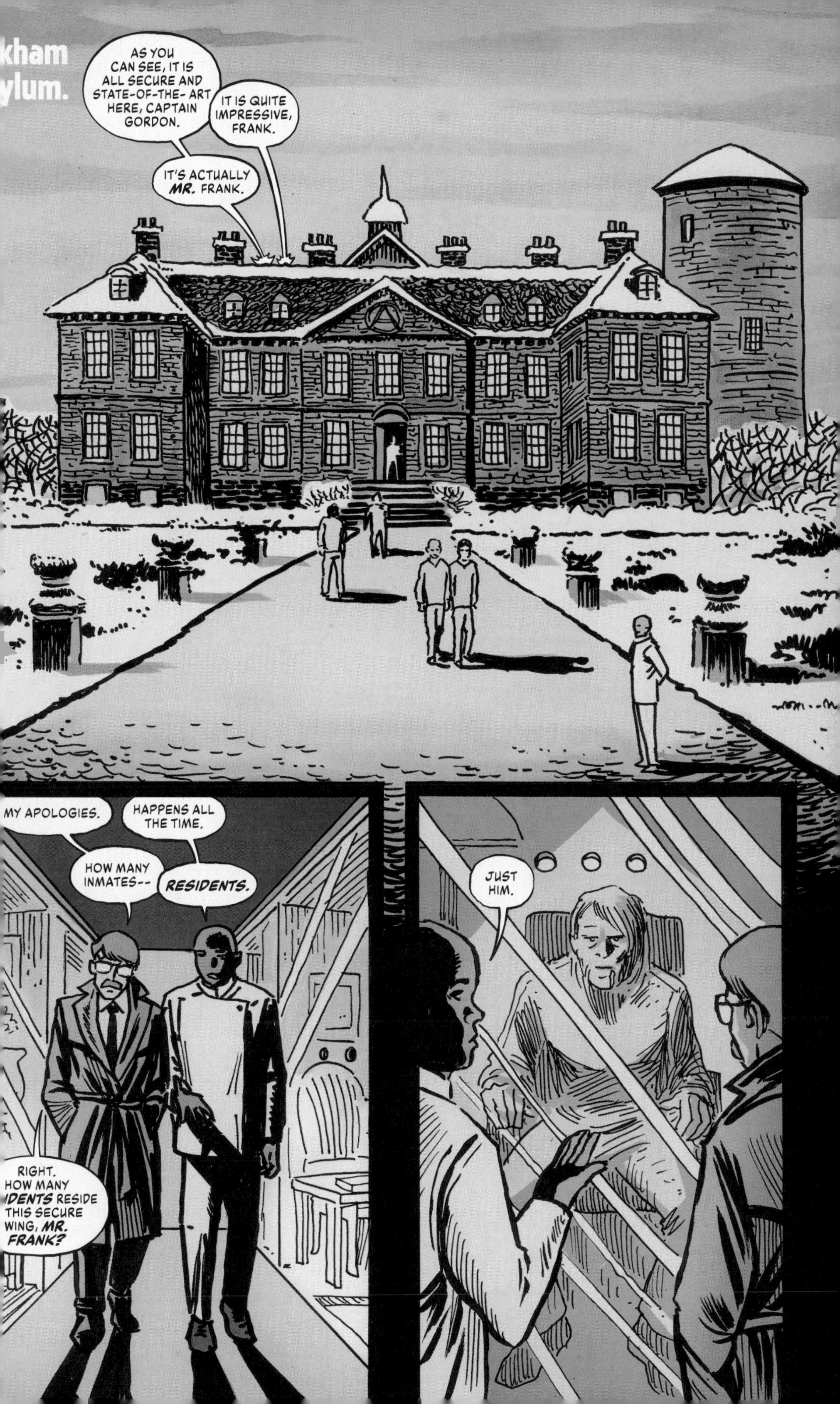
kham
ylum.
AS YOU CAN SEE, IT IS ALL SECURE AND STATE-OF-THE- ART HERE, CAPTAIN GORDON.
IT IS QUITE IMPRESSIVE, FRANK.
IT'S ACTUALLY *MR.* FRANK.
MY APOLOGIES.
HAPPENS ALL THE TIME.
HOW MANY INMATES--
RESIDENTS.
RIGHT. HOW MANY *IDENTS* RESIDE THIS SECURE WING, *MR. FRANK?*
JUST HIM.

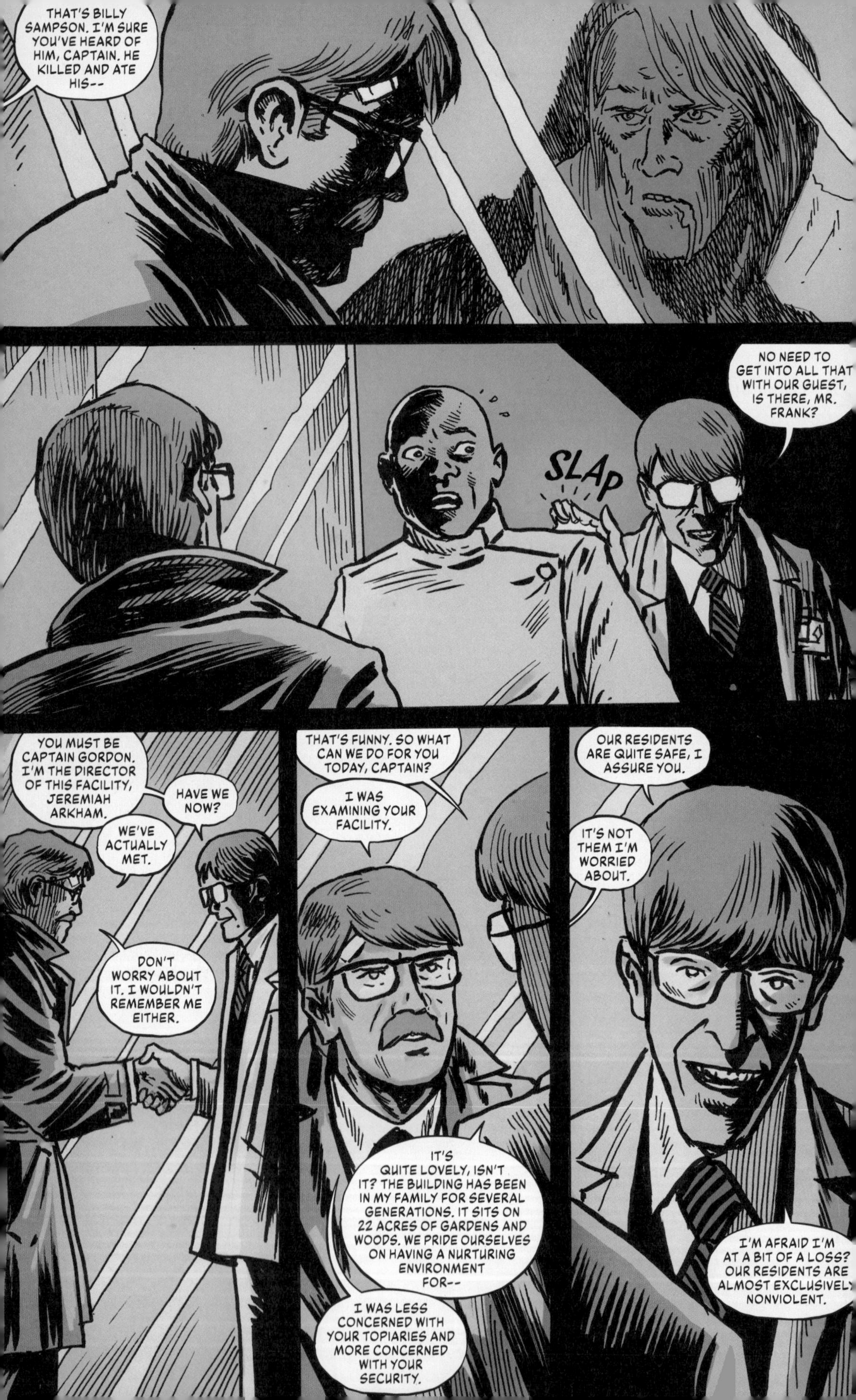
THAT'S BILLY SAMPSON. I'M SURE YOU'VE HEARD OF HIM, CAPTAIN. HE KILLED AND ATE HIS--
NO NEED TO GET INTO ALL THAT WITH OUR GUEST, IS THERE, MR. FRANK?
SLAP
YOU MUST BE CAPTAIN GORDON. I'M THE DIRECTOR OF THIS FACILITY, JEREMIAH ARKHAM.
WE'VE ACTUALLY MET.
HAVE WE NOW?
DON'T WORRY ABOUT IT. I WOULDN'T REMEMBER ME EITHER.
THAT'S FUNNY. SO WHAT CAN WE DO FOR YOU TODAY, CAPTAIN?
I WAS EXAMINING YOUR FACILITY.
IT'S QUITE LOVELY, ISN'T IT? THE BUILDING HAS BEEN IN MY FAMILY FOR SEVERAL GENERATIONS. IT SITS ON 22 ACRES OF GARDENS AND WOODS. WE PRIDE OURSELVES ON HAVING A NURTURING ENVIRONMENT FOR--
I WAS LESS CONCERNED WITH YOUR TOPIARIES AND MORE CONCERNED WITH YOUR SECURITY.
OUR RESIDENTS ARE QUITE SAFE, I ASSURE YOU.
IT'S NOT THEM I'M WORRIED ABOUT.
I'M AFRAID I'M AT A BIT OF A LOSS? OUR RESIDENTS ARE ALMOST EXCLUSIVELY NONVIOLENT.

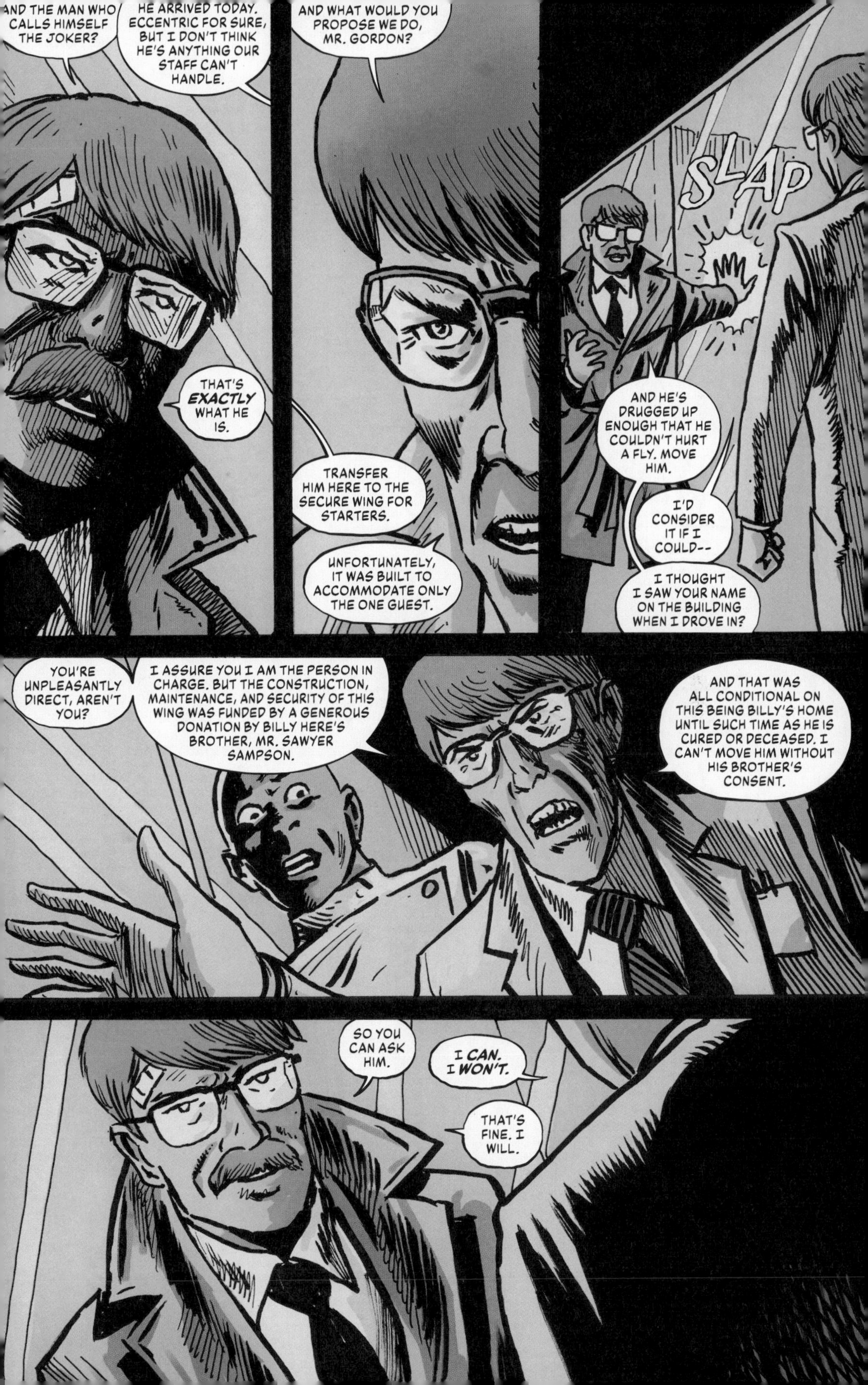
AND THE MAN WHO CALLS HIMSELF THE JOKER?
HE ARRIVED TODAY. ECCENTRIC FOR SURE, BUT I DON'T THINK HE'S ANYTHING OUR STAFF CAN'T HANDLE.
THAT'S EXACTLY WHAT HE IS.
AND WHAT WOULD YOU PROPOSE WE DO, MR. GORDON?
TRANSFER HIM HERE TO THE SECURE WING FOR STARTERS.
UNFORTUNATELY, IT WAS BUILT TO ACCOMMODATE ONLY THE ONE GUEST.
SLAP
AND HE'S DRUGGED UP ENOUGH THAT HE COULDN'T HURT A FLY. MOVE HIM.
I'D CONSIDER IT IF I COULD--
I THOUGHT I SAW YOUR NAME ON THE BUILDING WHEN I DROVE IN?
YOU'RE UNPLEASANTLY DIRECT, AREN'T YOU?
I ASSURE YOU I AM THE PERSON IN CHARGE. BUT THE CONSTRUCTION, MAINTENANCE, AND SECURITY OF THIS WING WAS FUNDED BY A GENEROUS DONATION BY BILLY HERE'S BROTHER, MR. SAWYER SAMPSON.
AND THAT WAS ALL CONDITIONAL ON THIS BEING BILLY'S HOME UNTIL SUCH TIME AS HE IS CURED OR DECEASED. I CAN'T MOVE HIM WITHOUT HIS BROTHER'S CONSENT.
SO YOU CAN ASK HIM.
I CAN. I WON'T.
THAT'S FINE. I WILL.

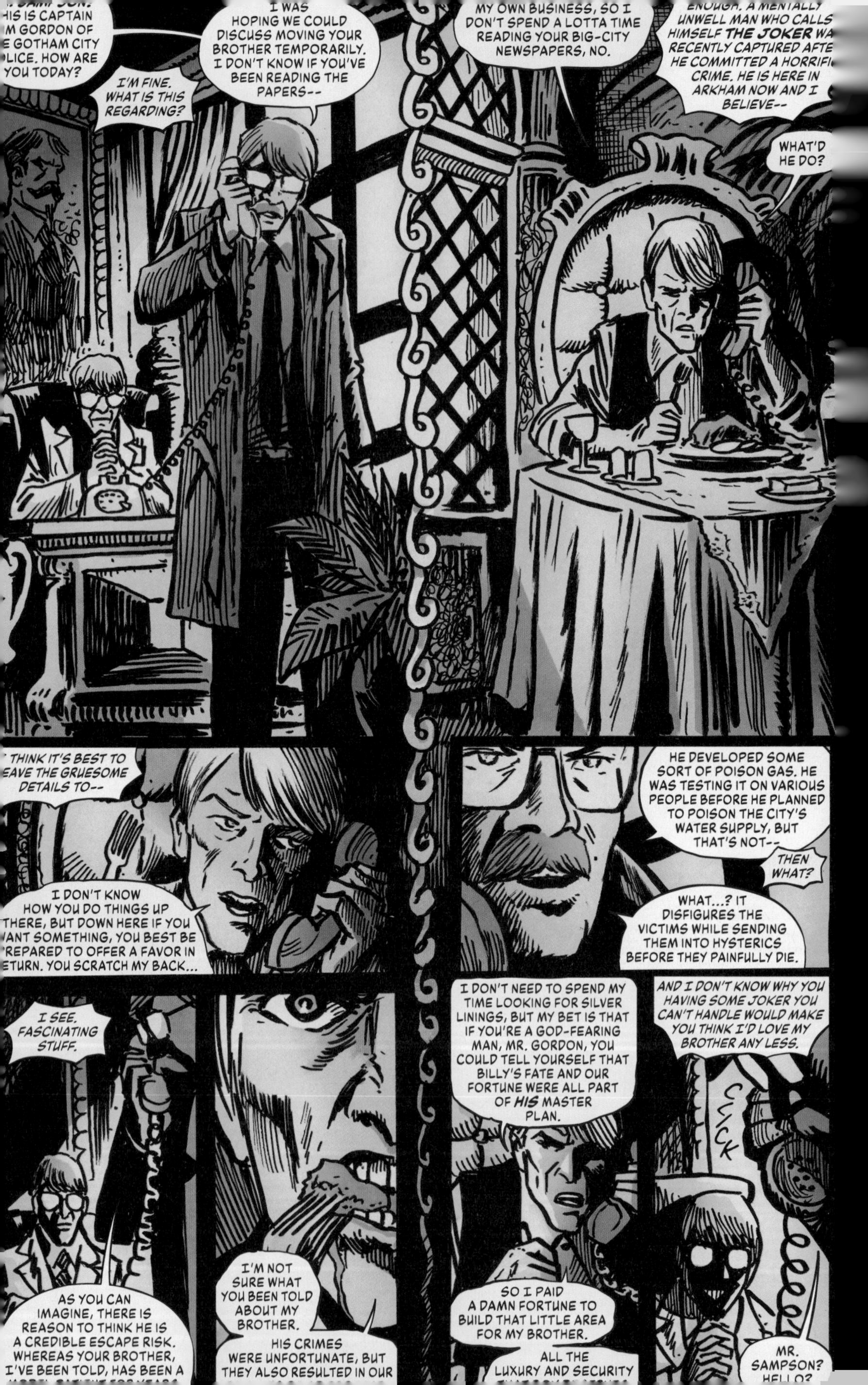
HIS IS CAPTAIN
M GORDON OF
E GOTHAM CITY
LICE. HOW ARE
YOU TODAY?
I'M FINE. WHAT IS THIS REGARDING?
I WAS HOPING WE COULD DISCUSS MOVING YOUR BROTHER TEMPORARILY. I DON'T KNOW IF YOU'VE BEEN READING THE PAPERS--
MY OWN BUSINESS, SO I DON'T SPEND A LOTTA TIME READING YOUR BIG-CITY NEWSPAPERS, NO.
ENOUGH. A MENTALLY UNWELL MAN WHO CALLS HIMSELF THE JOKER WA RECENTLY CAPTURED AFTE HE COMMITTED A HORRIFI CRIME. HE IS HERE IN ARKHAM NOW AND I BELIEVE--
WHAT'D HE DO?
THINK IT'S BEST TO EAVE THE GRUESOME DETAILS TO--
I DON'T KNOW HOW YOU DO THINGS UP THERE, BUT DOWN HERE IF YOU ANT SOMETHING, YOU BEST BE PREPARED TO OFFER A FAVOR IN ETURN. YOU SCRATCH MY BACK...
HE DEVELOPED SOME SORT OF POISON GAS. HE WAS TESTING IT ON VARIOUS PEOPLE BEFORE HE PLANNED TO POISON THE CITY'S WATER SUPPLY, BUT THAT'S NOT--
THEN WHAT?
WHAT...? IT DISFIGURES THE VICTIMS WHILE SENDING THEM INTO HYSTERICS BEFORE THEY PAINFULLY DIE.
I SEE. FASCINATING STUFF.
AS YOU CAN IMAGINE, THERE IS REASON TO THINK HE IS A CREDIBLE ESCAPE RISK. WHEREAS YOUR BROTHER, I'VE BEEN TOLD, HAS BEEN A
I'M NOT SURE WHAT YOU BEEN TOLD ABOUT MY BROTHER.
HIS CRIMES WERE UNFORTUNATE, BUT THEY ALSO RESULTED IN OUR
I DON'T NEED TO SPEND MY TIME LOOKING FOR SILVER LININGS, BUT MY BET IS THAT IF YOU'RE A GOD-FEARING MAN, MR. GORDON, YOU COULD TELL YOURSELF THAT BILLY'S FATE AND OUR FORTUNE WERE ALL PART OF HIS MASTER PLAN.
SO I PAID A DAMN FORTUNE TO BUILD THAT LITTLE AREA FOR MY BROTHER.
ALL THE LUXURY AND SECURITY
AND I DON'T KNOW WHY YOU HAVING SOME JOKER YOU CAN'T HANDLE WOULD MAKE YOU THINK I'D LOVE MY BROTHER ANY LESS.
CLICK
MR. SAMPSON?

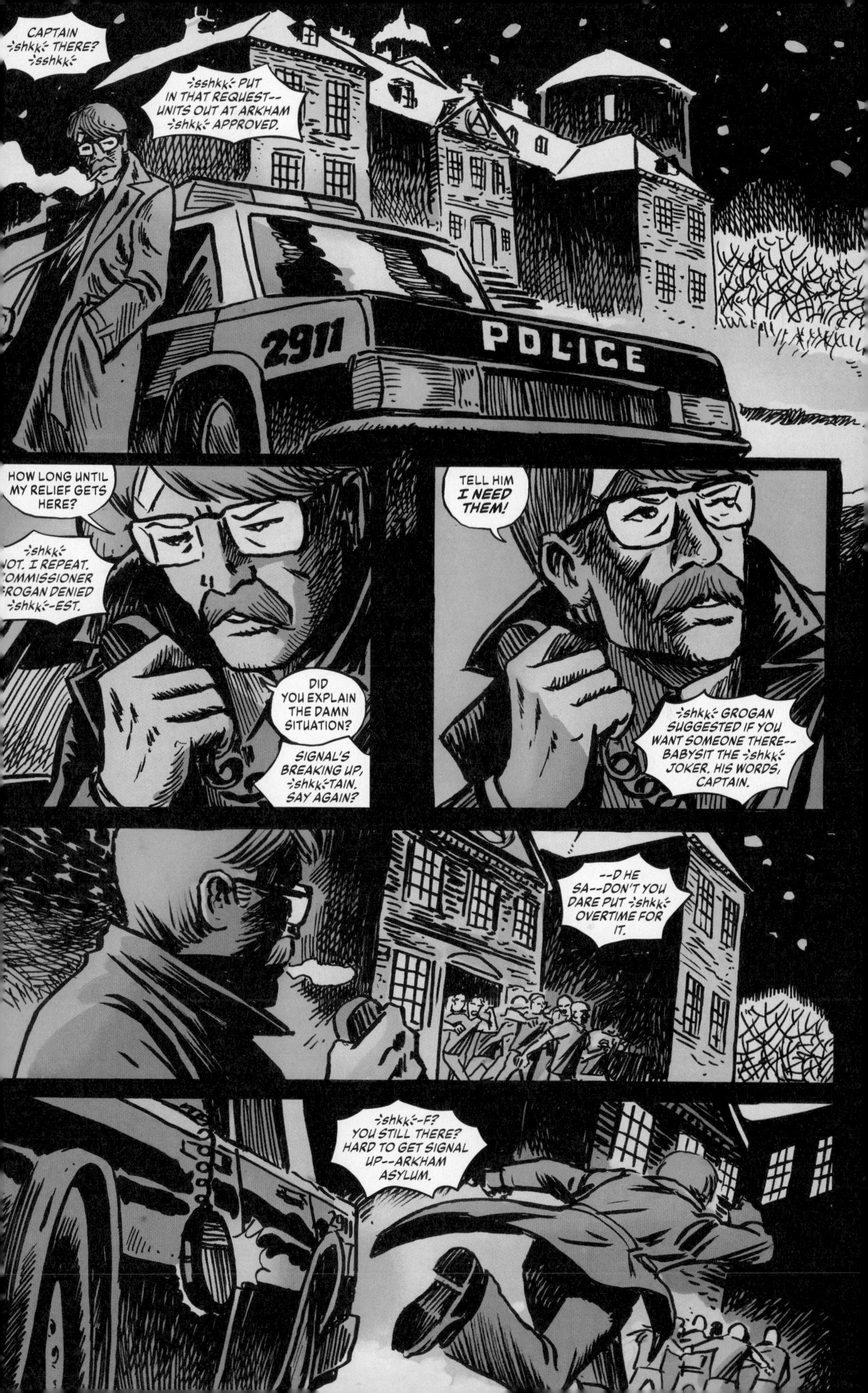
CAPTAIN -shkk- THERE? -sshkk-
-sshkk- PUT IN THAT REQUEST-- UNITS OUT AT ARKHAM -shkk- APPROVED.
2911
POLICE
HOW LONG UNTIL MY RELIEF GETS HERE?
-shkk- NOT. I REPEAT. COMMISSIONER GROGAN DENIED -shkk- -EST.
DID YOU EXPLAIN THE DAMN SITUATION?
SIGNAL'S BREAKING UP, -shkk- TAIN. SAY AGAIN?
TELL HIM I NEED THEM!
-shkk- GROGAN SUGGESTED IF YOU WANT SOMEONE THERE-- BABYSIT THE -shkk- JOKER. HIS WORDS, CAPTAIN.
--D HE SA--DON'T YOU DARE PUT -shkk- OVERTIME FOR IT.
-shkk- -F? YOU STILL THERE? HARD TO GET SIGNAL UP--ARKHAM ASYLUM.
2911

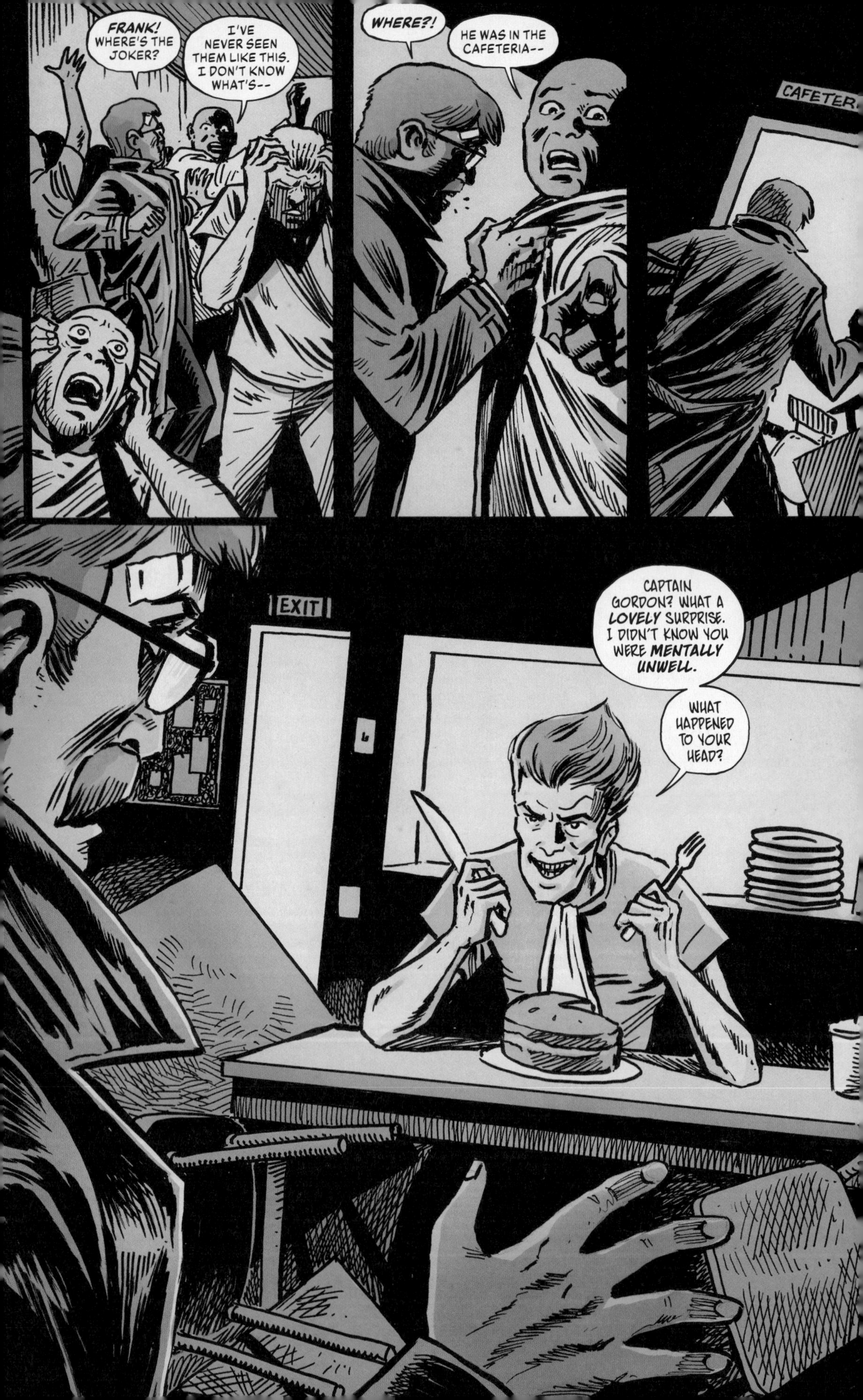
FRANK! WHERE'S THE JOKER?
I'VE NEVER SEEN THEM LIKE THIS. I DON'T KNOW WHAT'S--
WHERE?!
HE WAS IN THE CAFETERIA--
CAFETER
EXIT
CAPTAIN GORDON? WHAT A LOVELY SURPRISE. I DIDN'T KNOW YOU WERE MENTALLY UNWELL.
WHAT HAPPENED TO YOUR HEAD?

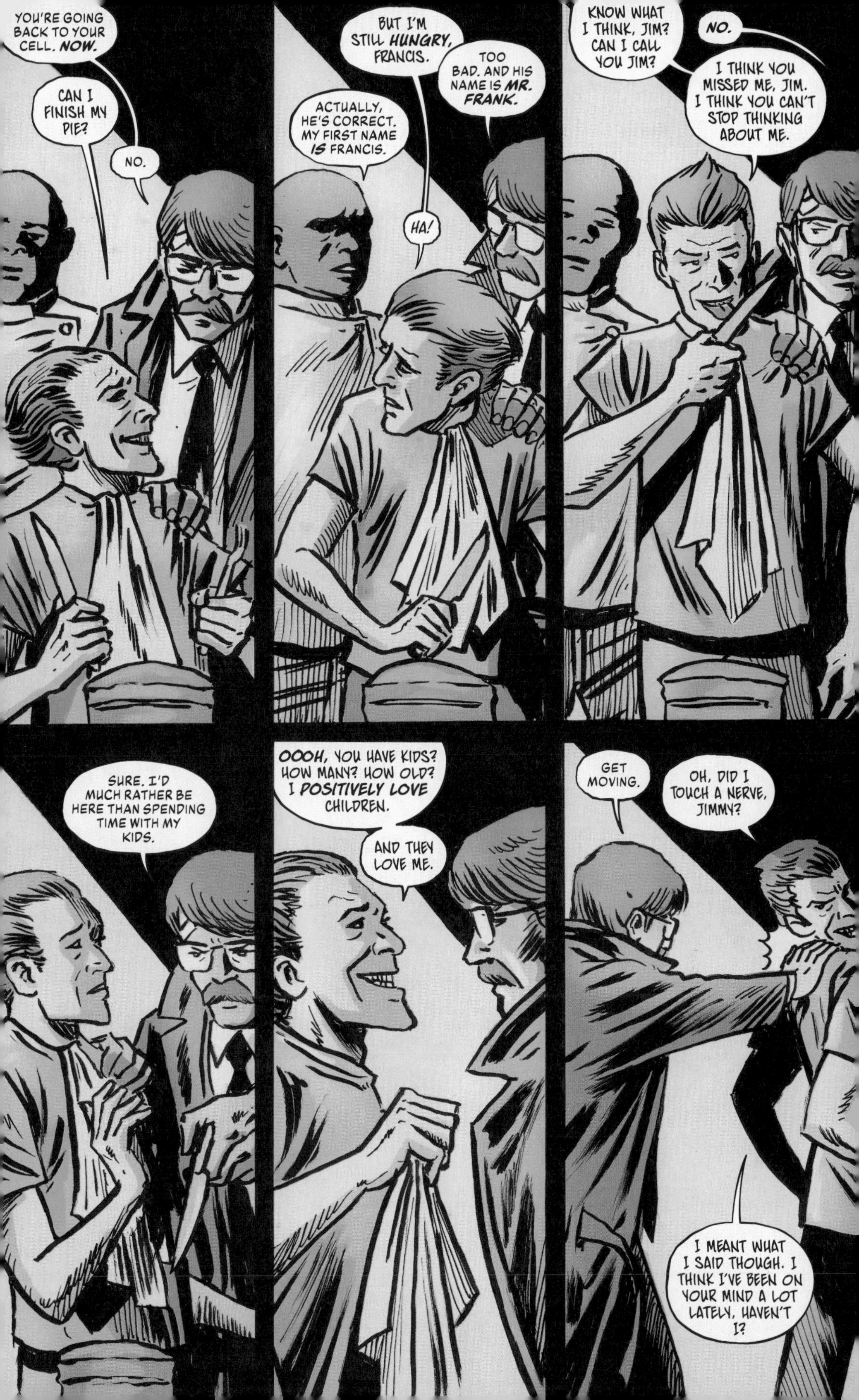
YOU'RE GOING BACK TO YOUR CELL. NOW.
CAN I FINISH MY PIE?
NO.
BUT I'M STILL HUNGRY, FRANCIS.
TOO BAD. AND HIS NAME IS MR. FRANK.
ACTUALLY, HE'S CORRECT. MY FIRST NAME IS FRANCIS.
HA!
KNOW WHAT I THINK, JIM? CAN I CALL YOU JIM?
NO.
I THINK YOU MISSED ME, JIM. I THINK YOU CAN'T STOP THINKING ABOUT ME.
SURE. I'D MUCH RATHER BE HERE THAN SPENDING TIME WITH MY KIDS.
OOOH, YOU HAVE KIDS? HOW MANY? HOW OLD? I POSITIVELY LOVE CHILDREN.
AND THEY LOVE ME.
GET MOVING.
OH, DID I TOUCH A NERVE, JIMMY?
I MEANT WHAT I SAID THOUGH. I THINK I'VE BEEN ON YOUR MIND A LOT LATELY, HAVEN'T I?

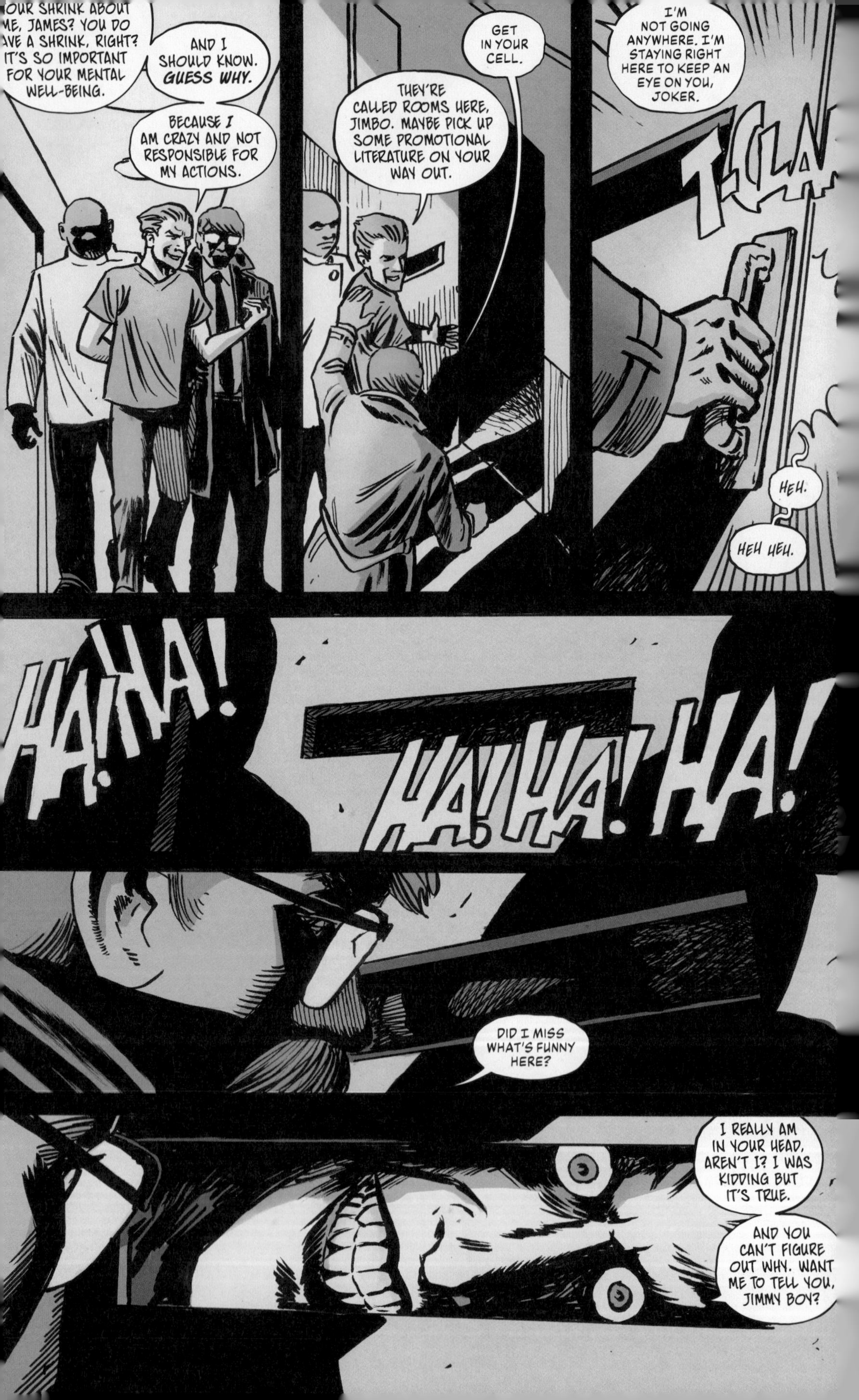
OUR SHRINK ABOUT ME, JAMES? YOU DO AVE A SHRINK, RIGHT? IT'S SO IMPORTANT FOR YOUR MENTAL WELL-BEING.
AND I SHOULD KNOW. GUESS WHY.
BECAUSE I AM CRAZY AND NOT RESPONSIBLE FOR MY ACTIONS.
GET IN YOUR CELL.
THEY'RE CALLED ROOMS HERE, JIMBO. MAYBE PICK UP SOME PROMOTIONAL LITERATURE ON YOUR WAY OUT.
I'M NOT GOING ANYWHERE. I'M STAYING RIGHT HERE TO KEEP AN EYE ON YOU, JOKER.
T-CLA
HEH.
HEH HEH.
HA! HA! HA!
HA! HA! HA! HA!
DID I MISS WHAT'S FUNNY HERE?
I REALLY AM IN YOUR HEAD, AREN'T I? I WAS KIDDING BUT IT'S TRUE.
AND YOU CAN'T FIGURE OUT WHY. WANT ME TO TELL YOU, JIMMY BOY?

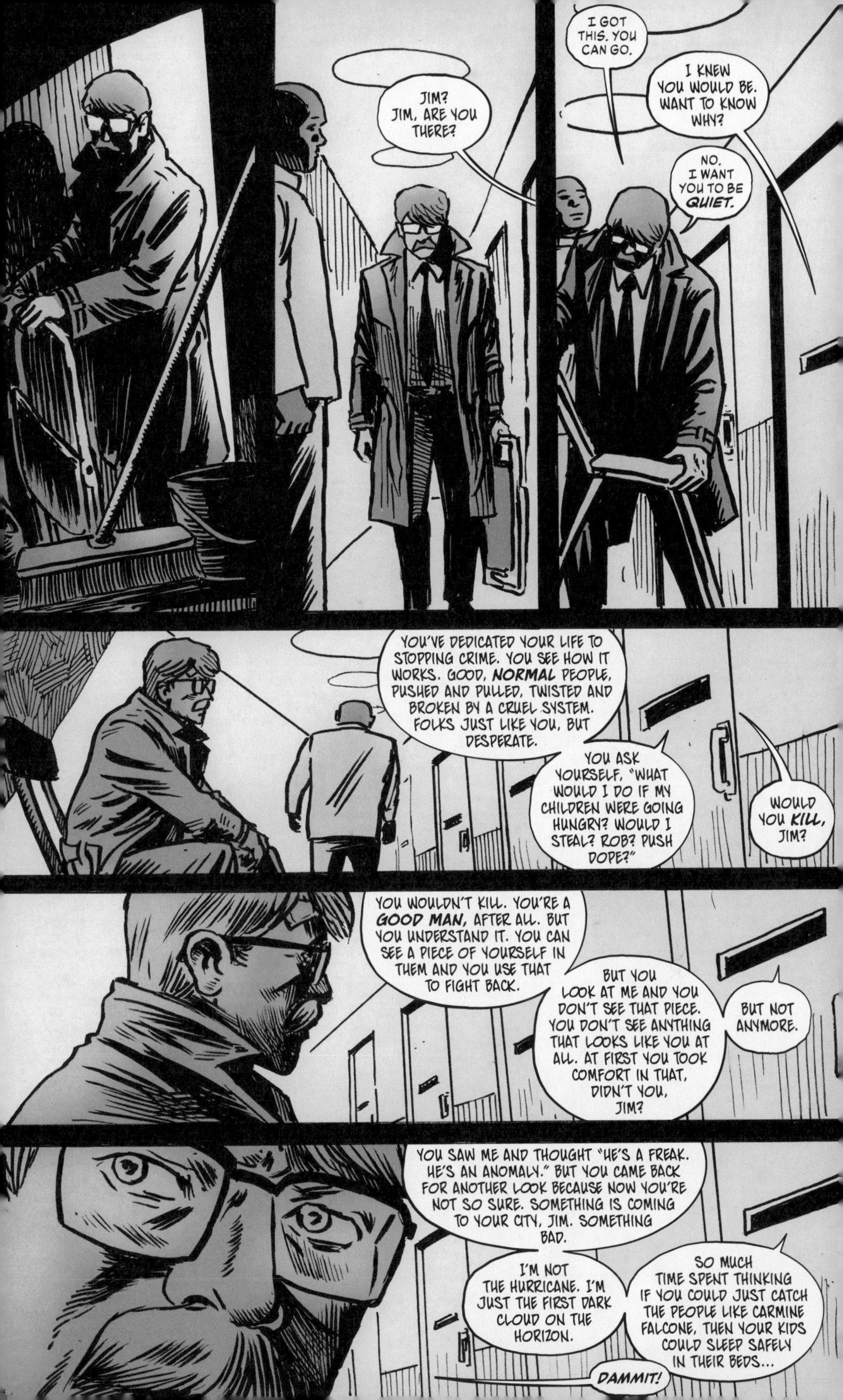
JIM? JIM, ARE YOU THERE?
I GOT THIS. YOU CAN GO.
I KNEW YOU WOULD BE. WANT TO KNOW WHY?
NO. I WANT YOU TO BE **QUIET.**
YOU'VE DEDICATED YOUR LIFE TO STOPPING CRIME. YOU SEE HOW IT WORKS. GOOD, **NORMAL** PEOPLE, PUSHED AND PULLED, TWISTED AND BROKEN BY A CRUEL SYSTEM. FOLKS JUST LIKE YOU, BUT DESPERATE.
YOU ASK YOURSELF, "WHAT WOULD I DO IF MY CHILDREN WERE GOING HUNGRY? WOULD I STEAL? ROB? PUSH DOPE?"
WOULD YOU **KILL,** JIM?
YOU WOULDN'T KILL. YOU'RE A **GOOD MAN,** AFTER ALL. BUT YOU UNDERSTAND IT. YOU CAN SEE A PIECE OF YOURSELF IN THEM AND YOU USE THAT TO FIGHT BACK.
BUT YOU LOOK AT ME AND YOU DON'T SEE THAT PIECE. YOU DON'T SEE ANYTHING THAT LOOKS LIKE YOU AT ALL. AT FIRST YOU TOOK COMFORT IN THAT, DIDN'T YOU, JIM?
BUT NOT ANYMORE.
YOU SAW ME AND THOUGHT "HE'S A FREAK. HE'S AN ANOMALY." BUT YOU CAME BACK FOR ANOTHER LOOK BECAUSE NOW YOU'RE NOT SO SURE. SOMETHING IS COMING TO YOUR CITY, JIM. SOMETHING BAD.
I'M NOT THE HURRICANE. I'M JUST THE FIRST DARK CLOUD ON THE HORIZON.
SO MUCH TIME SPENT THINKING IF YOU COULD JUST CATCH THE PEOPLE LIKE CARMINE FALCONE, THEN YOUR KIDS COULD SLEEP SAFELY IN THEIR BEDS...
DAMMIT!

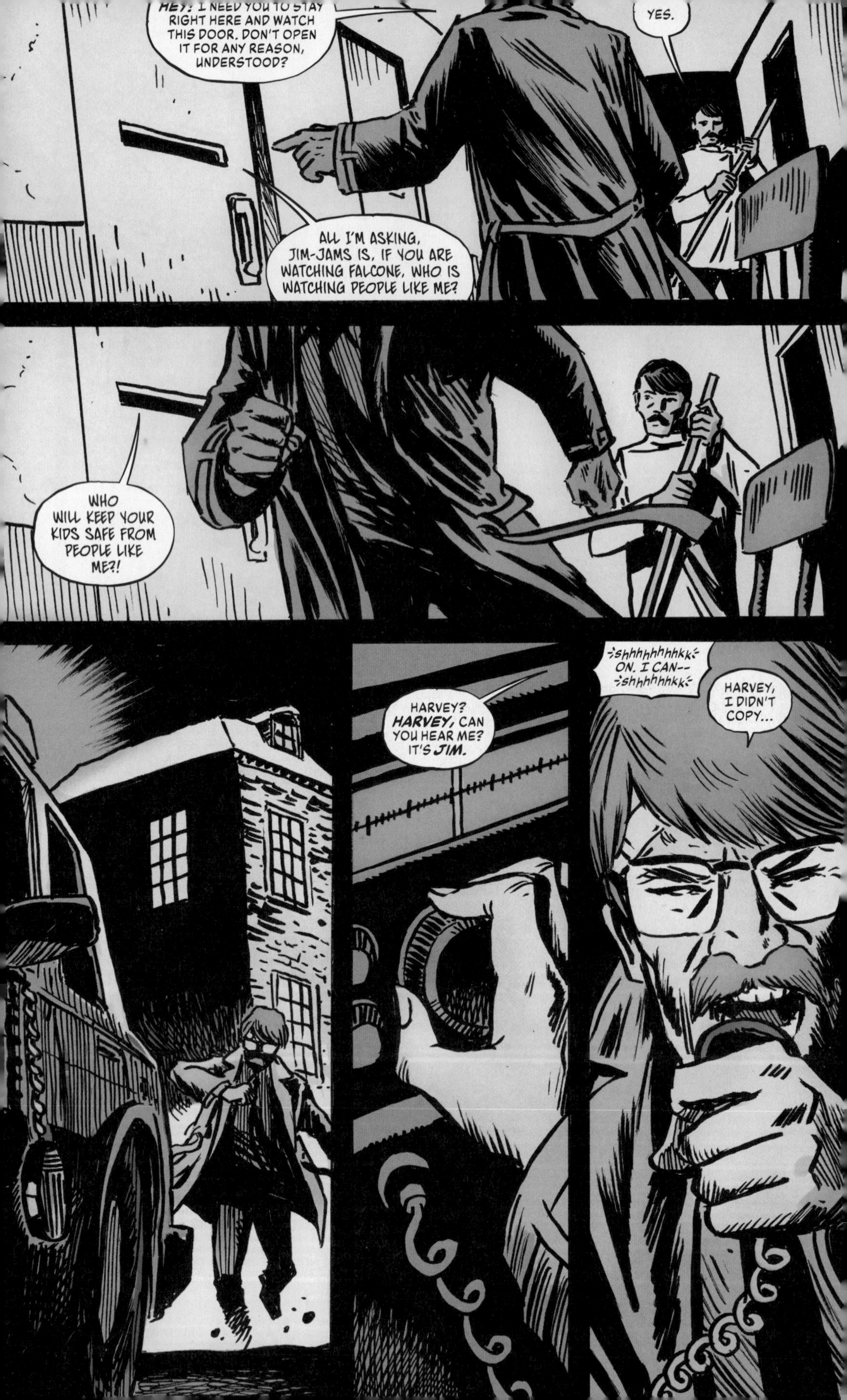
HEY! I NEED YOU TO STAY RIGHT HERE AND WATCH THIS DOOR. DON'T OPEN IT FOR ANY REASON, UNDERSTOOD?
YES.
ALL I'M ASKING, JIM-JAMS IS, IF YOU ARE WATCHING FALCONE, WHO IS WATCHING PEOPLE LIKE ME?
WHO WILL KEEP YOUR KIDS SAFE FROM PEOPLE LIKE ME?!
HARVEY? HARVEY, CAN YOU HEAR ME? IT'S JIM.
shhhhhhhhkk ON. I CAN-- shhhhhhkk
HARVEY, I DIDN'T COPY...

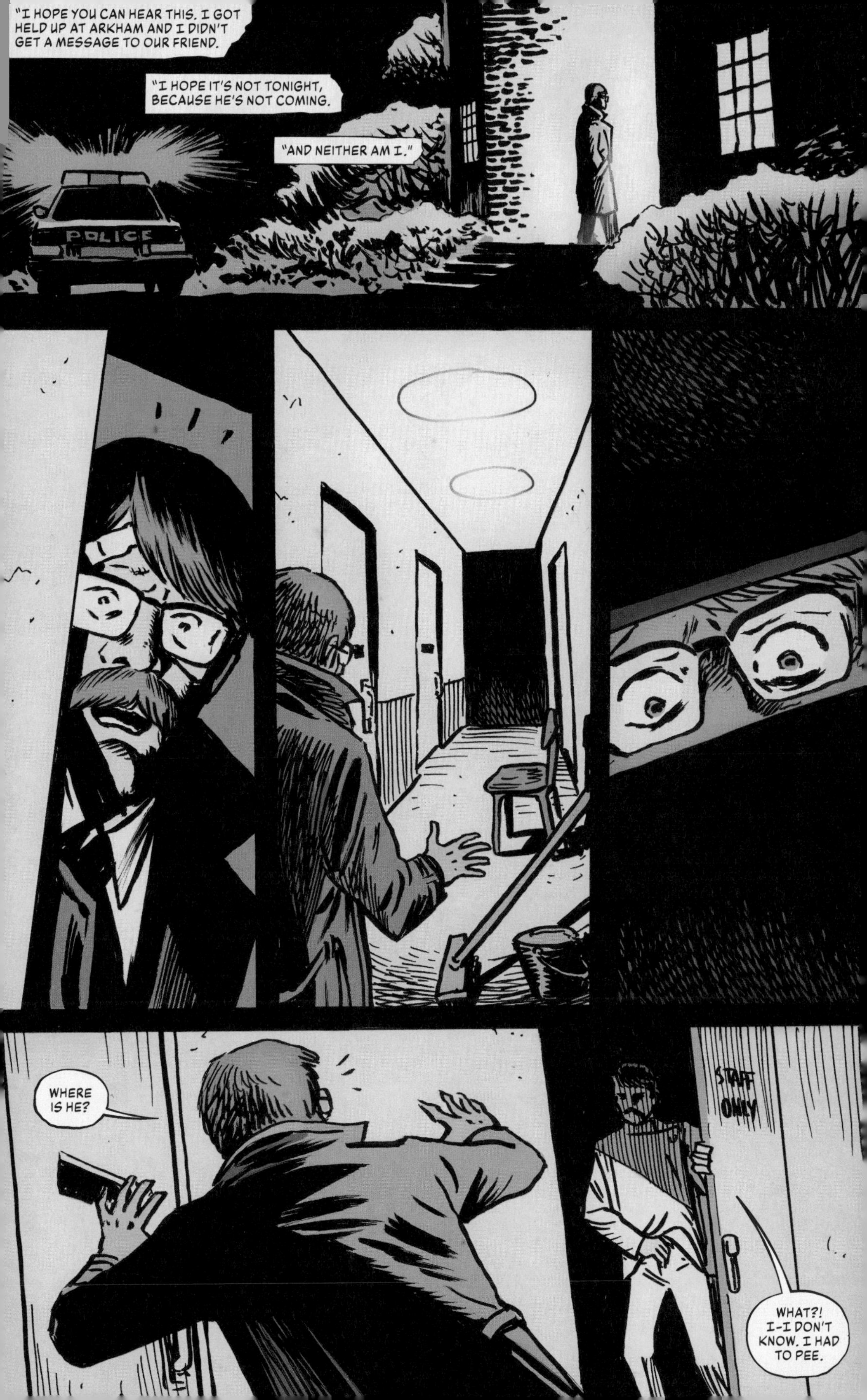
"I HOPE YOU CAN HEAR THIS. I GOT HELD UP AT ARKHAM AND I DIDN'T GET A MESSAGE TO OUR FRIEND.
"I HOPE IT'S NOT TONIGHT, BECAUSE HE'S NOT COMING.
"AND NEITHER AM I."
POLICE
WHERE IS HE?
STAFF ONLY
WHAT?! I-I DON'T KNOW. I HAD TO PEE.

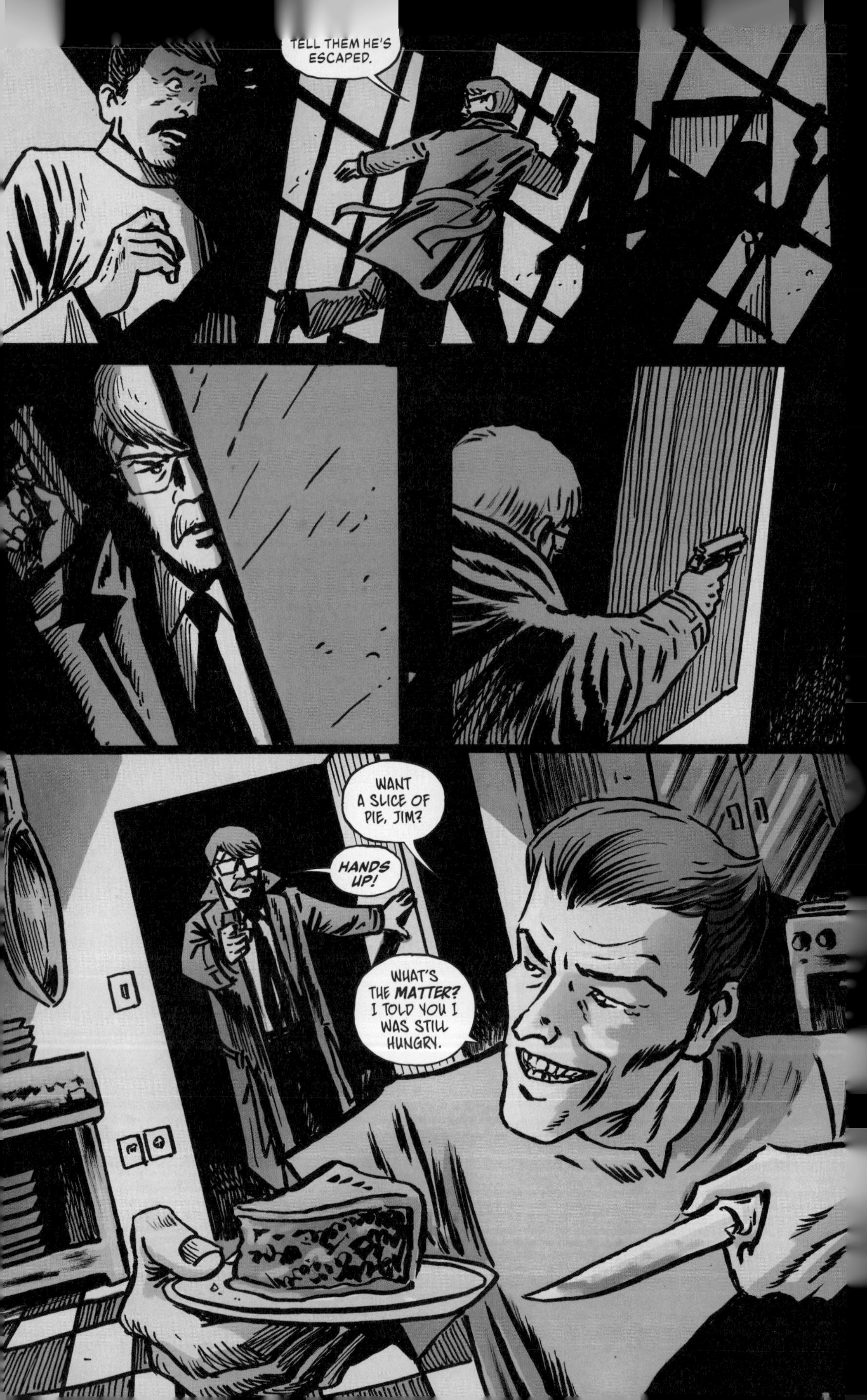
TELL THEM HE'S ESCAPED.
WANT A SLICE OF PIE, JIM?
HANDS UP!
WHAT'S THE MATTER? I TOLD YOU I WAS STILL HUNGRY.

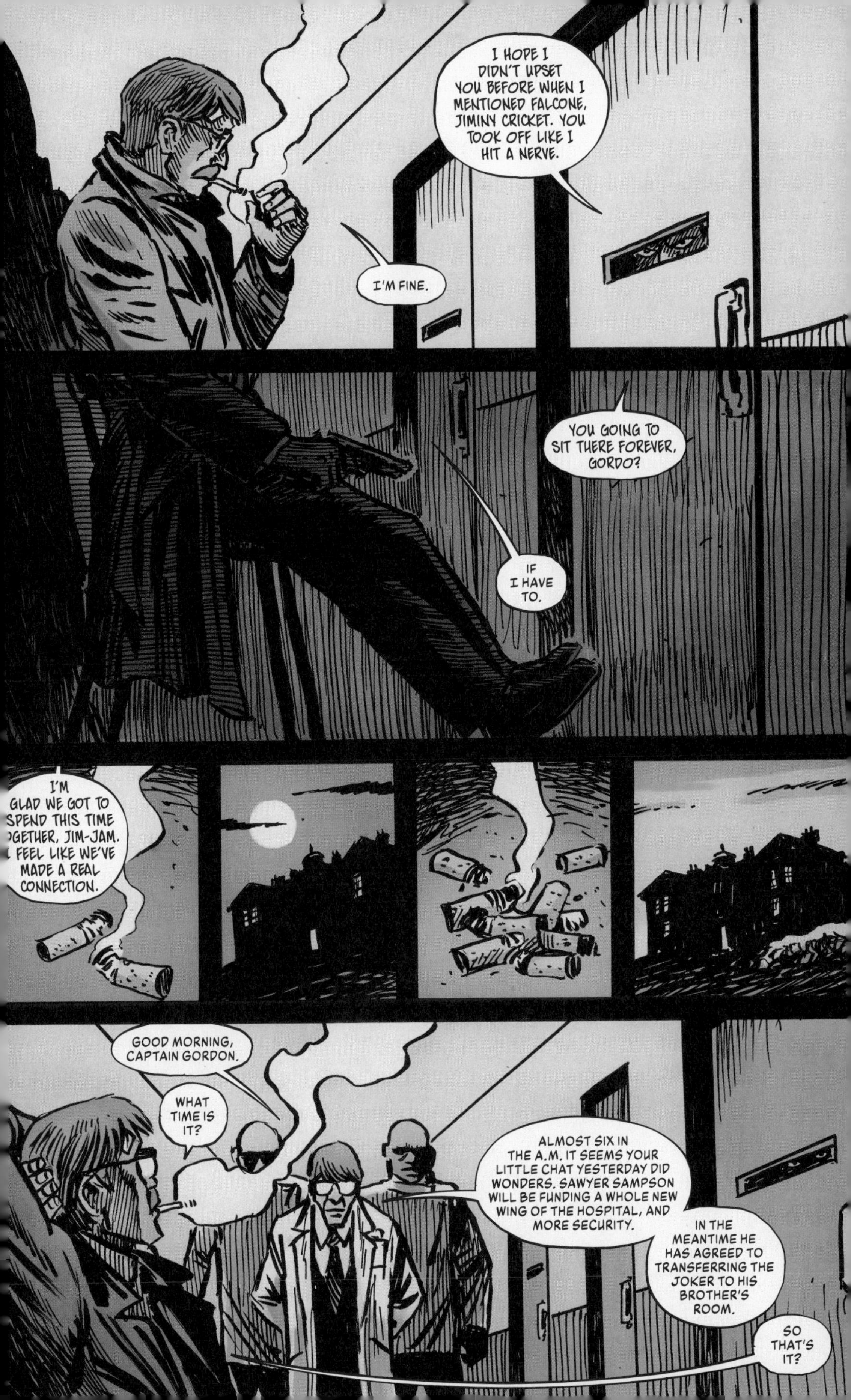
I HOPE I DIDN'T UPSET YOU BEFORE WHEN I MENTIONED FALCONE, JIMINY CRICKET. YOU TOOK OFF LIKE I HIT A NERVE.
I'M FINE.
YOU GOING TO SIT THERE FOREVER, GORDO?
IF I HAVE TO.
I'M GLAD WE GOT TO SPEND THIS TIME TOGETHER, JIM-JAM. I FEEL LIKE WE'VE MADE A REAL CONNECTION.
GOOD MORNING, CAPTAIN GORDON.
WHAT TIME IS IT?
ALMOST SIX IN THE A.M. IT SEEMS YOUR LITTLE CHAT YESTERDAY DID WONDERS. SAWYER SAMPSON WILL BE FUNDING A WHOLE NEW WING OF THE HOSPITAL, AND MORE SECURITY.
IN THE MEANTIME HE HAS AGREED TO TRANSFERRING THE JOKER TO HIS BROTHER'S ROOM.
SO THAT'S IT?

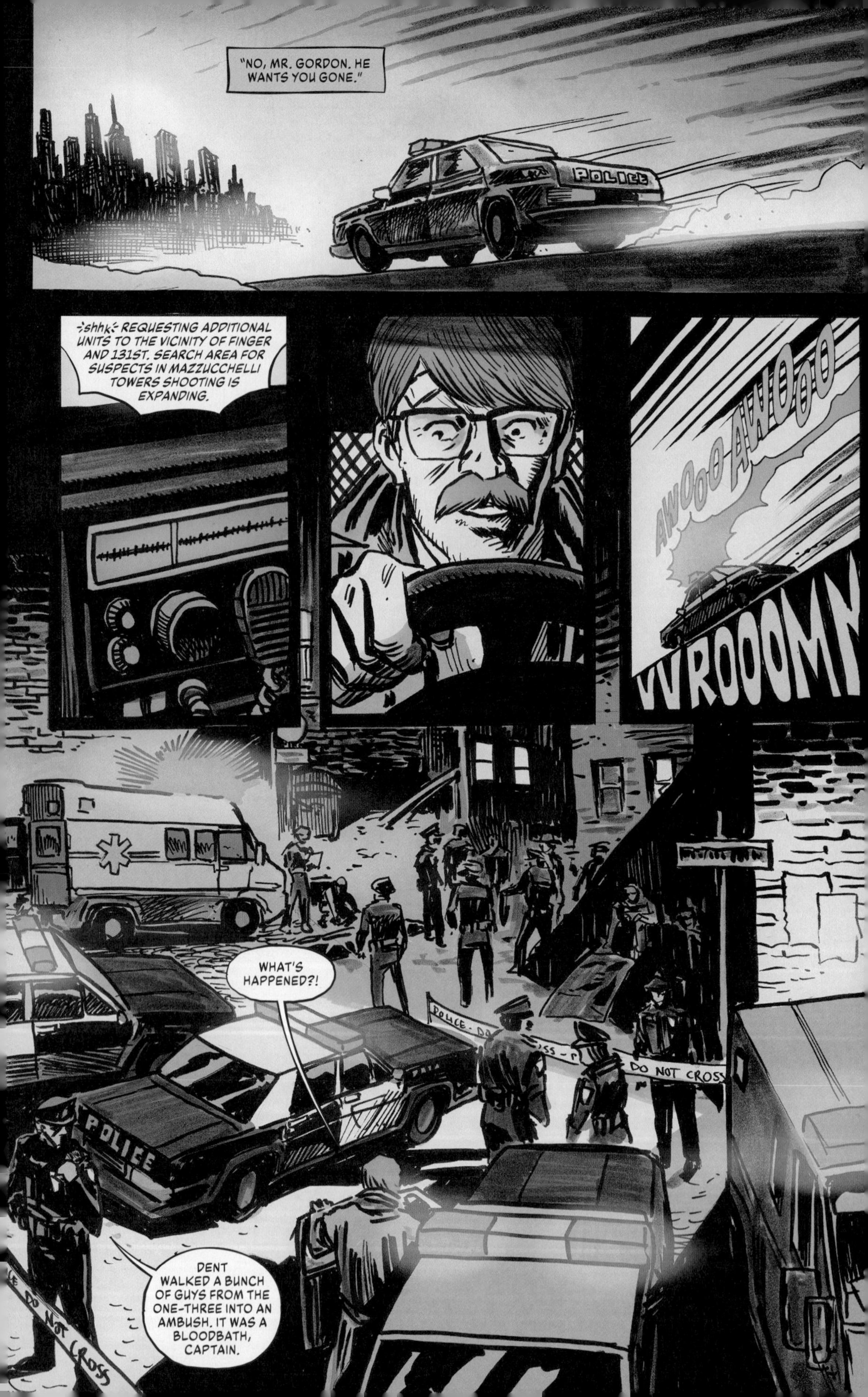
"NO, MR. GORDON. HE WANTS YOU GONE."
POLICE
shhk REQUESTING ADDITIONAL UNITS TO THE VICINITY OF FINGER AND 131ST. SEARCH AREA FOR SUSPECTS IN MAZZUCCHELLI TOWERS SHOOTING IS EXPANDING.
AWOOO AWOOO AWOOO
VVROOOMN
WHAT'S HAPPENED?!
POLICE
DO NOT CROSS
DENT WALKED A BUNCH OF GUYS FROM THE ONE-THREE INTO AN AMBUSH. IT WAS A BLOODBATH, CAPTAIN.

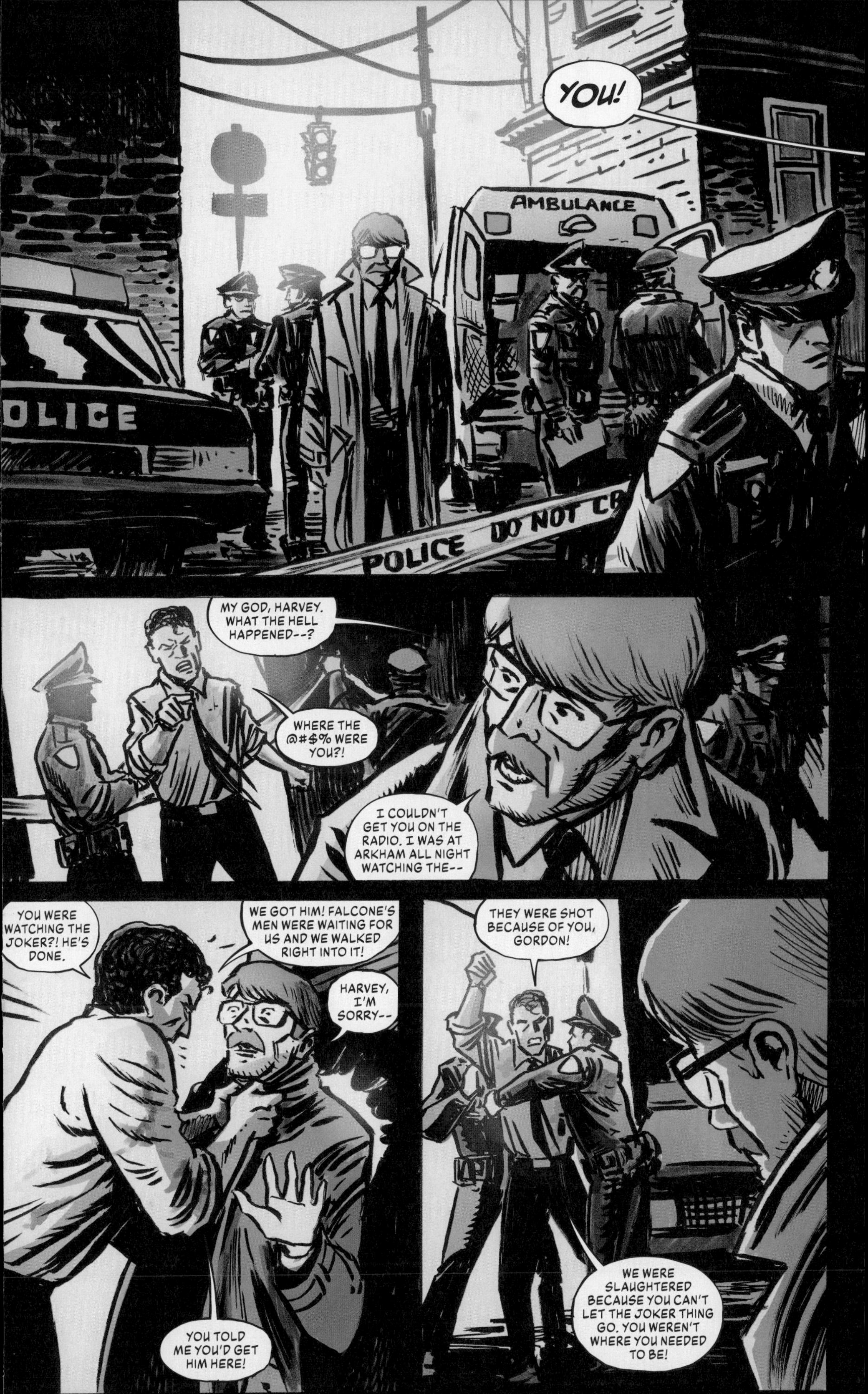
YOU!
AMBULANCE
POLICE
POLICE DO NOT CR
MY GOD, HARVEY. WHAT THE HELL HAPPENED--?
WHERE THE @#$% WERE YOU?!
I COULDN'T GET YOU ON THE RADIO. I WAS AT ARKHAM ALL NIGHT WATCHING THE--
YOU WERE WATCHING THE JOKER?! HE'S DONE.
WE GOT HIM! FALCONE'S MEN WERE WAITING FOR US AND WE WALKED RIGHT INTO IT!
HARVEY, I'M SORRY--
YOU TOLD ME YOU'D GET HIM HERE!
THEY WERE SHOT BECAUSE OF YOU, GORDON!
WE WERE SLAUGHTERED BECAUSE YOU CAN'T LET THE JOKER THING GO. YOU WEREN'T WHERE YOU NEEDED TO BE!

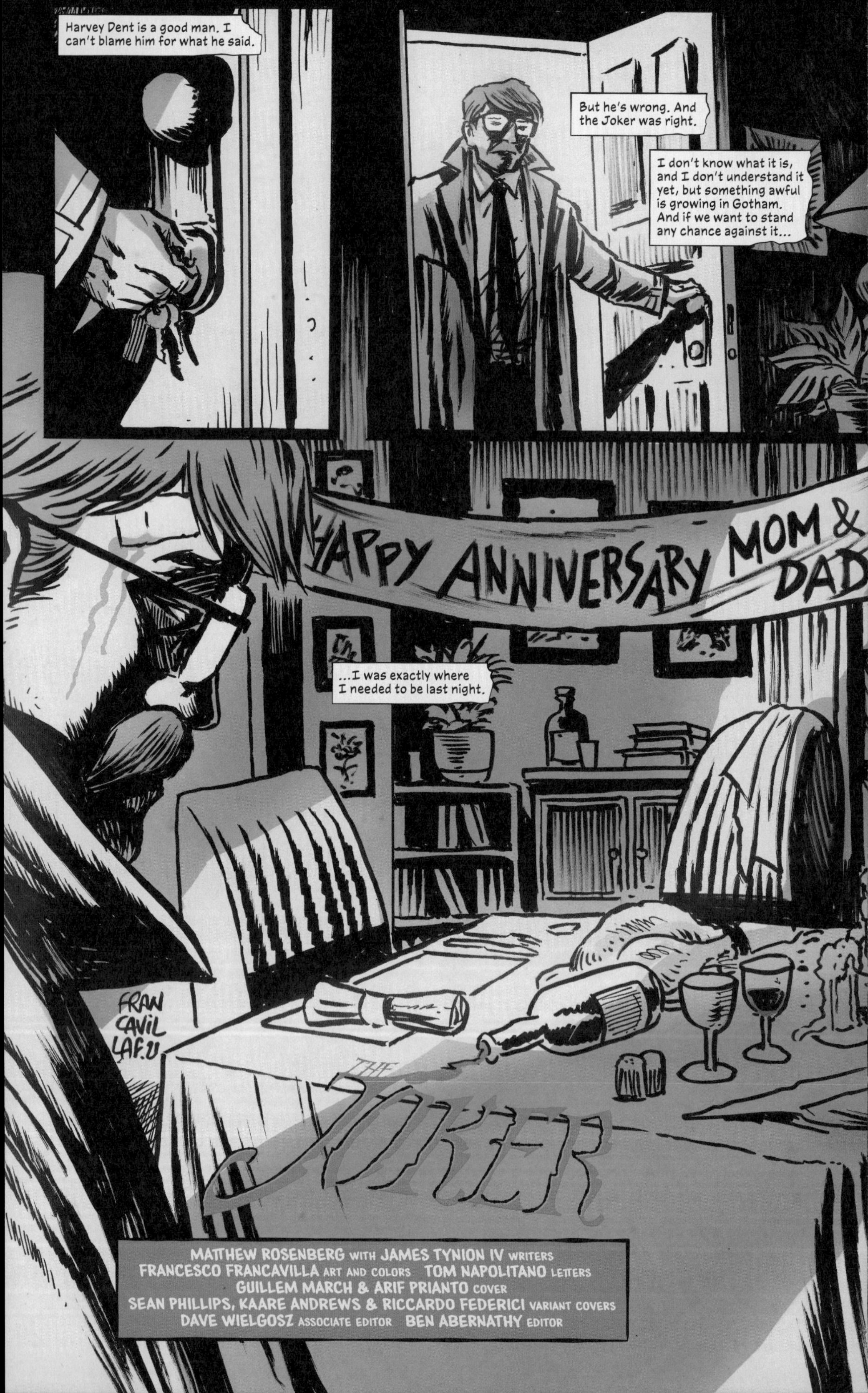
Harvey Dent is a good man. I can't blame him for what he said.
But he's wrong. And the Joker was right.
I don't know what it is, and I don't understand it yet, but something awful is growing in Gotham. And if we want to stand any chance against it...
HAPPY ANNIVERSARY MOM & DAD
...I was exactly where I needed to be last night.
FRAN CAVIL LAF.21
THE JOKER
MATTHEW ROSENBERG WITH JAMES TYNION IV WRITERS
FRANCESCO FRANCAVILLA ART AND COLORS TOM NAPOLITANO LETTERS
GUILLEM MARCH & ARIF PRIANTO COVER
SEAN PHILLIPS, KAARE ANDREWS & RICCARDO FEDERICI VARIANT COVERS
DAVE WIELGOSZ ASSOCIATE EDITOR BEN ABERNATHY EDITOR

Batman: The Joker War Zone
Cover Art by Ben Oliver

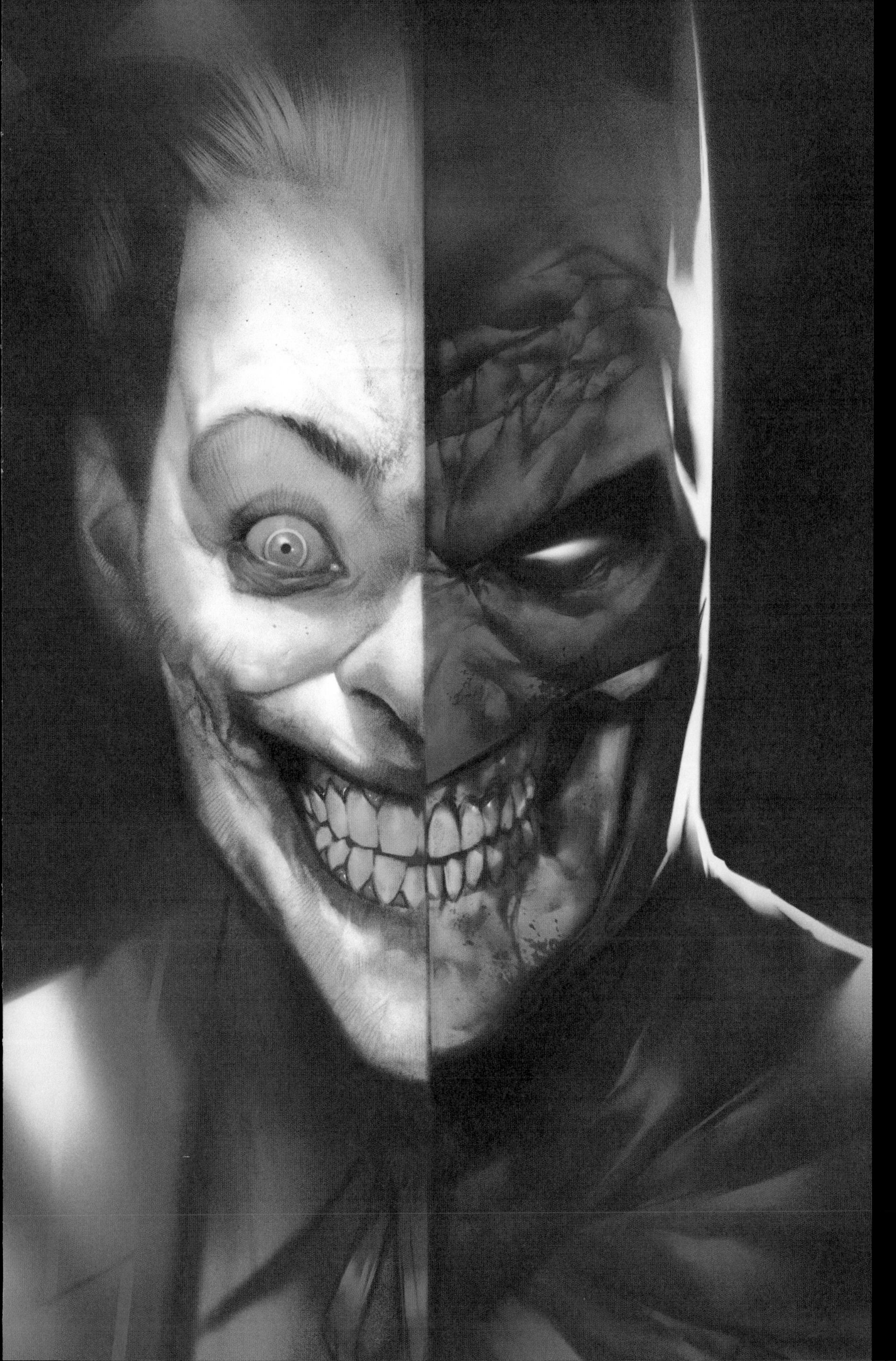

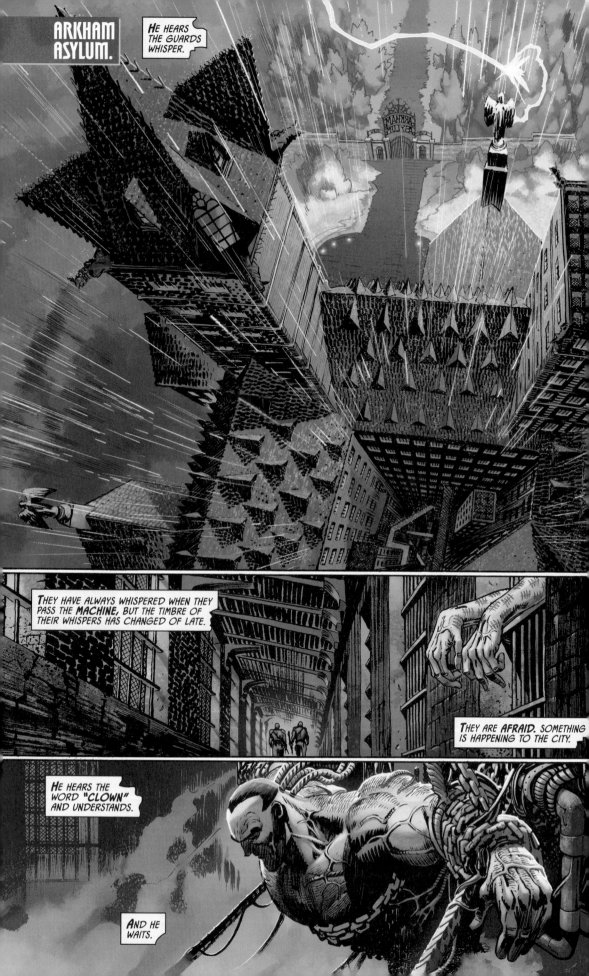

ARKHAM ASYLUM.

HE HEARS THE GUARDS WHISPER.

THEY HAVE ALWAYS WHISPERED WHEN THEY PASS THE *MACHINE*, BUT THE TIMBRE OF THEIR WHISPERS HAS CHANGED OF LATE.

THEY ARE *AFRAID*. SOMETHING IS HAPPENING TO THE CITY.

HE HEARS THE WORD *"CLOWN"* AND UNDERSTANDS.

AND HE WAITS.

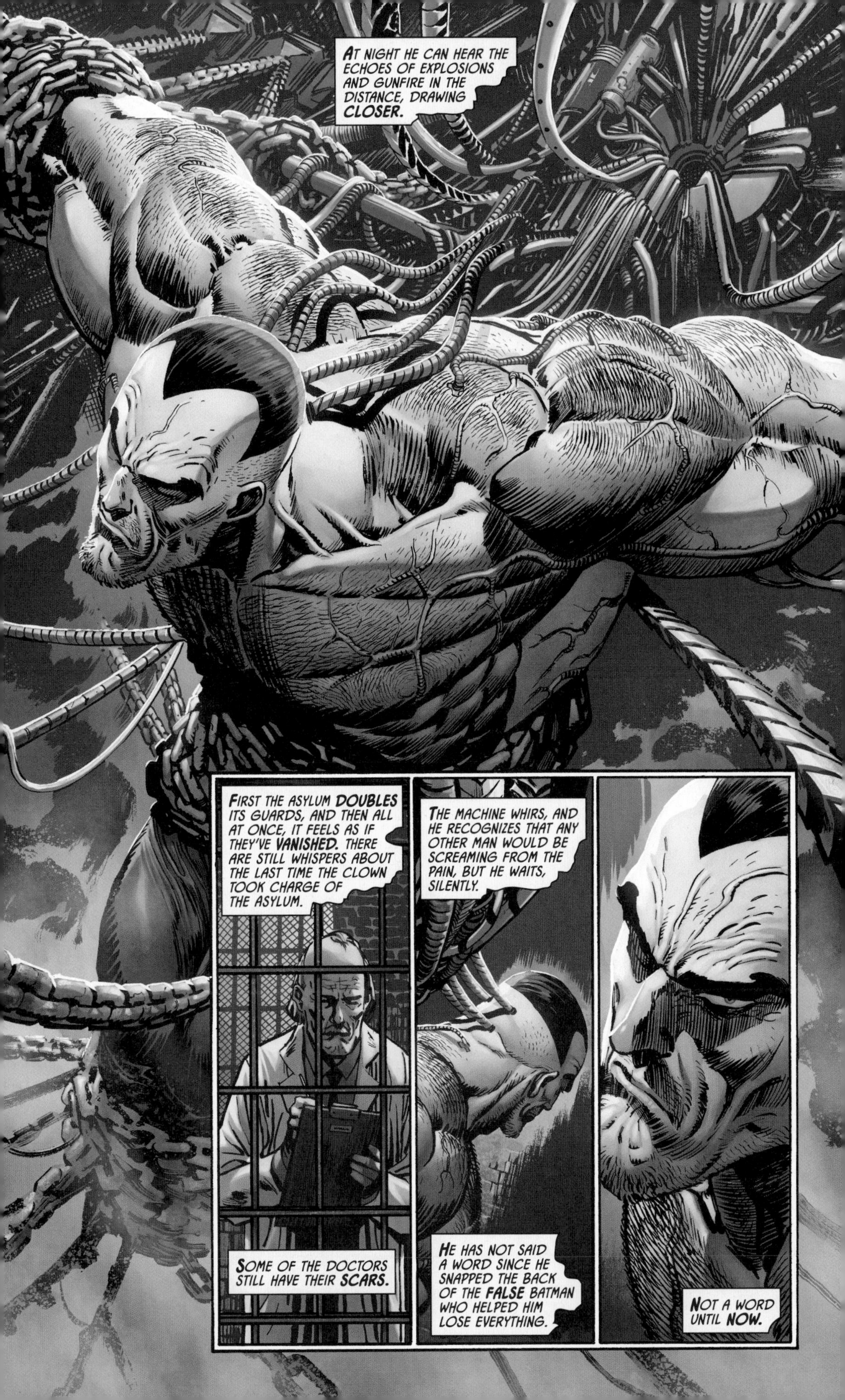
AT NIGHT HE CAN HEAR THE ECHOES OF EXPLOSIONS AND GUNFIRE IN THE DISTANCE, DRAWING CLOSER.
FIRST THE ASYLUM DOUBLES ITS GUARDS, AND THEN ALL AT ONCE, IT FEELS AS IF THEY'VE VANISHED. THERE ARE STILL WHISPERS ABOUT THE LAST TIME THE CLOWN TOOK CHARGE OF THE ASYLUM.
SOME OF THE DOCTORS STILL HAVE THEIR SCARS.
THE MACHINE WHIRS, AND HE RECOGNIZES THAT ANY OTHER MAN WOULD BE SCREAMING FROM THE PAIN, BUT HE WAITS, SILENTLY.
HE HAS NOT SAID A WORD SINCE HE SNAPPED THE BACK OF THE FALSE BATMAN WHO HELPED HIM LOSE EVERYTHING.
NOT A WORD UNTIL NOW.

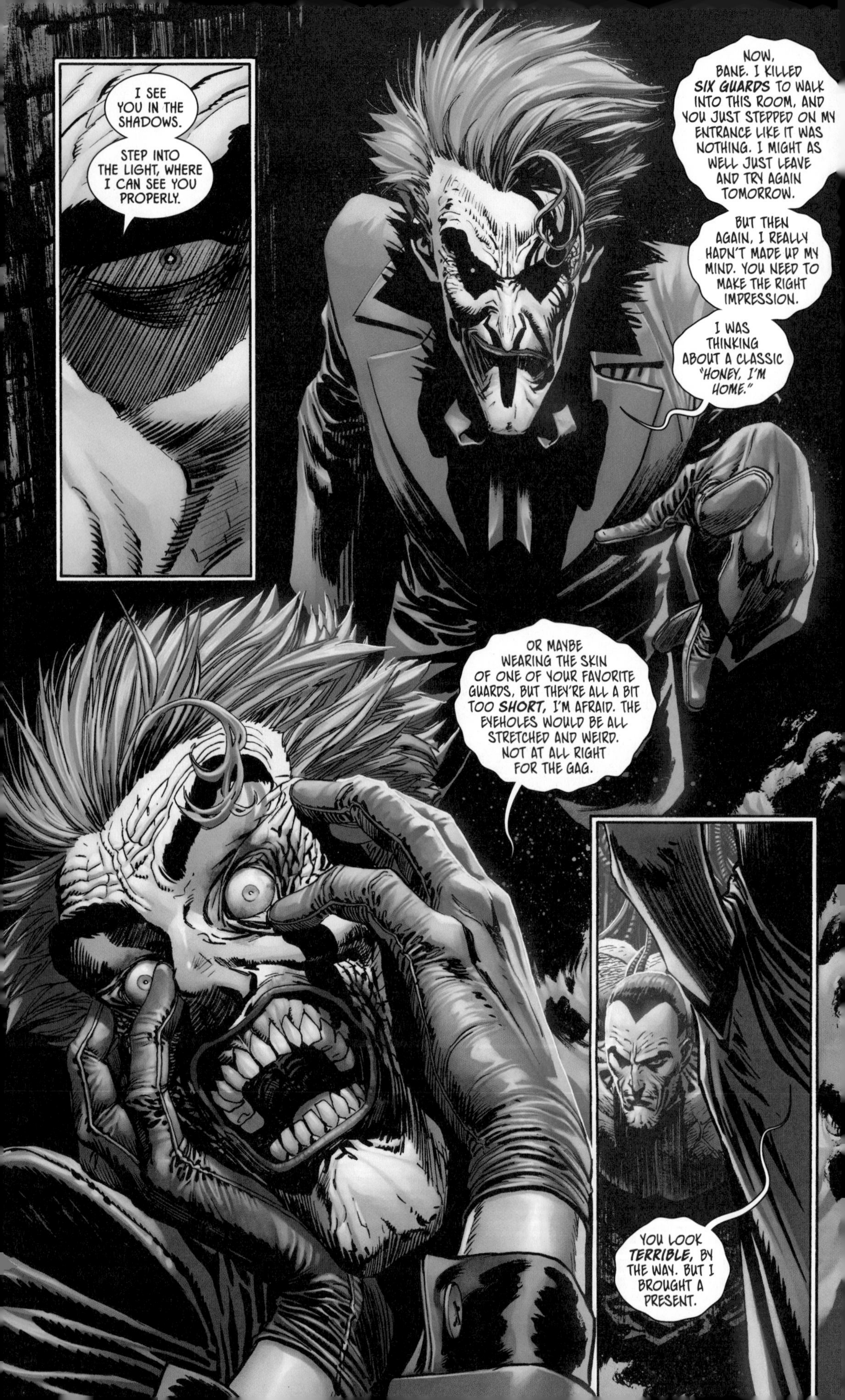
I SEE YOU IN THE SHADOWS.
STEP INTO THE LIGHT, WHERE I CAN SEE YOU PROPERLY.
NOW, BANE. I KILLED **SIX GUARDS** TO WALK INTO THIS ROOM, AND YOU JUST STEPPED ON MY ENTRANCE LIKE IT WAS NOTHING. I MIGHT AS WELL JUST LEAVE AND TRY AGAIN TOMORROW.
BUT THEN AGAIN, I REALLY HADN'T MADE UP MY MIND. YOU NEED TO MAKE THE RIGHT IMPRESSION.
I WAS THINKING ABOUT A CLASSIC *"HONEY, I'M HOME."*
OR MAYBE WEARING THE SKIN OF ONE OF YOUR FAVORITE GUARDS, BUT THEY'RE ALL A BIT TOO **SHORT,** I'M AFRAID. THE EYEHOLES WOULD BE ALL STRETCHED AND WEIRD. NOT AT ALL RIGHT FOR THE GAG.
YOU LOOK **TERRIBLE,** BY THE WAY. BUT I BROUGHT A PRESENT.

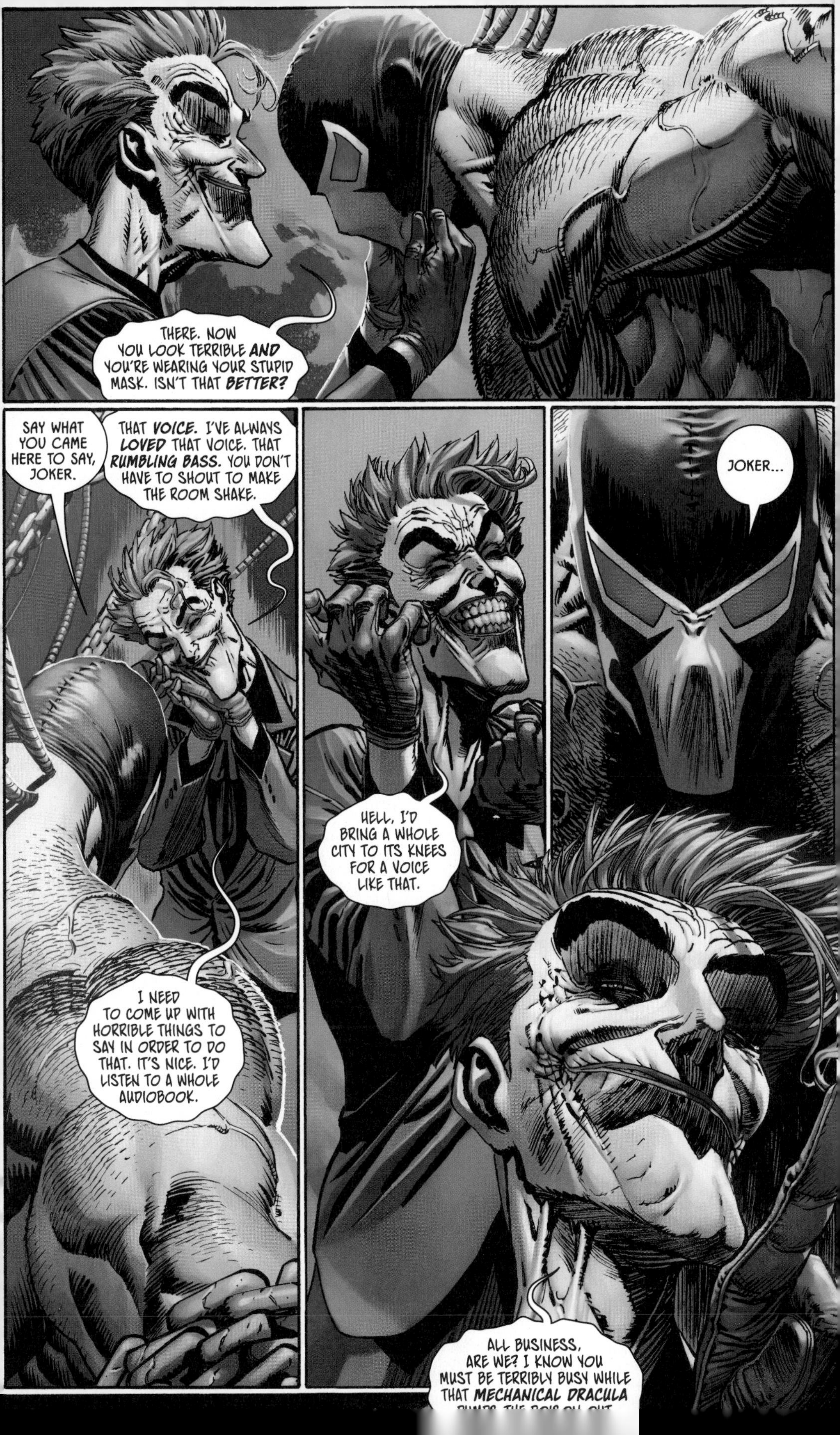
THERE. NOW YOU LOOK TERRIBLE AND YOU'RE WEARING YOUR STUPID MASK. ISN'T THAT BETTER?
SAY WHAT YOU CAME HERE TO SAY, JOKER.
THAT VOICE. I'VE ALWAYS LOVED THAT VOICE. THAT RUMBLING BASS. YOU DON'T HAVE TO SHOUT TO MAKE THE ROOM SHAKE.
I NEED TO COME UP WITH HORRIBLE THINGS TO SAY IN ORDER TO DO THAT. IT'S NICE. I'D LISTEN TO A WHOLE AUDIOBOOK.
HELL, I'D BRING A WHOLE CITY TO ITS KNEES FOR A VOICE LIKE THAT.
JOKER...
ALL BUSINESS, ARE WE? I KNOW YOU MUST BE TERRIBLY BUSY WHILE THAT MECHANICAL DRACULA

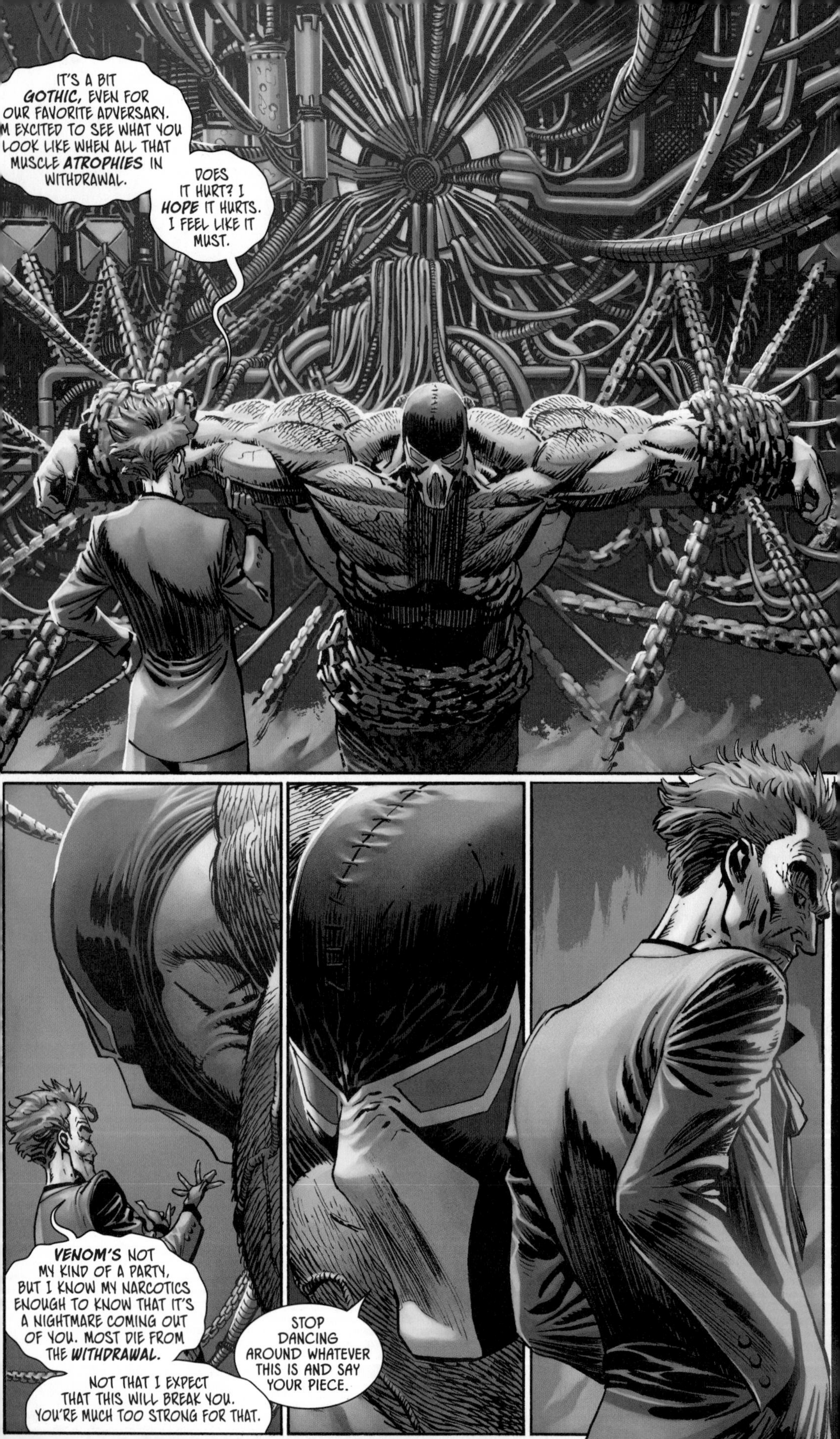
IT'S A BIT GOTHIC, EVEN FOR OUR FAVORITE ADVERSARY. I'M EXCITED TO SEE WHAT YOU LOOK LIKE WHEN ALL THAT MUSCLE ATROPHIES IN WITHDRAWAL.
DOES IT HURT? I HOPE IT HURTS. I FEEL LIKE IT MUST.
VENOM'S NOT MY KIND OF A PARTY, BUT I KNOW MY NARCOTICS ENOUGH TO KNOW THAT IT'S A NIGHTMARE COMING OUT OF YOU. MOST DIE FROM THE WITHDRAWAL.
NOT THAT I EXPECT THAT THIS WILL BREAK YOU. YOU'RE MUCH TOO STRONG FOR THAT.
STOP DANCING AROUND WHATEVER THIS IS AND SAY YOUR PIECE.

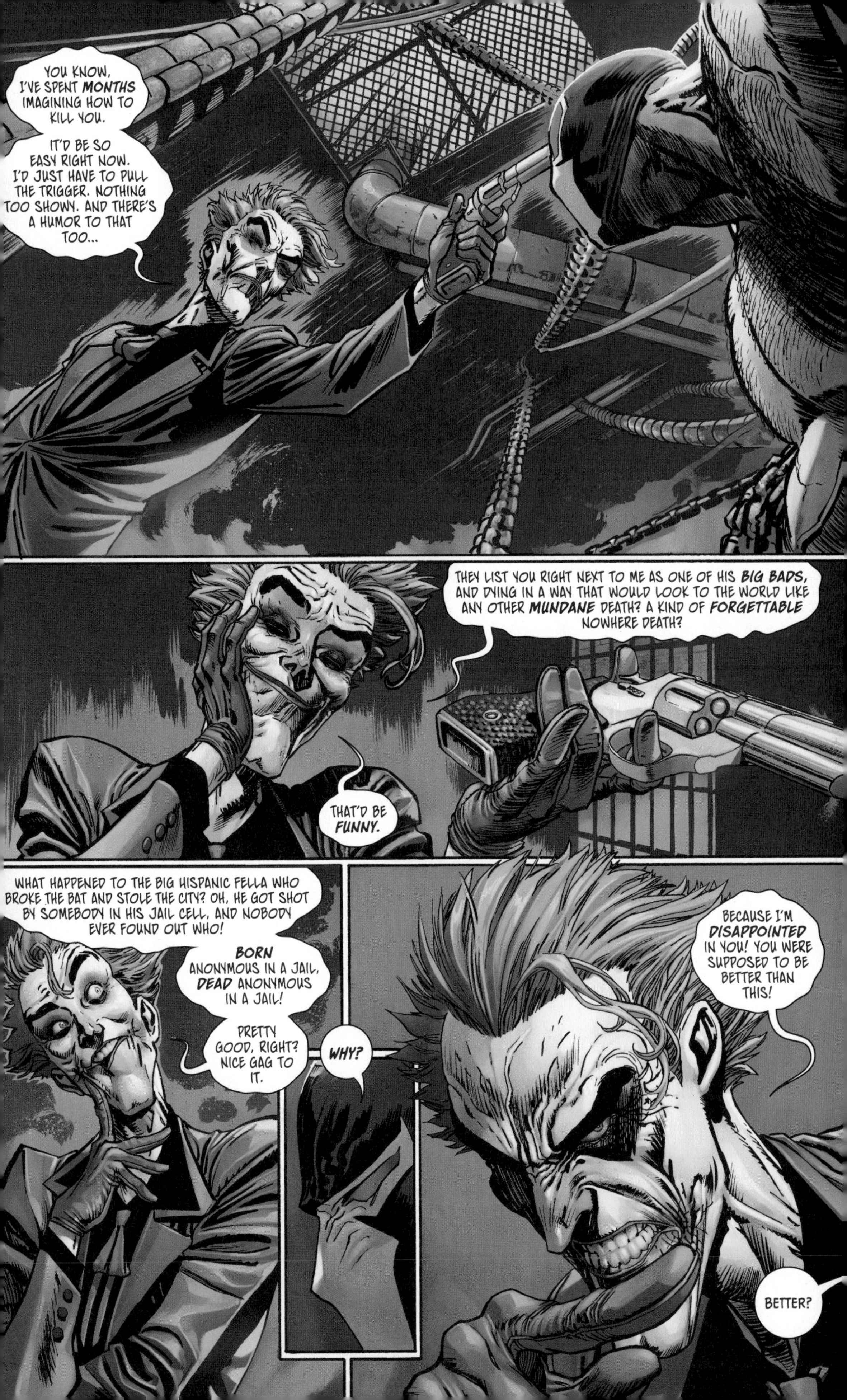
YOU KNOW, I'VE SPENT MONTHS IMAGINING HOW TO KILL YOU.
IT'D BE SO EASY RIGHT NOW. I'D JUST HAVE TO PULL THE TRIGGER. NOTHING TOO SHOWY. AND THERE'S A HUMOR TO THAT TOO...
THEY LIST YOU RIGHT NEXT TO ME AS ONE OF HIS BIG BADS, AND DYING IN A WAY THAT WOULD LOOK TO THE WORLD LIKE ANY OTHER MUNDANE DEATH? A KIND OF FORGETTABLE NOWHERE DEATH?
THAT'D BE FUNNY.
WHAT HAPPENED TO THE BIG HISPANIC FELLA WHO BROKE THE BAT AND STOLE THE CITY? OH, HE GOT SHOT BY SOMEBODY IN HIS JAIL CELL, AND NOBODY EVER FOUND OUT WHO!
BORN ANONYMOUS IN A JAIL, DEAD ANONYMOUS IN A JAIL!
PRETTY GOOD, RIGHT? NICE GAG TO IT.
WHY?
BECAUSE I'M DISAPPOINTED IN YOU! YOU WERE SUPPOSED TO BE BETTER THAN THIS!
BETTER?

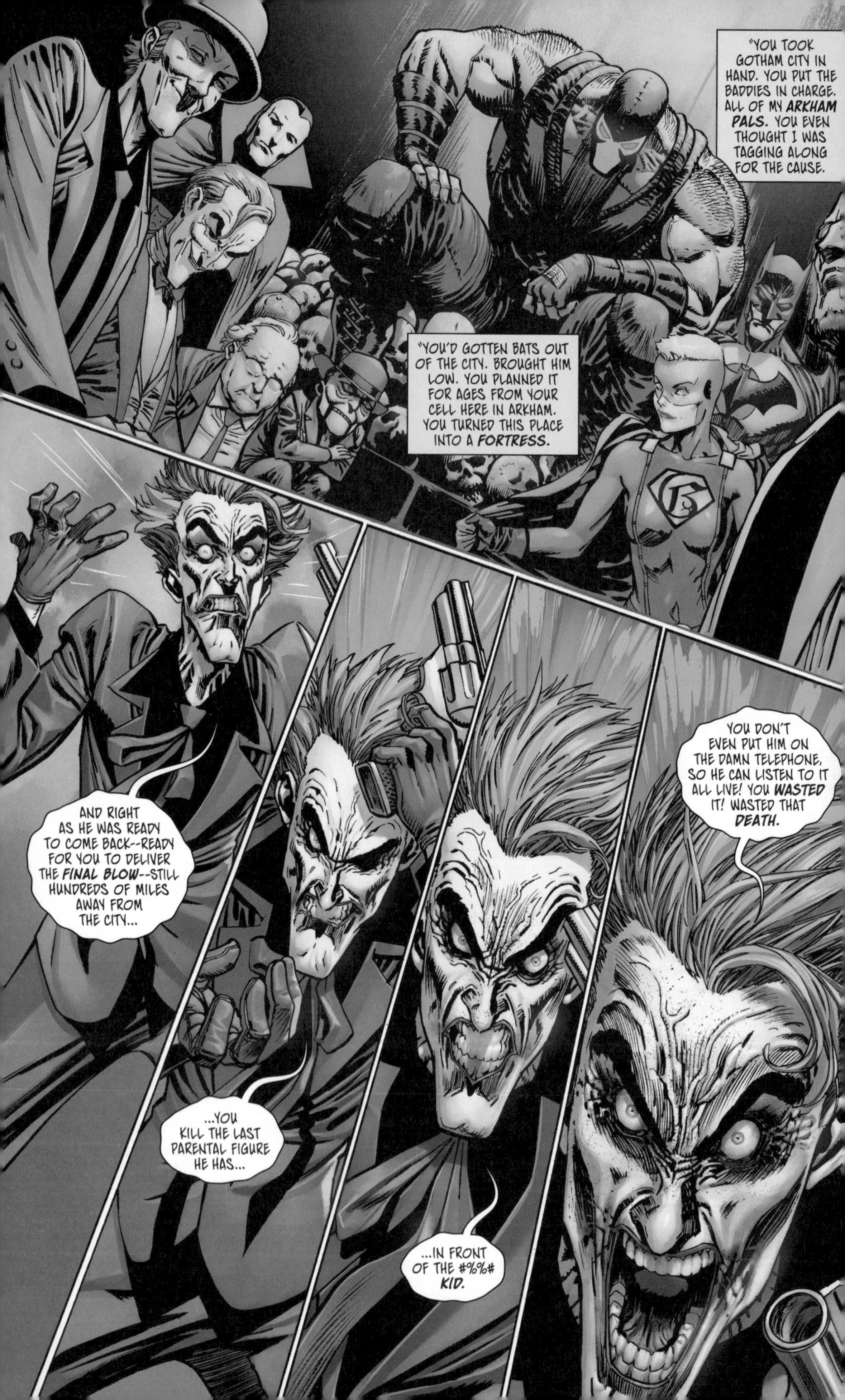
"YOU TOOK GOTHAM CITY IN HAND. YOU PUT THE BADDIES IN CHARGE. ALL OF MY ARKHAM PALS. YOU EVEN THOUGHT I WAS TAGGING ALONG FOR THE CAUSE.
"YOU'D GOTTEN BATS OUT OF THE CITY. BROUGHT HIM LOW. YOU PLANNED IT FOR AGES FROM YOUR CELL HERE IN ARKHAM. YOU TURNED THIS PLACE INTO A FORTRESS.
AND RIGHT AS HE WAS READY TO COME BACK--READY FOR YOU TO DELIVER THE FINAL BLOW--STILL HUNDREDS OF MILES AWAY FROM THE CITY...
...YOU KILL THE LAST PARENTAL FIGURE HE HAS...
...IN FRONT OF THE #%%# KID.
YOU DON'T EVEN PUT HIM ON THE DAMN TELEPHONE, SO HE CAN LISTEN TO IT ALL LIVE! YOU WASTED IT! WASTED THAT DEATH.

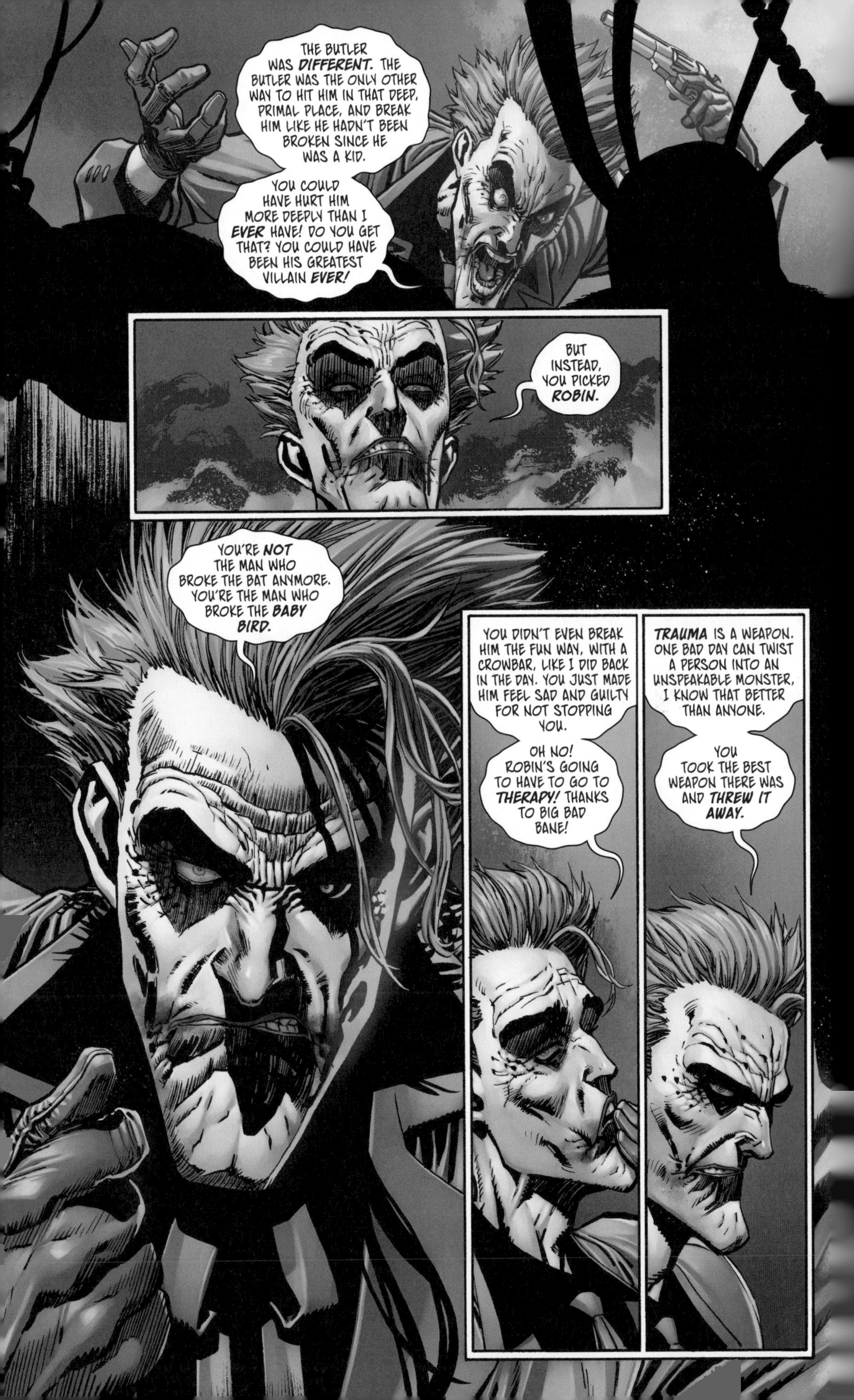
THE BUTLER WAS ***DIFFERENT.*** THE BUTLER WAS THE ONLY OTHER WAY TO HIT HIM IN THAT DEEP, PRIMAL PLACE, AND BREAK HIM LIKE HE HADN'T BEEN BROKEN SINCE HE WAS A KID.
YOU COULD HAVE HURT HIM MORE DEEPLY THAN I ***EVER*** HAVE! DO YOU GET THAT? YOU COULD HAVE BEEN HIS GREATEST VILLAIN ***EVER!***
BUT INSTEAD, YOU PICKED ***ROBIN.***
YOU'RE ***NOT*** THE MAN WHO BROKE THE BAT ANYMORE. YOU'RE THE MAN WHO BROKE THE ***BABY BIRD.***
YOU DIDN'T EVEN BREAK HIM THE FUN WAY, WITH A CROWBAR, LIKE I DID BACK IN THE DAY. YOU JUST MADE HIM FEEL SAD AND GUILTY FOR NOT STOPPING YOU.
OH NO! ROBIN'S GOING TO HAVE TO GO TO ***THERAPY!*** THANKS TO BIG BAD BANE!
TRAUMA IS A WEAPON. ONE BAD DAY CAN TWIST A PERSON INTO AN UNSPEAKABLE MONSTER, I KNOW THAT BETTER THAN ANYONE.
YOU TOOK THE BEST WEAPON THERE WAS AND ***THREW IT AWAY.***

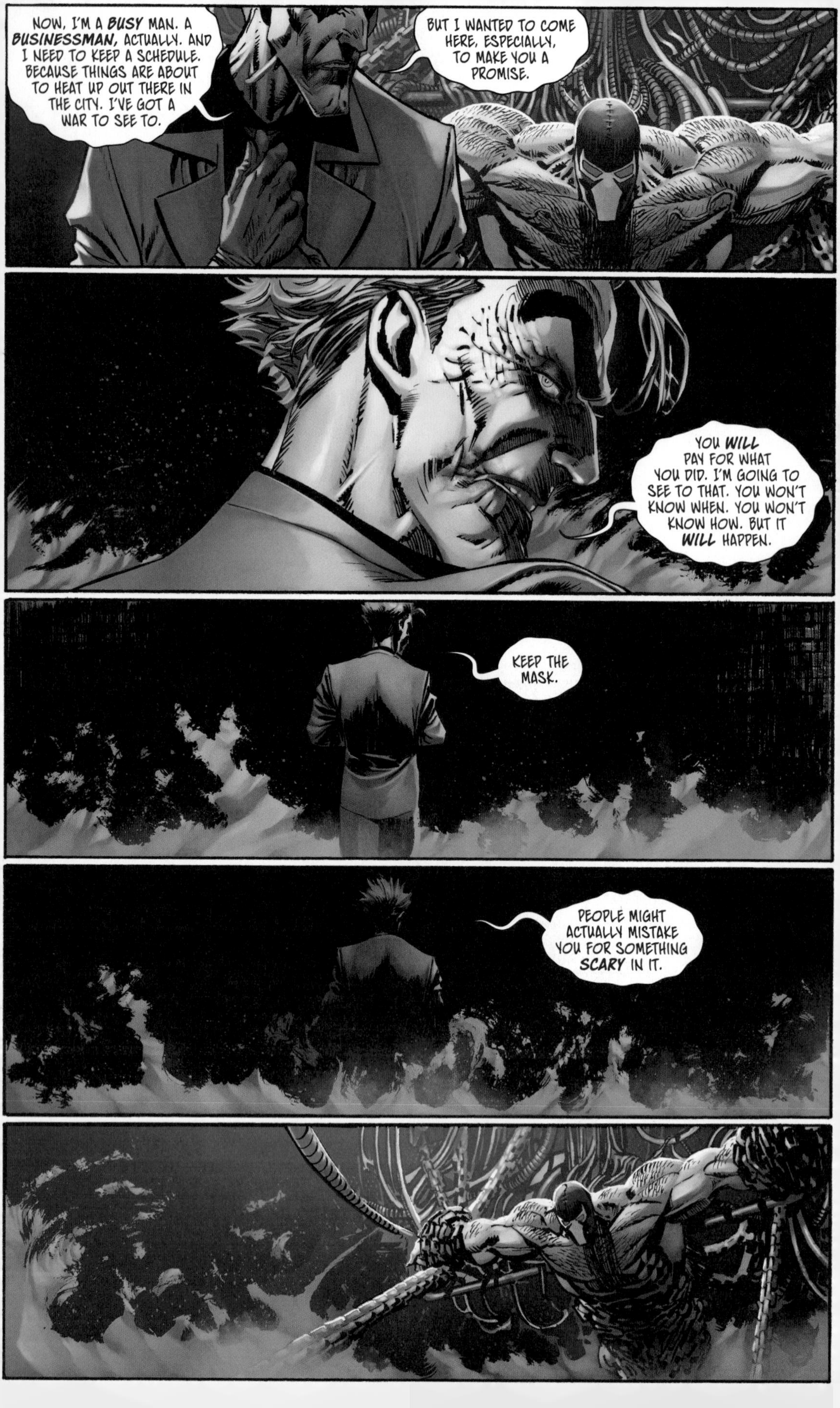
NOW, I'M A **BUSY** MAN. A **BUSINESSMAN,** ACTUALLY. AND I NEED TO KEEP A SCHEDULE. BECAUSE THINGS ARE ABOUT TO HEAT UP OUT THERE IN THE CITY. I'VE GOT A WAR TO SEE TO.
BUT I WANTED TO COME HERE, ESPECIALLY, TO MAKE YOU A PROMISE.
YOU **WILL** PAY FOR WHAT YOU DID. I'M GOING TO SEE TO THAT. YOU WON'T KNOW WHEN. YOU WON'T KNOW HOW. BUT IT **WILL** HAPPEN.
KEEP THE MASK.
PEOPLE MIGHT ACTUALLY MISTAKE YOU FOR SOMETHING **SCARY** IN IT.

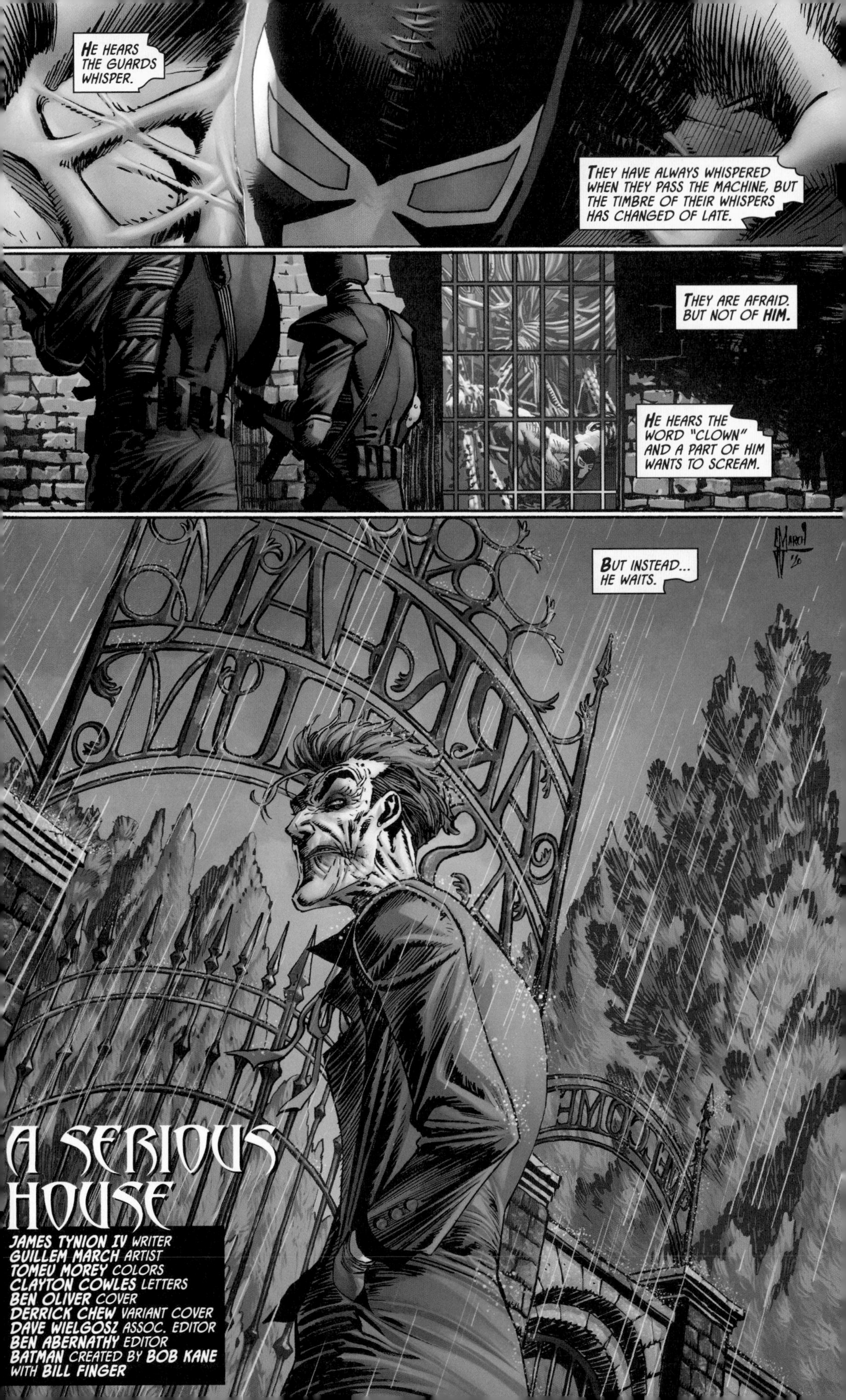
HE HEARS THE GUARDS WHISPER.
THEY HAVE ALWAYS WHISPERED WHEN THEY PASS THE MACHINE, BUT THE TIMBRE OF THEIR WHISPERS HAS CHANGED OF LATE.
THEY ARE AFRAID. BUT NOT OF HIM.
HE HEARS THE WORD "CLOWN" AND A PART OF HIM WANTS TO SCREAM.
BUT INSTEAD... HE WAITS.
A SERIOUS HOUSE
JAMES TYNION IV WRITER
GUILLEM MARCH ARTIST
TOMEU MOREY COLORS
CLAYTON COWLES LETTERS
BEN OLIVER COVER
DERRICK CHEW VARIANT COVER
DAVE WIELGOSZ ASSOC. EDITOR
BEN ABERNATHY EDITOR
BATMAN CREATED BY BOB KANE WITH BILL FINGER

Batman #100
Cover Art by Jorge Jimenez
Colors by Tomeu Morey

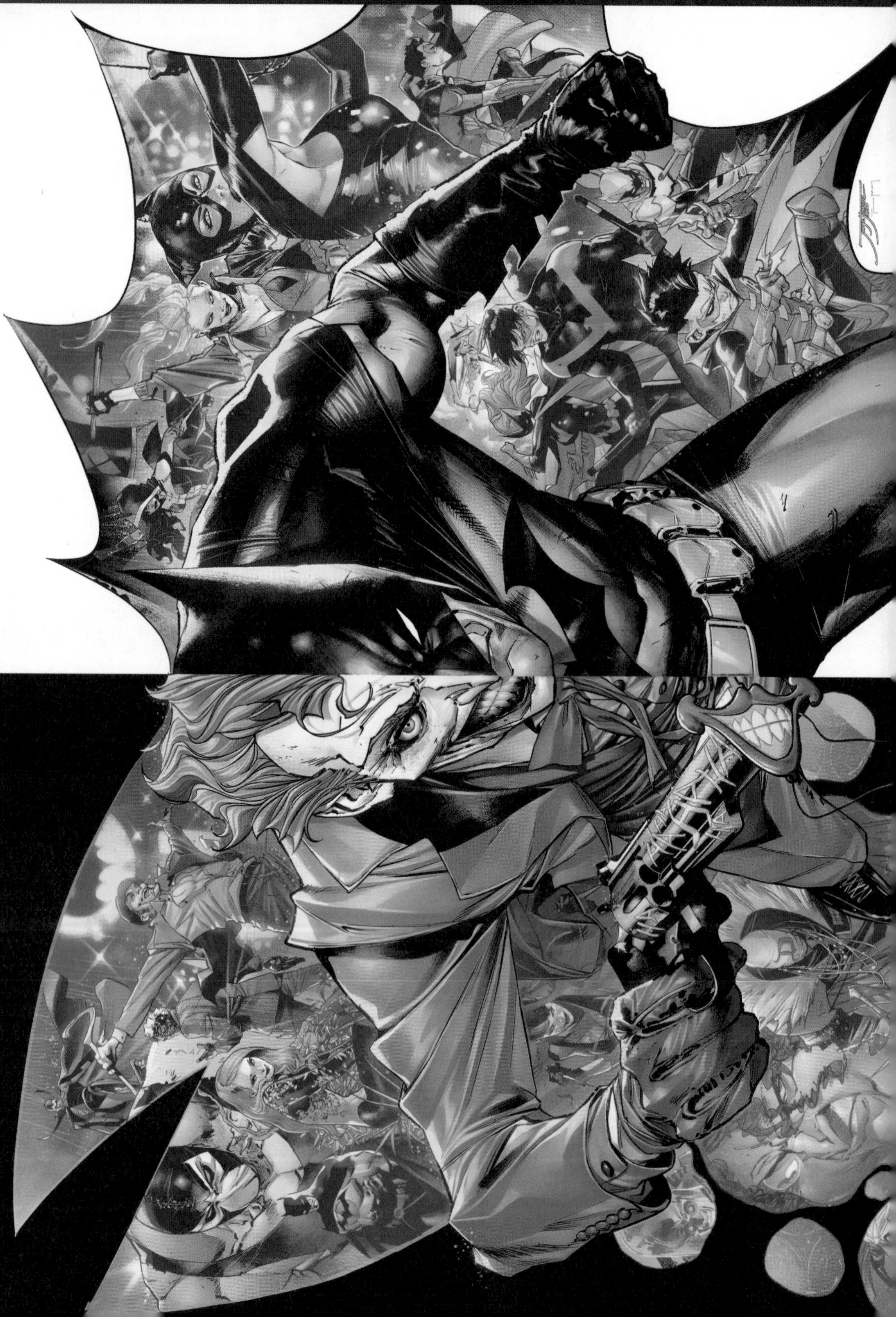

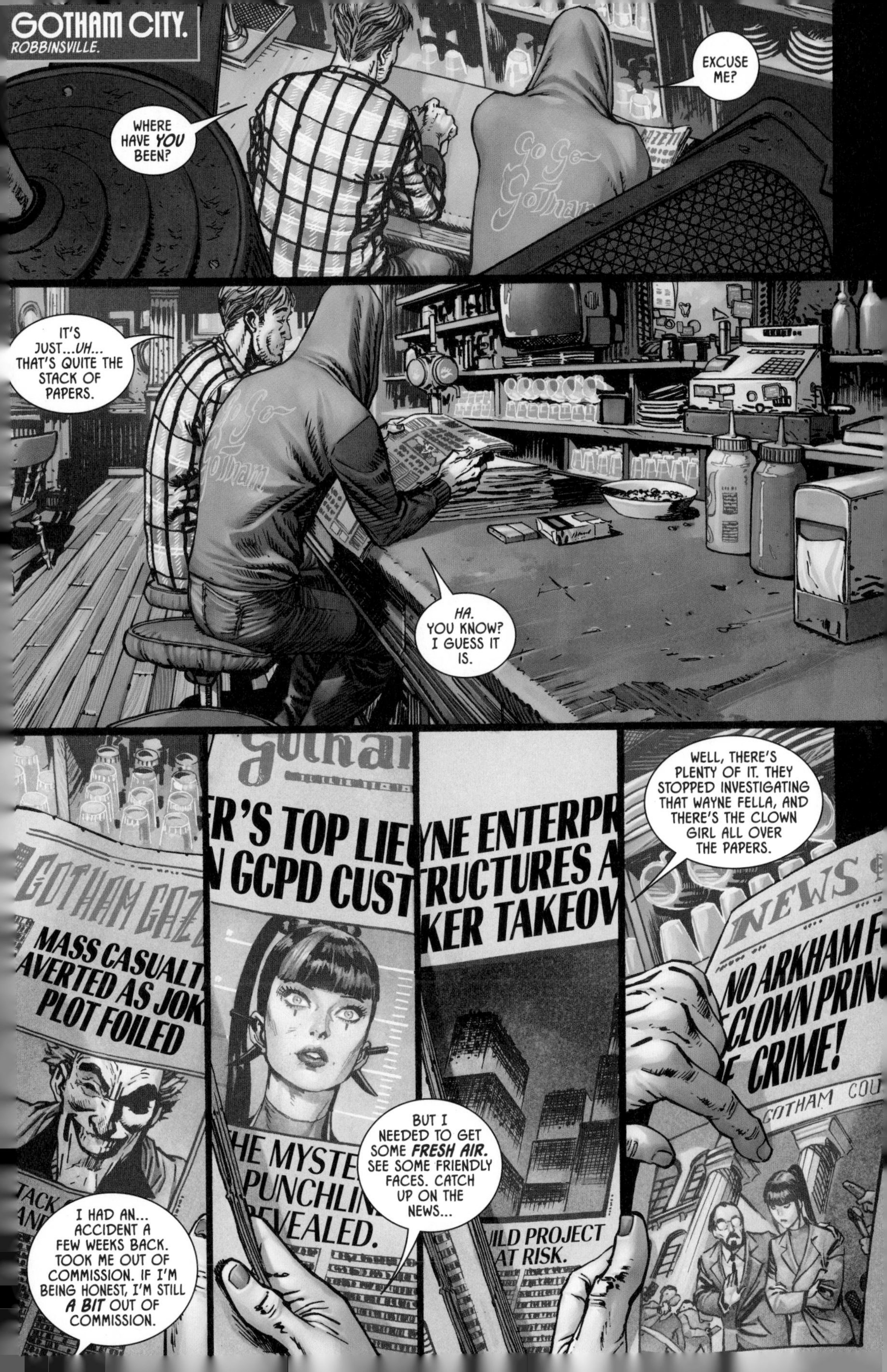
GOTHAM CITY.
ROBBINSVILLE.
WHERE HAVE YOU BEEN?
EXCUSE ME?
IT'S JUST...UH... THAT'S QUITE THE STACK OF PAPERS.
HA. YOU KNOW? I GUESS IT IS.
GOTHAM GAZ
MASS CASUALT AVERTED AS JOK PLOT FOILED
I HAD AN... ACCIDENT A FEW WEEKS BACK. TOOK ME OUT OF COMMISSION. IF I'M BEING HONEST, I'M STILL A BIT OUT OF COMMISSION.
R'S TOP LIE N GCPD CUST
HE MYSTE PUNCHLIN EVEALED.
BUT I NEEDED TO GET SOME FRESH AIR. SEE SOME FRIENDLY FACES. CATCH UP ON THE NEWS...
YNE ENTERPR TRUCTURES A KER TAKEOV
UILD PROJECT AT RISK.
WELL, THERE'S PLENTY OF IT. THEY STOPPED INVESTIGATING THAT WAYNE FELLA, AND THERE'S THE CLOWN GIRL ALL OVER THE PAPERS.
NEWS
NO ARKHAM F CLOWN PRIN F CRIME!
GOTHAM COU

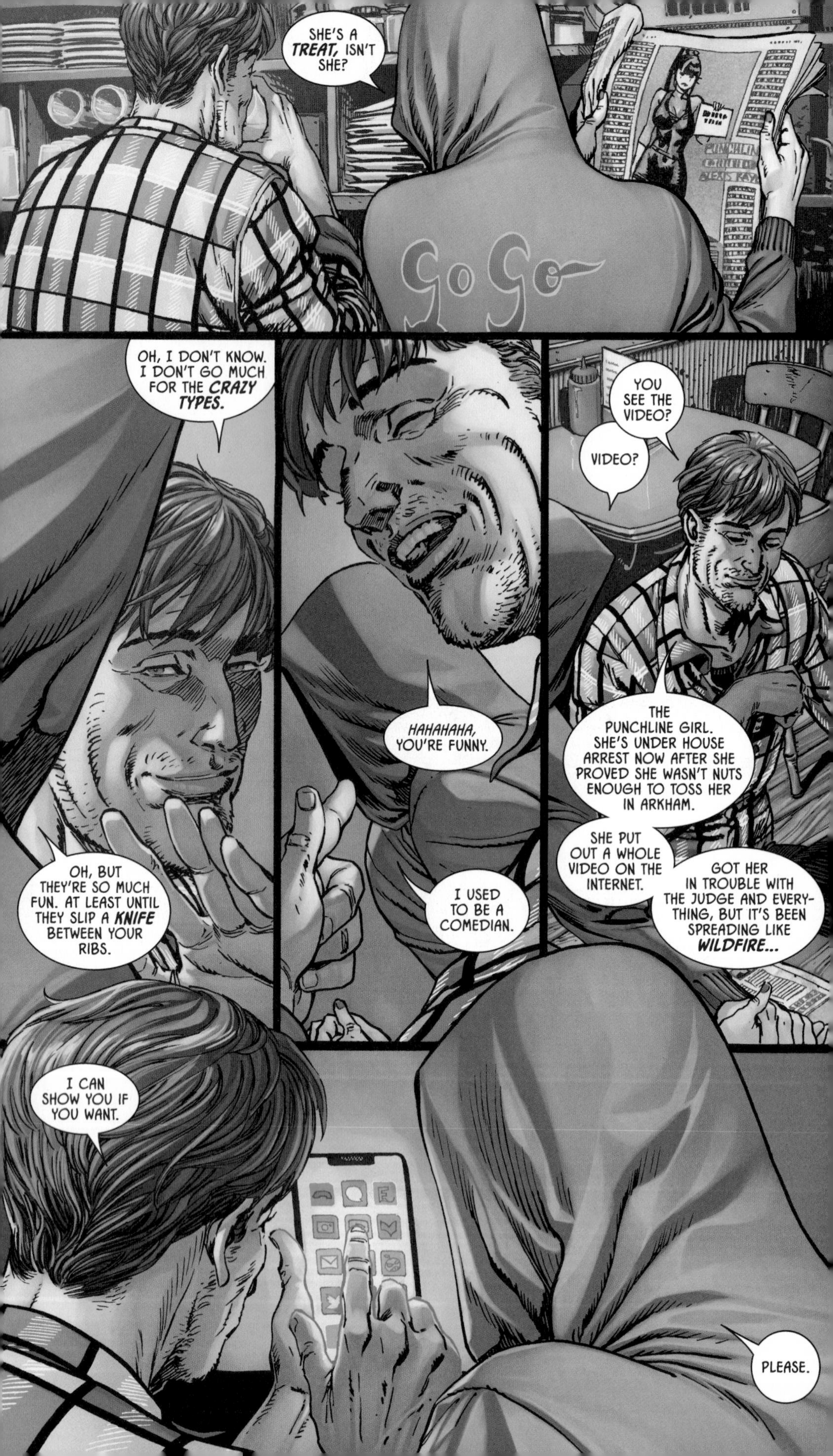
SHE'S A TREAT, ISN'T SHE?
OH, I DON'T KNOW. I DON'T GO MUCH FOR THE CRAZY TYPES.
OH, BUT THEY'RE SO MUCH FUN. AT LEAST UNTIL THEY SLIP A KNIFE BETWEEN YOUR RIBS.
HAHAHAHA, YOU'RE FUNNY.
I USED TO BE A COMEDIAN.
YOU SEE THE VIDEO?
VIDEO?
THE PUNCHLINE GIRL. SHE'S UNDER HOUSE ARREST NOW AFTER SHE PROVED SHE WASN'T NUTS ENOUGH TO TOSS HER IN ARKHAM.
SHE PUT OUT A WHOLE VIDEO ON THE INTERNET.
GOT HER IN TROUBLE WITH THE JUDGE AND EVERYTHING, BUT IT'S BEEN SPREADING LIKE WILDFIRE...
I CAN SHOW YOU IF YOU WANT.
PLEASE.

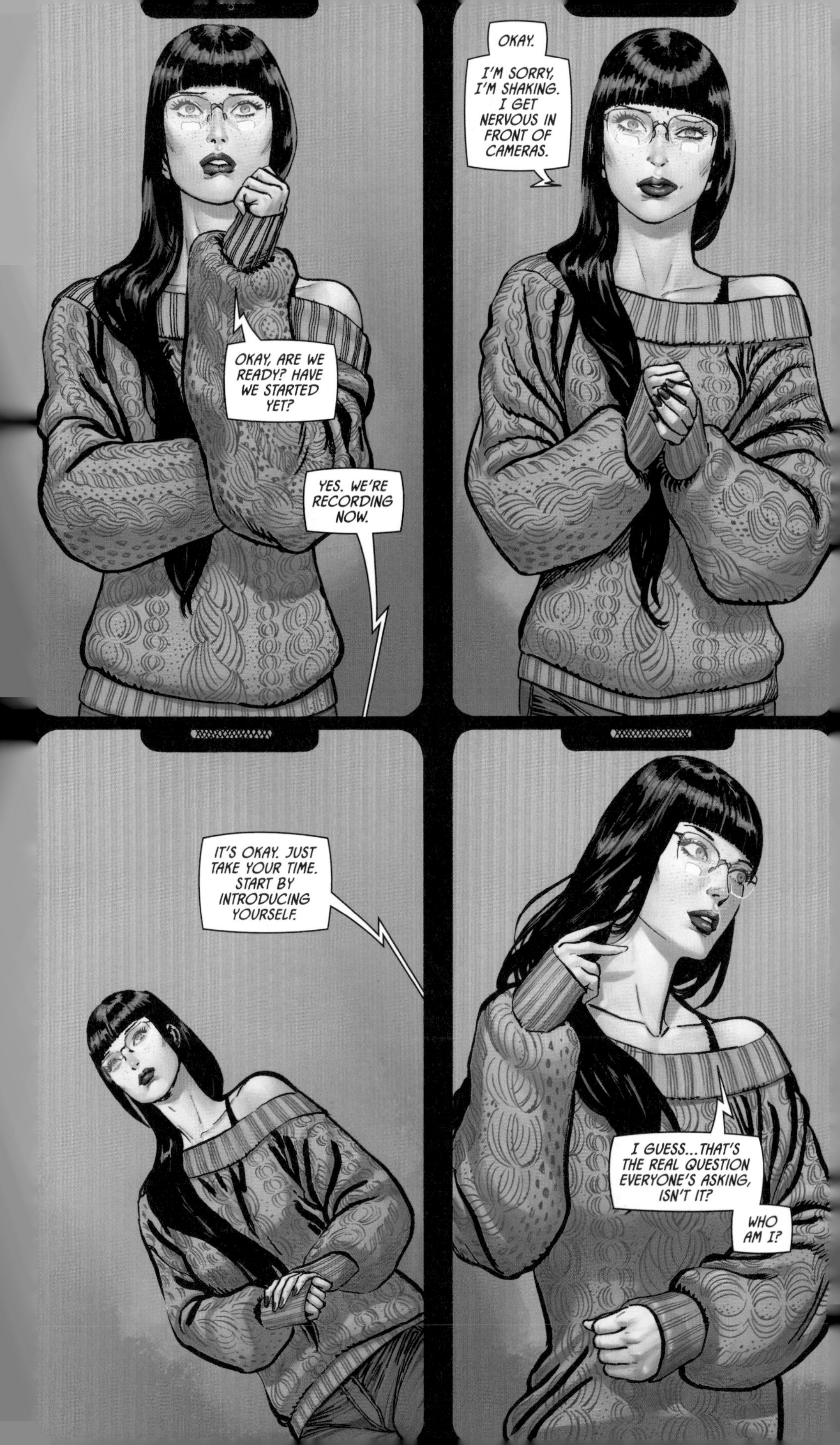
OKAY, ARE WE READY? HAVE WE STARTED YET?
YES. WE'RE RECORDING NOW.
OKAY.
I'M SORRY, I'M SHAKING. I GET NERVOUS IN FRONT OF CAMERAS.
IT'S OKAY. JUST TAKE YOUR TIME. START BY INTRODUCING YOURSELF.
I GUESS...THAT'S THE REAL QUESTION EVERYONE'S ASKING, ISN'T IT?
WHO AM I?

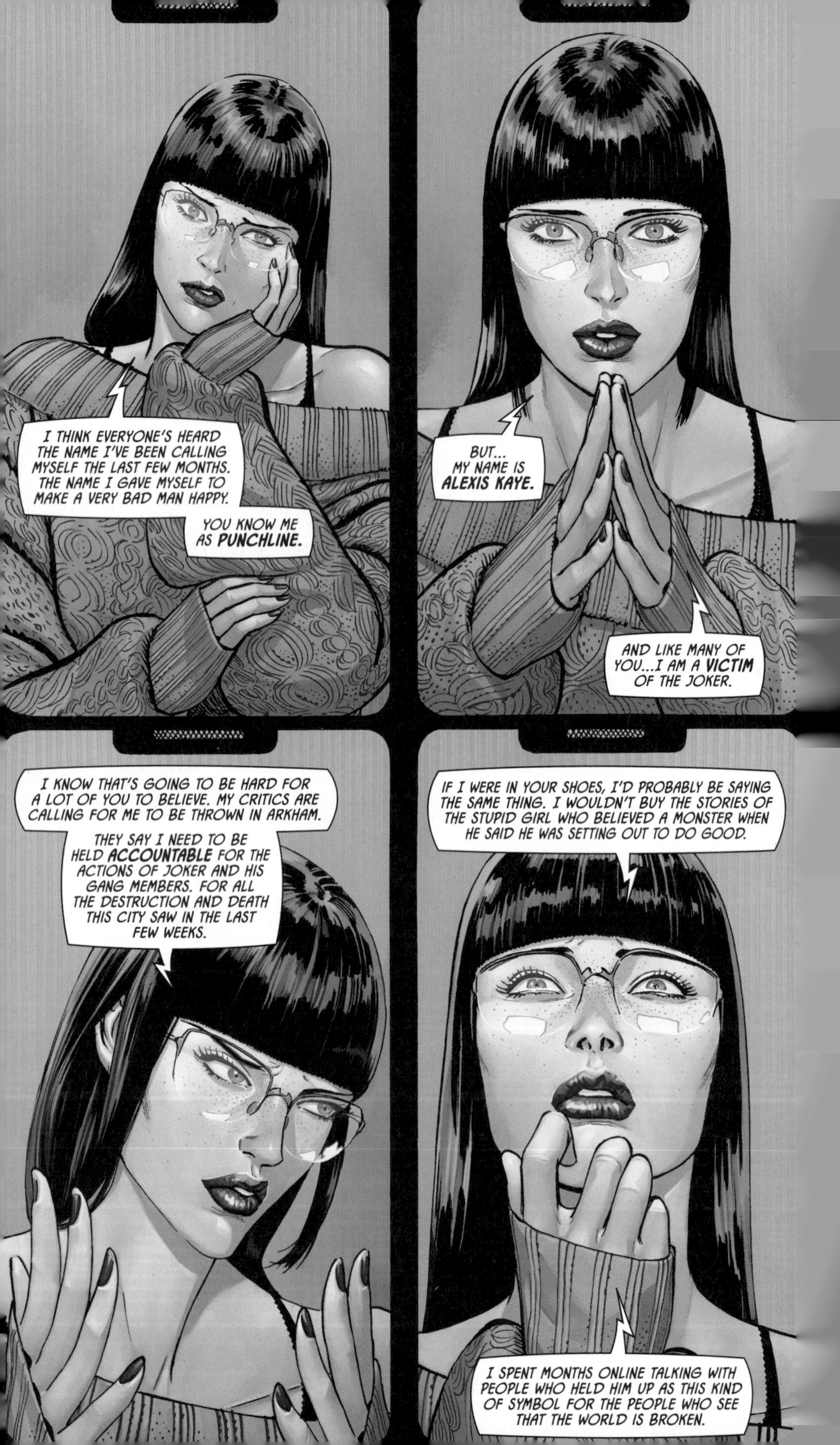
I THINK EVERYONE'S HEARD THE NAME I'VE BEEN CALLING MYSELF THE LAST FEW MONTHS. THE NAME I GAVE MYSELF TO MAKE A VERY BAD MAN HAPPY.
YOU KNOW ME AS PUNCHLINE.
BUT... MY NAME IS ALEXIS KAYE.
AND LIKE MANY OF YOU...I AM A VICTIM OF THE JOKER.
I KNOW THAT'S GOING TO BE HARD FOR A LOT OF YOU TO BELIEVE. MY CRITICS ARE CALLING FOR ME TO BE THROWN IN ARKHAM.
THEY SAY I NEED TO BE HELD ACCOUNTABLE FOR THE ACTIONS OF JOKER AND HIS GANG MEMBERS. FOR ALL THE DESTRUCTION AND DEATH THIS CITY SAW IN THE LAST FEW WEEKS.
IF I WERE IN YOUR SHOES, I'D PROBABLY BE SAYING THE SAME THING. I WOULDN'T BUY THE STORIES OF THE STUPID GIRL WHO BELIEVED A MONSTER WHEN HE SAID HE WAS SETTING OUT TO DO GOOD.
I SPENT MONTHS ONLINE TALKING WITH PEOPLE WHO HELD HIM UP AS THIS KIND OF SYMBOL FOR THE PEOPLE WHO SEE THAT THE WORLD IS BROKEN.

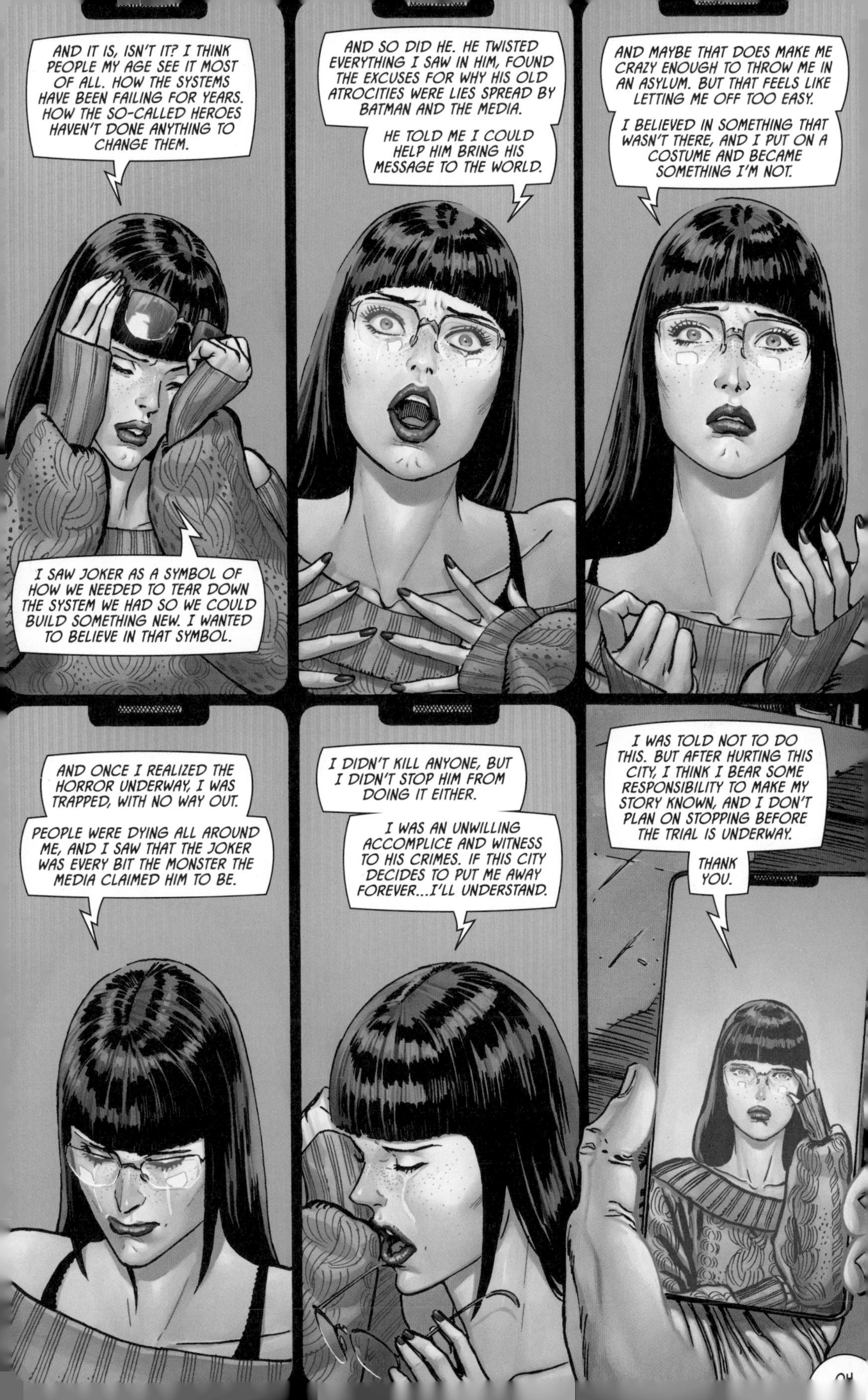
AND IT IS, ISN'T IT? I THINK PEOPLE MY AGE SEE IT MOST OF ALL. HOW THE SYSTEMS HAVE BEEN FAILING FOR YEARS. HOW THE SO-CALLED HEROES HAVEN'T DONE ANYTHING TO CHANGE THEM.
I SAW JOKER AS A SYMBOL OF HOW WE NEEDED TO TEAR DOWN THE SYSTEM WE HAD SO WE COULD BUILD SOMETHING NEW. I WANTED TO BELIEVE IN THAT SYMBOL.
AND SO DID HE. HE TWISTED EVERYTHING I SAW IN HIM, FOUND THE EXCUSES FOR WHY HIS OLD ATROCITIES WERE LIES SPREAD BY BATMAN AND THE MEDIA.
HE TOLD ME I COULD HELP HIM BRING HIS MESSAGE TO THE WORLD.
AND MAYBE THAT DOES MAKE ME CRAZY ENOUGH TO THROW ME IN AN ASYLUM. BUT THAT FEELS LIKE LETTING ME OFF TOO EASY.
I BELIEVED IN SOMETHING THAT WASN'T THERE, AND I PUT ON A COSTUME AND BECAME SOMETHING I'M NOT.
AND ONCE I REALIZED THE HORROR UNDERWAY, I WAS TRAPPED, WITH NO WAY OUT.
PEOPLE WERE DYING ALL AROUND ME, AND I SAW THAT THE JOKER WAS EVERY BIT THE MONSTER THE MEDIA CLAIMED HIM TO BE.
I DIDN'T KILL ANYONE, BUT I DIDN'T STOP HIM FROM DOING IT EITHER.
I WAS AN UNWILLING ACCOMPLICE AND WITNESS TO HIS CRIMES. IF THIS CITY DECIDES TO PUT ME AWAY FOREVER...I'LL UNDERSTAND.
I WAS TOLD NOT TO DO THIS. BUT AFTER HURTING THIS CITY, I THINK I BEAR SOME RESPONSIBILITY TO MAKE MY STORY KNOWN, AND I DON'T PLAN ON STOPPING BEFORE THE TRIAL IS UNDERWAY.
THANK YOU.

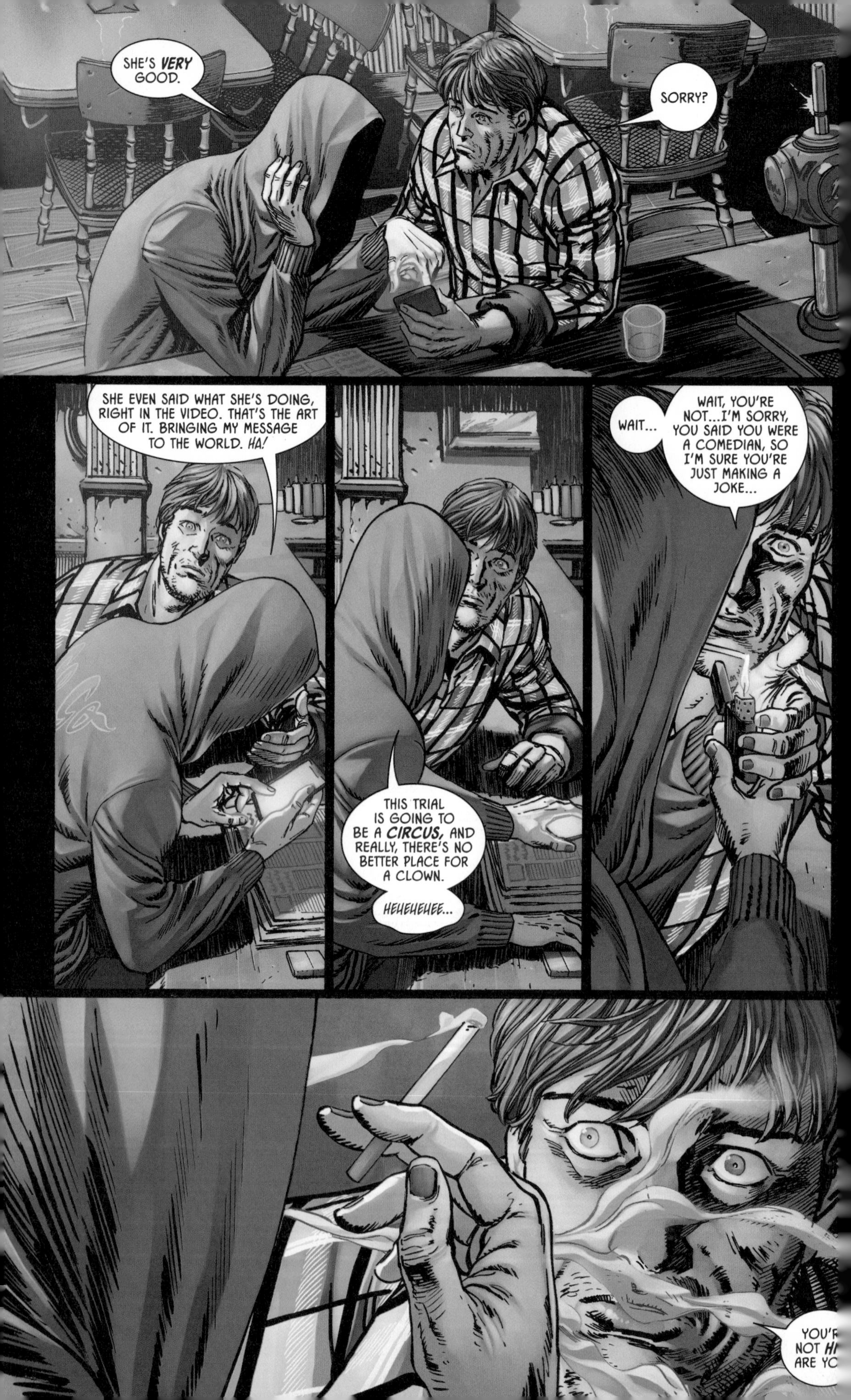
SHE'S VERY GOOD.
SORRY?
SHE EVEN SAID WHAT SHE'S DOING, RIGHT IN THE VIDEO. THAT'S THE ART OF IT. BRINGING MY MESSAGE TO THE WORLD. HA!
THIS TRIAL IS GOING TO BE A CIRCUS, AND REALLY, THERE'S NO BETTER PLACE FOR A CLOWN.
HEHEHEHEE...
WAIT...
WAIT, YOU'RE NOT...I'M SORRY, YOU SAID YOU WERE A COMEDIAN, SO I'M SURE YOU'RE JUST MAKING A JOKE...

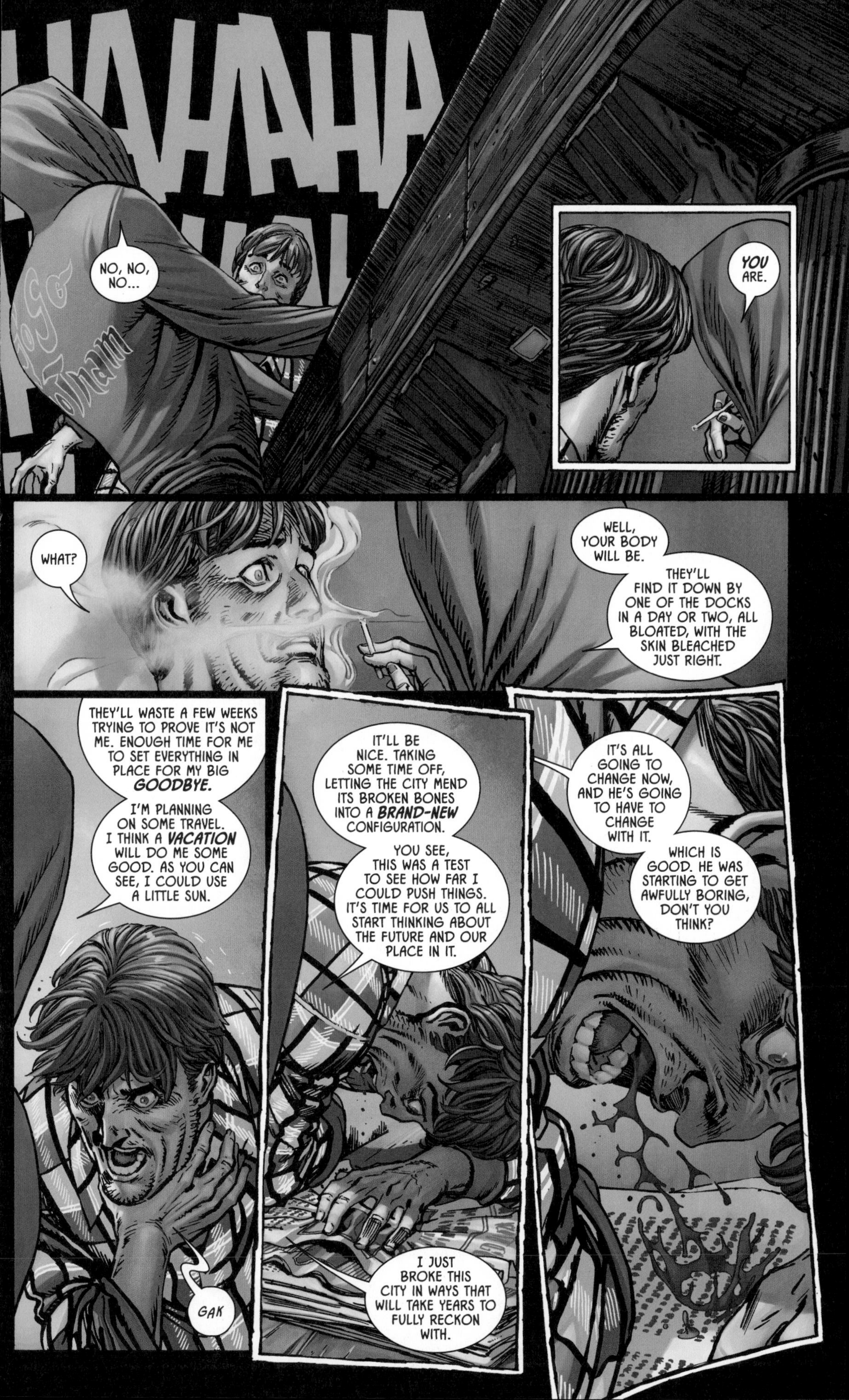

HAHAHA
NO, NO, NO...
YOU ARE.
WHAT?
WELL, YOUR BODY WILL BE.
THEY'LL FIND IT DOWN BY ONE OF THE DOCKS IN A DAY OR TWO, ALL BLOATED, WITH THE SKIN BLEACHED JUST RIGHT.
THEY'LL WASTE A FEW WEEKS TRYING TO PROVE IT'S NOT ME. ENOUGH TIME FOR ME TO SET EVERYTHING IN PLACE FOR MY BIG GOODBYE.
I'M PLANNING ON SOME TRAVEL. I THINK A VACATION WILL DO ME SOME GOOD. AS YOU CAN SEE, I COULD USE A LITTLE SUN.
GAK
IT'LL BE NICE. TAKING SOME TIME OFF, LETTING THE CITY MEND ITS BROKEN BONES INTO A BRAND-NEW CONFIGURATION.
YOU SEE, THIS WAS A TEST TO SEE HOW FAR I COULD PUSH THINGS. IT'S TIME FOR US TO ALL START THINKING ABOUT THE FUTURE AND OUR PLACE IN IT.
I JUST BROKE THIS CITY IN WAYS THAT WILL TAKE YEARS TO FULLY RECKON WITH.
IT'S ALL GOING TO CHANGE NOW, AND HE'S GOING TO HAVE TO CHANGE WITH IT.
WHICH IS GOOD. HE WAS STARTING TO GET AWFULLY BORING, DON'T YOU THINK?

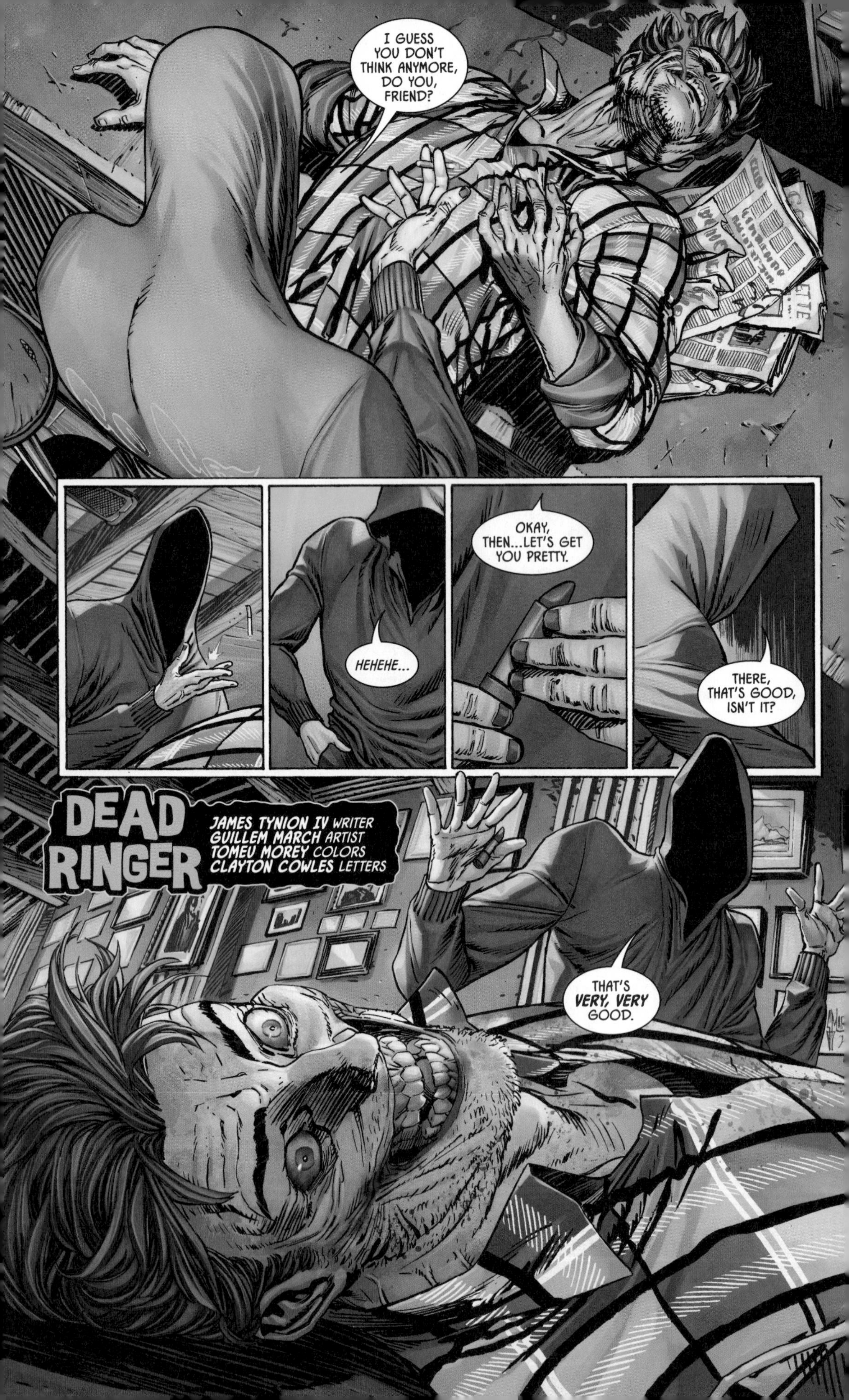
I GUESS YOU DON'T THINK ANYMORE, DO YOU, FRIEND?
HEHEHE...
OKAY, THEN...LET'S GET YOU PRETTY.
THERE, THAT'S GOOD, ISN'T IT?
DEAD RINGER
JAMES TYNION IV WRITER
GUILLEM MARCH ARTIST
TOMEU MOREY COLORS
CLAYTON COWLES LETTERS
THAT'S VERY, VERY GOOD.